VV Jones Ministries

Healing and Deliverance by the Finger of God

Learning to Develop a Viable Prayer Life

Virgil Jones
September, 2011

Healing and Deliverance by the Finger of God
Learning to Develop a Viable Prayer Life

Copyright © 2011
Virgil V. Jones
First Edition 2011

Unless otherwise stated, Scripture quotations
Are taken from the New King James Version
Of the Holy Bible Copyright 2011, Logos Publishing

Published
By
Virgil Jones/VVJones Ministries

Printed in the United States by Morris Publishing®
3212 East Highway 30
Kearney, NE 68847
1-800-650-7888

Images by:
Clark Graphic Images
11815 S. Menlo Ave.
Los Angeles, CA 90044
(323) 755-0474

Images within: Clark Graphic Images

ISBN: 978-0-9832229-0-3
Library of Congress Control Number: 2011916885

TABLE OF CONTENTS

OUTLINE

A. Preface. Thesis Statement: Healing and Deliverance Ministry is viable in this current age and is needed if the spread of the Gospel of Jesus Christ is to have any lasting impact on the world at large.

B What is healing?
- When people say they have been healed, what do they mean?
- How does what they say compare to science and reason?
- How does the church view healing in the context of miracles?

C. What is deliverance?
When people say they have been delivered, what do they mean?
- How does what they say compare to science and reason?
- How does the church view deliverance in the context of miracles?

D. How does healing and deliverance relate to the culture of today?
- Who are the supporters and what is their argument?
- Who are the naysayers and what is their argument?
- What does the Bible say?

E. Given the data contained herein, one must decide where one stands and live with the consequences or benefits of having made that decision.

PREFACE

The purpose of this writing is to address the subject of Healing and Deliverance Ministry. The preliminary pages will reflect a third-person writing formula to engage the student in an environment that is normative. Due to the size and scope of the argument, some presumptions must be made. One presumption includes the inerrancy and authority of Scripture. Another presumption includes categorizing those who support healing and deliverance ministry in the present age and those who do not. Differences of opinion abound from person to person. Two seminary vernaculars will be featured in this discussion. Continuation Theology will refer to the doctrine that supports Healing and Deliverance Ministry in this current age. Cessation Theology will refer to the doctrine that does not support Healing and Deliverance Ministry in this current age. No other grouping will be mentioned.

In choosing this assignment, there has been comprehensive research on the subject of healing and deliverance. The extensive bibliography bears this out and hopes to leave no stone unturned. There is another issue that needs to be addressed before going further. The material presented herein is not intended to replace or deny the use of doctors. The medical profession is available as part of the environment that brings health and wholeness and is an invaluable resource that cannot be overlooked. The human body is designed to heal itself. Diet, exercise, rehabilitation, rest and medicine all aim to maintain wellness. If none of these works, God does make provisions by using Healing and Deliverance Ministry as one of His tools.

Finally, if reading in the third person is difficult, do not panic. Only the first chapter is written in such a way. Since this book will be used by the college and seminary student, there needs to be a clear indication that the author is aware of the Turabian writing style. The first chapter was written originally using end notes but due to the formatting of this book, all notes will be formatted as footnotes. First and second person references will flow from chapter two and beyond. It is advisable not to skip over the first chapter because some presumptions will be made in the latter chapters that are founded on chapter one.

Enjoy the ride!

Introduction

A Preliminary Essay

Preliminary Introduction

One of the most frustrating experiences a person can have is a condition that no medical treatment can solve. When sickness happens, people usually go to the doctor, get medicine, take the medicine and eventually get well. If the condition does not have a medical remedy, there is trouble. The aim of this discussion has to do with bringing one back to health and wholeness. To do that requires either healing or deliverance.

What is Healing?

Before going further a few definitions are in order. *The New Dictionary of Theology* suggests that sickness is the result of the inability of humanity to obey God.[1] *The Baker Encyclopedia of the Bible* links disease to sickness, illness, torment and affliction.[2] These two bibliographic entries suggest that after God had finished making and creating everything He

---

[1] Sinclair B. Ferguson, David F. Wright, and J. I. Packer, eds., *New Dictionary of Theology* (Downers Grove, IL: InterVarsity Press, 1978), 287.

[2] W. A. Elwell and B. J. Beitzel, *Baker Encyclopedia of the Bible* (Grand Rapids: Baker Book House, 1988), 633.

had made, all was well. In fact, the Bible declares that everything was good. Everything existed in harmony and there was only goodness and wellness upon the face of the earth. Humanity could experience only good things so long as the will and plan of God were followed. There was no sickness, disease or death. When humanity sinned everything changed. Accordingly, sickness and disease were punishments for disobedience to the purpose and plan of God and became a result of the fall of man in the Garden of Eden. Millard Erickson suggests, "When sin entered the human race, a curse (actually a series of curses) was pronounced on humanity; diseases were part of that curse."[3] The resultant trouble of maintaining good health makes healing a necessity for humanity.

Sickness and disease come in multiple forms. There is a temporary form like that of a simple virus or in the form of

---

[3] Millard J. Erickson, *Christian Theology* (Grand Rapids: Baker Academics, 1998), 853.

something more severe which has the capacity to debilitate a person until death. It all depends.

After the creation, everything was made with a purpose. The whole of creation can be reduced to single cell organisms. Each cell replicates to form a particular organism, both animate and inanimate. Cells form something as complex as the human being or as simple as an amoeba, (a single cell organism). The fall of man caused the ground to be cursed. From here, good things turned bad. Even simple life forms like bacteria became affected. D.G. Lindsay agrees, "All bacteria was created with some purpose. Bacteria is both helpful and harmful to man; circumstances dictate its effects. Research indicates that it is not that new viruses and bacteria are materializing, but that life forms on the Earth are growing steadily more susceptible to their harmful effects." [4] Humanity is still feeling the effects of the fall and the only remedy in these cases is God Himself.

---

[4] D. G. Lindsay, *Harmony of Science and Scripture* (Dallas: Christ for the Nations, 1998), n .p.

Healing, as presented by the *New International Encyclopedia of Biblical Words,* aims to restore one completely in harmony with God where one receives benefits of wholeness.[5] Everything depends on the relationship one has with God. Harmony with God often results in wellness. Disharmony with God generally results in sickness and disease

When a person says they have been healed, what does this mean? It means that whatever ailment, illness, sickness or disease they had is now gone. Their healing has happened to them by medical or non-medical means. Whatever condition they had is no longer present. In other words, they are free from everything that made them sick.

Healing is viewed by science as the use of medical or dietary aids to make a person well. According to the *Merriam-Webster Dictionary,* when a person is made whole, it means

---

[5] Lawrence O. Richards, ed., *New International Encyclopedia of Biblical Words* (Grand Rapids: Zondervan Publishing House, 1996), 329.

he/she is cured.[6] The *Oxford Dictionary and Thesaurus* suggests the meaning that the person has become sound or healthy again.[7] The medical profession aims at making sick people well. Marilyn Schlitz affirms, "Integral medicine embraces the recognition that human beings possess emotional, spiritual, and relational dimensions that are essential in the diagnosis and treatment of disease and the cultivation of wellness."[8] The general consensus then is that a healthy person is one whose mind, body, soul and spirit function in socially acceptable ways with no restrictions. How a person gets to be whole is a different matter altogether.

---

[6] Merriam-Webster, Inc. *The Merriam-Webster Collegiate Dictionary – 10th ed.* (Springfield, MA: Merriam-Webster, 1996), 523.

[7] Oxford University Press, Inc. *The Oxford Dictionary and Thesaurus* (Oxford; New York: Oxford University Press, 1996), 676.

[8] Marilyn Schlitz, "Consciousness and Healing." October 2004, *The American Journal of Medicine – Book Index on Healing 2005* http://www.elsevier.com/wps/find/simple_search.cws_home?boost=true&needs_keyword=true&adv=false&action=simple_search&default=default&keywords=healing (April 2011)

13

What makes a person well or whole is a subject full of

opinion. The *New Dictionary of Theology* suggests that healing,

redemption and restoration will happen during the time of

resurrection and rapture at the Second Coming of Jesus Christ.[9]

This would be what is common in Cessation Theology which

views healing and deliverance as something to look forward to in

the end of time. Cessationists believe that miracles of this sort

are not for today. Continuation Theology disagrees.

Continuation Theology believes healing and miracles are for

today. According to Erickson, the miracles of Jesus did not

cease. Then and now, the supernatural invades the natural.[10] J.

Rodman Williams offers a similar sentiment. He states that the

sovereignty of God does not preclude Him from impacting any

---

[9] Sinclair B. Ferguson, David F. Wright, and J. I. Packer, eds., *New Dictionary of Theology* (Downers Grove, IL: InterVarsity Press, 1978), 288.

[10] Millard J. Erickson, *Christian Theology* (Grand Rapids: Baker Academics, 1998), 857-858.

aspect of the created world.[11] That God moves in and out of the natural via supernatural means shows He is concerned with the wellbeing of humanity today. What about deliverance?

What is Deliverance?

Deliverance requires an understanding of some basic definitions. *The Wycliffe Bible Encyclopedia* shares that "Freedom is exemption or release of one personality from domination by or obligation to another."[12] *The Tyndale Bible Dictionary* suggests that deliverance has come when a person has come to redeem or release another.[13]

When a person says they have been delivered, what does this mean? It means that whatever had them bound, no longer affects them. The thing or entity they refer to in this case is usually a

---

[11] J. Rodman Williams, *Renewal Theology* (Grand Rapids: Zondervan Publishing House, 1996), 144-145.

[12] Charles F. Pfeiffer, Howard F. Vos and John Rea, eds., *The Wycliffe Bible Encyclopedia – Volumes I & II* (Chicago: Moody Press, 1975), 637.

[13] Walter A. Elwell, and Philip Wesley Comfort *Tyndale Bible Dictionary – Tyndale Reference Library* (Wheaton: Tyndale House Publishers, 2001), 371.

sinister presence better known as a demonic spirit. The demonic spirit manifests in different ways and the main function of that spirit is to destroy the host. According to Francis MacNutt, a delivered person has an inner healing that leaves no room for a demonic spirit.[14] A delivered person is a free person.

The world of science and reason has a different understanding of deliverance. Science and medicine diagnoses most demonic manifestations as mental illness, "a disorder of the mind."[15] Other diagnoses refer to Multiple Personality Disorder (M.P.D.), Dissociative Identity Disorder (D.I.D.) or Schizophrenia to name a few. Merriam-Webster defines M.P.D. as a disconnect between the primary personality and the other personalities where one interchangeably dominates the others.[16]

---

[14] Francis McNutt, *Deliverance from Evil Spirits* (Grand Rapids: Chosen Books, 2009), 189.

[15] Oxford University Press, Inc. *The Oxford Dictionary and Thesaurus* (Oxford; New York: Oxford University Press, 1996), 936.

[16] *The Merriam-Webster Collegiate Dictionary – Electronic 11th ed.* (Springfield, MA: Merriam-Webster, 1996), n. p.

James Friesen suggests each personality that manifests itself will dominate all the others.[17] Friesen goes on to say that D.I.D. is best understood independently functioning mental processes.[18] Each of these conditions is generally handled via medicinal aids and psychotherapy.

Deliverance ministry is often linked with healing ministry as stated above and theologians do not mind weighing in on the topic. Deliverance ministry has to do with removing the demonic presence from a person.

Demonology comes in the form of possession or influence. *Lewis Sperry Chafer Systematic Theology* suggests that there is a difference between demon possession and demon influence. Demonic possession has to do with a demon entering a person, whereas demonic influence has to do with a demon impacting a

---

[17] James G. Friesen, *Uncovering the Mystery of M.P.D – Its Shocking Origins…Its Shocking Cure* (San Bernardino: Here's Life Publishers, 1991), 43.

[18] Ibid., 115.

person.[19] In other words, possession identifies a presence within. Influence identifies a presence without. Each of these is removed by the power of God.

Healing and Deliverance in the Twenty-first Century

The culture of today is antagonistic to the Christian Church. One reason is probably because the Church is split where she should be unified. Some churches agree in healing and deliverance ministry while others do not. In either case, the answer lies in the beginning. It was in the beginning where God created everything. Humanity was part of the creative plan of God. Because of the fall, sickness and death has haunted man ever since. That humanity is split on the subject of healing and deliverance is no surprise. In spite of the debate, the Holy Bible is a great resource book that contains stories of individuals who have struggled with many of the issues people face today. God has already seen and handled it all. The earthly ministry of Jesus

---

[19] John E. Walvoord, Donald K. Campbell and Roy B. Zuck, eds., *Lewis Sperry Chafer Systematic Theology – Volumes I & II* (Wheaton: Victor Books, 1984), 321.

was not out of necessity or obligation but out of love and genuine concern for the individual.

The ministry of Jesus included the message and the miracle. Howard Ervin states, "The sign and the message complement each other. The sign confirms the message. The message authenticates the sign, for no miracle is self-authenticating."[20] A message without a sign loses drawing power. A sign with no message draws people for the wrong reasons. Jesus often challenged people to come to God the right way. According to Ervin, "the way Jesus healed can be found in three categories: (1) healing miracles that took place in response to Jesus' spoken word; (2) healing miracles that were communicated by a physical touch; and (3) the use of a material substance."[21] Charles Kraft adds, "In the encounter itself...whether we seek healing or deliverance – we take the authority we have been

---

[20] Howard M. Ervin, *Healing – Sign of the Kingdom* (Peabody, MA: Hendrickson Publishers, Inc., 2002), 2.

[21] Ibid., 34.

given and command the condition to be gone."[22] Jesus was often

quoted saying, "I do what I see My Father doing and I say what I

hear My Father saying." A faithful follower of Christ will do

what Jesus did.

Initial Concluding Thought

Given the current discussion, one must decide what to do

with sickness, disease or demonization. Whether one chooses to

support or deny the existence of miracles in the twenty-first

century is of no real consequence. God is still sovereign. He will

do whatever He desires. God is neither dead nor aloof. He is as

concerned about His creation today as He was in Bible days. The

stories of Naaman in 2 Kings 5, the Syro-Phoenician Woman in

Mark 7, the Woman with the Issue of Blood in Luke 8 and

current testimonies all bear the record that God is interested in

His creation. Supernatural healing or deliverance still gets

attention and tranforms many a skeptic. It is therefore best to

---

[22] Charles H. Kraft, *Christianity with Power* (Ann Arbor: Vine Books, 1989), 149.

listen to the voice of God and follow the will of God and let the rest take care of itself. *He that hath an ear let him hear what the Spirit is saying to the churches.*

Chapter 1

My First Encounter

I was about five or six years old. I remember this event as vividly as if it happened this morning. It was a crisp Saturday morning. My parents had not yet found their first cup of coffee but I was outside already. The birds were chirping. There was a gentle breeze. A few children were outside but not the normal crowd. Soon the street would be filled with the noise of children playing on both sides of the street.

It was a small neighborhood where everybody knew each other. We lived at 630 E. 109th Street in Los Angeles. We lived just a stone's throw from the newly built Alain Leroy Locke Senior High School where my aunts and uncle would attend. I was in my early matriculation years at 109th Street Elementary School where most of the children who would come out to play that day would attend.

Notwithstanding the dismal showing that morning, I was out early with my skate board. It was a wooden board with metal wheels. It was the same metal wheels usually found on the metal skates. These were the same wheels that would eventually shear in pieces long before the skates or skateboards were fully used up. There I was on my skateboard riding it the way my mother warned me, standing straight up. She had earlier seen me riding it on one knee with my two hands grabbing the front of the board and suggested it was too dangerous. She said something about how I could cut or scrape my hand riding the board that way.

Nevertheless there I was riding my board *her* way until I got a brilliant idea. I want to ride the board *my* way for a while. After all, what harm could it do? No one is watching. I bet I could take a few spins without anyone ever being the wiser. I'm sure you know what I did next. I looked to the left. I looked to the right. I looked behind me. No one of substance was paying any attention to me. So I bent down, placed my left knee on the board, collected my ten fingers on the front of the board and away I went. The more I pushed off with my right foot, the faster I'd go. The wind was blowing in my hair as I picked up speed.

This was the life! I did this a few times. I'd go to the end of the block, turn around and ride the board right back. This was sure fun. I liked riding my skateboard this way. That nagging overprotective mother of mine did not know what was best for me.

After a few good runs without incident, I remember thinking, "I better not try my luck too much. The nosey neighbors might see and rat me out to my parents." Yes, we lived in a neighborhood like this. All the parents on the block seemed to be nosey meddling parents. I decided I would make one last run before I went back to my mother's way of riding my skateboard. I will forever the fate of that decision. As I rode past our house, I was moving from east to west. A kid came riding past me on a bike. There was more than enough room for her to pass by so I was not worried or bothered. At the house adjacent to ours was a neighbor who was especially close to our family. They loved my baby brother and showered him with gifts as he was the newest addition to our family by then. Life was so great on 109th Street until *he* came along!

There I was, moving westbound on the sidewalk when I saw it. It was a used tin can with the jagged top still attached by just a piece of tin. I had rode past it several times that day without incident but this time was different. It was as if I was being drawn to it like a magnet draws metal. The more I tried to steer to the right of it, I kept veering left until it happened. I ran aground and cut myself on that old rusty can. I fell off my board and looked at my thumb. The sight was unbearable. I removed the dirt and grass from the fresh wound and went running to the garden hose to rinse the wound. After this I ran inside to wash it further and wrap it up. Boy, I escaped without getting caught and my wound is clean and healing, so I thought.

I do not know when my sister who was less than a year older than I found out but she made me pay the price. I had to do her chores and her bidding. If I did not do what she said, she would tell mom how my thumb got messed up. I did not want our mom to find out because if she did, I knew there was a spanking waiting for me.

My sister was a rough task master. I had to do her chores along with my own. I had to find a way to empty the trash with one hand; wash dishes with one hand; wipe down countertops and tables with one hand; make her a sandwich with one hand. Life for me was tough. This was not the way my life was supposed to be. I finally got tired and began complaining. I do not know if you have a sibling like mine but when she felt her control slipping out of her hands, she began to get loud. "If you don't do what I say, I'm going to tell mom about your hand!" Before I could respond in walked mother. She overheard the commotion and came to see what it was all about. "What hand?! Let me see your hand!"

As tears welled up in my eyes, I gently took my hand from behind my back. There it was, wrapped carefully in band aids, bathroom tissue and Kleenex. By now a week had passed and my left thumb had swollen to twice its size. It was painful to the slightest touch. When my mother began to unwrap it, she saw the blood, swollenness and discoloration and quickly responded, "Let's go!" We all knew what that meant. She scooped up my baby brother and off we went.

We knew the trip to Doctor Ines Office all too well. Every year we'd head over to his office to be inoculated. His office was near the familiar projects just a few miles away. As soon as we made that right turn, we'd begin a concert of weeping and wailing that would make any blue grass singer proud. This time the only one crying was me because I had to go see Doctor Ines.

Once we got inside and sat down in his patient chair, he asked me what happened. As soon as I told him, I could see my mother's anger and concern conflict her. In one sense I deserved a spanking, in another sense I was getting my punishment. In one sense I needed a scolding, in another sense the pain was all the scolding I could handle. My mother stood there in the examination room against the pristine white ceramic tiled walls holding my sister's hand with one hand and my baby brother in her other arm. Her concern and agitation showed clearly on her face. The familiar nurse tried to console all of us to no avail.

As Doctor Ines began unwrapping by left thumb, it was a grotesque sight. My thumb was badly swollen and horribly discolored. The tissue was stuck to infected skin and as he removed it, he dislodged skin as well. It was so bad that the nurse left the room. It was too much for her to bear. My sister started crying. She and I together made Beethoven's 5th Symphony pale in comparison our concerto. "Wah-wa-wa-waaahhhh! Wah-wah-wa-waaahhh!"

After a thorough look, Doctor Ines gave my mother his prognosis. "I think he is going to lose his thumb. I do not believe we can save it. It is badly infected. I have never seen an infection this bad in all my years as a general practitioner." As he looked into my mother's pleading eyes, he said, "I'll do what I can." I have no doubt that the infection had gotten so bad that losing my thumb was a foregone conclusion. I may have been five or six but I knew what I saw and heard that day.

My mother started to pray. I had heard her pray before at the dinner table and at church but this was different. This was not one of those simple cookie-cutter prayers. She prayed as if her son was dying. She called on the Lord as I had never heard her call on Him before. Her eyes looked toward heaven. He face shined as though she was in the presence of the Almighty. Her countenance seemed bright as if angels were surrounding us and the room appeared to glow. My mother was "in the zone" and she was bending God's ear.

While she prayed, Doctor Ines took a long needle full of a clear fluid and emptied it in my left thumb. Then he started squeezing my thumb. The pain was so unbearable that I can go back to that moment right now and find a tear welling up in my eye. As he squeezed, so many different color fluids exited my left thumb. I cried so long and so loud that I had nothing left in me. I was all cried out. Soon he finished, cleaned the wound, put some antibiotics on it, wrapped it with the proper gauze, then made a statement. "Let's hope God heard your prayer Mrs. Jones." After giving my mother some instructions on dressing the wound and giving me medication, he sent us on our way.

Needless to say, I did not lose my left thumb. I have a scar to prove that this is not some concocted story. More importantly, this was my first experience with healing and miraculous prayer. I pray as you read these pages that the Lord God will bring back an experience to you or touch your spirit as He did mine. I pray you become one of God's ambassadors for healing and deliverance ministry as I am. It is a journey well worth each step you make.

Setting the Stage

One of the most frustrating experiences a person can have is a condition that no medical treatment can handle. People who are not physically healthy do what most reasonable-minded persons do, go to the doctor. In many cases, they are diagnosed and helped by some form of medical intervention. This pattern of returning an ailing person to health and wholeness is well and

good until there is a problem that no doctor or medical treatment

can resolve. The scene goes something like this:

Patient: "Well doctor, have you found an answer to my
problem?"
Doctor: "Well, yes and no."
Patient: "What do you mean?"
Doctor: "We know what you have. We just can't find a cure for
it."
Patient: "What am I supposed to do then?"
Doctor: "I don't know."
The patient is left puzzled. The doctor is sitting in front of the

puzzled patient scratching his head and wringing his hands. The

patient then departs bewildered, frustrated and dejected. If there

is a loved one to share this experience with them, they are

fortunate. Sadly, this is not the norm. Often people go it alone

keeping it all in and hope for the best. This is not God's design.

He has the answer to every problem we will ever face. There is

no condition, He cannot handle. None of us is helpless or

hopeless because He provides help and hope.

Most often, those with strange conditions are without

hope because they have no one available to them who

understands how to function in healing and deliverance ministry. This document is a manual on how to tap into the power of God so that you can function and be used in healing and deliverance ministry. By the time you finish reading this book, you will have a basic blueprint for ministry that will bring you into an environment that is different from anything you have ever experienced. You will have the capacity to be gifted by God to enter into the realm of ministry where miracles are commonplace. It is from this position that you will offer help and hope to those bewildered persons to whom the doctor has thrown up his hands and said, "There is nothing else we can do."

The premise of this book is to place God back where He belongs – in front. He should not be our last resort but our first option. As in the case mentioned above, people will often consider trying God when all else fails. This is not the worst thing that can happen because God does work this way. The Bible offers plenty of examples that bear this out. The stories of Naaman (Old Testament) and the woman with the issue of blood

(New Testament) offer us sufficient proof that God is willing to be a last resort. These stories will be discussed in greater detail later.

While God is willing to be a last resort, His preference is to be first. His aim for humanity is to be the One we come to first and foremost for everything we need. Health and wholeness are part of what He offers us on a daily basis. Any area where health and wholeness are challenged is an area where God has sovereign rule. His authority has no limits therefore there is nothing He cannot do.

Within the scope of our discussion, we will present an area that gets little attention – undisclosed sin. Often, undisclosed sin is either forgotten about or pushed aside with devastating consequences. People become sick because of their unwillingness to admit or address a sin they have committed in the past. There is no prescription or medical treatment available for this except the power of repentance and forgiveness. God uses the power of repentance and forgiveness to deliver and/or heal the person to make them whole. In our discussion of repentance and forgiveness, we will provide steps and through reflection and strategy, and help hurting people overcome whatever is ailing them. For this book, my intention is to include the areas where an individual has been attacked or influenced by demons as a result of unrepentant sin or unresolved forgiveness issues. Unfortunately, many of the issues that cause illnesses are smoke screens because there is often a deeper underlying cause. This cause usually goes unnoticed because that which rises to the surface is a symptom rather than the root issue. This manual attempts to address the cause and effect or the stimulus and response relationship and set in order that which keeps an individual from truly being whole.

When I mention whole, I am referring to a person that looks, acts and speaks as a normal human being. People who are whole possess physical, social, mental, emotional and spiritual wellness. These attributes are necessary for us to be vibrant responsible and functioning adults. When either of these is misfiring, one is ill or influenced by some sort of demonic presence. When none of these is ailing, one is well and healthy. I will present in this document a methodology that can be used to establish a deliverance ministry in the area of forgiveness in the church and data that support said agenda.

There is one additional disclaimer that I need to address before going further. The material I am presenting is not intended to replace or deny the use of the medical profession. Physicians are available to us as part of the environment that brings us health and wholeness. The medical profession is an invaluable resource that cannot be overlooked. The human body is designed to heal itself. Diet, exercise, rehabilitation, rest and medicine all aim to bring about health and wholeness. If none of these works, the physician's "there's nothing more we can do" response often leads a person back to God. As mentioned above, God is more than willing to respond to their need. This is where healing and deliverance ministry becomes His tool to provide health and wellness to the ailing soul. I pray that you will enjoy the journey into *Healing and Deliverance by the Finger of God.*

In case you are wondering about the title of this book, I'd like to quickly offer this insight. When Jesus healed and delivered a sick man whose condition was caused by a demonic presence in Luke 11:14-26, He was accused of doing the work of Beelzebub by the Pharisees. The man was dumb or mute which meant that he was unable to talk. This story was recorded also in Matthew 9 and Mark 3. Matthew's version (9:34) says the Pharisees made the accusation. Mark's version (3:22) says the scribes made the accusation. Luke's version (11:15) says "some of them" made the accusation. It is safe to say that the scribes and Pharisees were the accusers here. Rather than rejoicing that the sick man was made whole, the scribes and Pharisees focused on making a damaging statement to question Jesus' authority and ruin His reputation. Here is a quick point to ponder: Anyone who dares to get involved in healing and deliverance ministry must be prepared to face those who will question their authority and attempt to ruin their reputation. Be encouraged. Jesus' response (in Luke 11:20) makes the bold claim that healing and deliverance ministry comes to us by the "finger of God" which acknowledges the presence of the Kingdom of God. Matthew's version (12:28) refers to the ministry as being led by the Spirit of God. Both of these statements provide the foundation and framework for this book. Healing and deliverance ministry is nothing without the finger and/or the Spirit of God. I hope this title does not scare you away. God does not stand in righteous indignation pointing at the sick and diseased. Jesus stood pointing at His accusers who would dare challenge the rightness or appropriateness of healing and deliverance ministry. *Healing and Deliverance by the Finger of God* is as precise as the ministry itself. If you are a Cessation Theorist, I hope and pray by the end of this book, you will either be convinced or converted.

Chapter 2

Chapter Two – My Story

I can remember when the Lord started speaking to me. I was still a child. What God said to me then was as clear as it is today. I will share a few of my stories, some of which are quite funny, in the interest of drawing you closer to Him. I suspect God has spoken to you as He did to me or that He is speaking to you now. If so, I hope you will gain strength from my testimony and research on healing and deliverance ministry.

As you read, you will discover that much of the data contained herein is found in the Bible. I have done extensive research on the subject of healing and deliverance ministry and have found encouraging support by various authors as to the validity of this ministry. They have included their personal testimonies in an attempt to show that God uses regular people to do miraculous things. Their testimonies and stories are amazing. I found myself writing in the margins of their books statements like "Wow" or "Oh, my God!" I have chosen a different path. I aim to minimize my stories so that you can maximize your story.

Each of us will have different testimonies as God uses us. Please do not make the mistake by assuming that I don't have any stories to tell. My stories are as numerous as those I have read in the bibliographies provided at the end of this book. I have included a few but they don't even scratch the surface. There is a purpose however. My hope is that you will see the simplicity of the power of God and prepare to be used by Him in healing and deliverance ministry. My prayer for you is that you will become a fearless faithful follower of Christ whose foundation is formed in Spirit-filled ministry that finds the fearful and offer them help and hope through *Healing and Deliverance by the Finger of God*.

The Inclination

I was maybe eight or ten when I first felt something unusual happening within. The Lord had given me something unique. I cannot explain it any better than this: I had the ability to see either the angel of death or the arena of death. I didn't have what M. Night Shyamalan called *The Sixth Sense* nor was I a funny looking kid who went around saying, "I see dead people." My ability was different. The way it worked was like this: I could look at a person and know that I would never see them alive again. It didn't matter where I was or what I was doing. When a particular person (usually a family member) was in the room, I had this sense that something ominous was present, something that spoke of death. It didn't matter how healthy a person appeared to be, if they had this "thing" on them, I knew I would never see them alive again. It could be a matter of days or months that news would come of their demise. A freak accident, a heart attack, stroke, or some other disease or event would move them from the land of the living to that invisible place called death. I never told anybody of this phenomenon I now know was the discernment of spirits. There are obvious reasons why.

It was not socially acceptable to tell a person something like this, "You're going to die soon." That statement doesn't even sound right and writing it doesn't feel right. But that's how

I felt as a kid. Death wasn't something adults spoke with kids about on a level as deep as this. Sure, the guppy died and got flushed or the dog went to doggie heaven and got buried in the backyard but this was different. My understanding was deeper than I let on.

In church, there was no real discussion on the subject of death. Only the cursory, "Sister Maggie went on to be with the Lord" would suffice. There was no comprehensive discussion on gifts of the Spirit outlined in 1 Corinthians 12. I was a Sunday school student, always present with my Sunday School book in tow. Our lessons didn't cover things like this for someone my age and I understand why. These are not subjects children normally discuss or understand. Most adults don't even understand it. Out of fear, I soon asked the Lord to take this gift away. In time, I learned that this gift was not taken away but simply suppressed until I became mature enough to handle it.

My Inquisition

My upbringing was in a traditional environment. Calvary Baptist Church of Los Angeles was a great place to learn. My pastor as a child was the late Rev. Dr. Manuel L. Scott Sr. who was one of America's great preachers of the twentieth century. As I processed through the youth department I was one of those students who asked questions. I was inquisitive. Many of my instructors have crossed over God's celestial shore but there are a few members today who still remember "little Virgil," much to my chagrin. As the Senior Pastor of the church in which I was reared, there are some things I'd like to forget that well-meaning Calvary constituents don't mind bringing up. My only response to their nostalgic knowledge is, "Yes, I remember doing that."

Here is a funny story that will bring my inquisitive nature to light. One Sunday, our lesson was about Jesus walking on water. It was an intriguing story that caught my attention because Peter also (briefly) walked on water. Here is the text found in Matthew 14:22-33.

[22] And straightway Jesus constrained his disciples to get into a ship, and to go before him unto the other side, while he sent the multitudes away. [23] And when he had sent the multitudes away, he went up into a mountain apart to pray: and when the evening was come, he was there alone. [24] But the ship was now in the midst of the sea, tossed with waves: for the wind was contrary. [25] And in the fourth watch of the night Jesus went unto them, walking on the sea. [26] And when the disciples saw him walking on the sea, they were troubled, saying, It is a spirit; and they cried out for fear. [27] But straightway Jesus spake unto them, saying, Be of good cheer; it is I; be not afraid. [28] And Peter answered him and said, Lord, if it be thou, bid me come unto thee on the water. [29] And he said, Come. And when Peter was come down out of the ship, he walked on the water, to go to Jesus. [30] But when he saw the wind boisterous, he was afraid; and beginning to sink, he cried, saying, Lord, save me. [31] And immediately Jesus stretched forth *his* hand, and caught him, and said unto him, O thou of little faith, wherefore didst thou doubt? [32] And when they were come into the ship, the wind ceased. [33] Then they that were in the ship came and worshipped him, saying, Of a truth thou art the Son of God.

My inquisitive nature got the best of me and my hand kept going up. The more my teacher read, the more I interrupted with my bevy of questions. This walking on water was fascinating to me. I had to ask if it were possible for us to do the same today, to which the teacher responded affirmatively. "All you need is faith, faith like Jesus and Peter and you can walk on water." Why did she tell me that? Of all persons, you don't tell "little Virgil" something like this without expecting a surprise.

Well, I couldn't rest. After Sunday School was over, the worship service began and I fidgeted all through service. I couldn't sit still. My mother who was singing in the choir that day had to give me one of those "Baptist Mother" looks from the choir stand, but that didn't appease my spirit much. My feet kept kicking even though my upper body stayed still. After service, we loaded in the car and headed home. I was bothered and buffeted by this Jesus and Peter walking on water. "All you need is faith, faith like Jesus and Peter and you can walk on water" played over and over in my mind.

When we arrived home, my brother and sisters quickly changed clothes and went outside to play, not me. I looked at that big swimming pool staring at me in our backyard. My first unction was to change clothes but my mind said, "That's not faith." My teacher's statement "All you need is faith, faith like

Jesus and Peter and you can walk on water" kept ringing in my head. I'm sure you know what happened next.

I opened the door, went outside and closed the door behind me. I walked to the edge of the pool. "All you need is faith, faith like Jesus and Peter and you can walk on water." There I was with my black suit, black shoes, black socks, white shirt and black tie standing on the edge of our pool. "All you need is faith, faith like Jesus and Peter and you can walk on water." There were no winds. There were no waves. It was daylight. Certainly, I have an advantage over Peter. I have faith without obstacles. "All you need is faith, faith like Jesus and Peter and you can walk on water." Well, I took a step on the glass-like substance that appeared to ripple from the gentle breeze – and SANK LIKE A BOAT ANCHOR! It was splish, splash! I went down so fast I bumped my head on the bottom of the pool.

Puzzled, I swam to the surface and climbed out. Right now my well pressed suit, is wet, shrinking. My sleeves that were once at my knuckles were now at my elbows. My cuffs that were at the tips of my toes were now at my knees. My tie became a noose. And my shoes were now squeaking and too small. I walked "squeaking" into my room and changed quickly before my mother found out that the suit she had purchased just a month or two earlier was now ruined. I put everything in the dryer and never did tell her what happened to my suit. To this day, my mind is still haunted by the carelessness of my teacher's statement, "All you need is faith, faith like Jesus and Peter and you can walk on water."

Chapter 3

Chapter Three – It's All about Us

Who We Are

To begin this discussion, it is necessary to discuss who we are. According to the first three chapters in Genesis, we are creatures formed by God in His image and likeness. We are the only ones into whom God breathed the breath of life thereby making us living souls. We are the only creatures designed with the capacity to freely choose our behaviors. We are not driven by animalistic instinct. We are free to make choices to even walk on water. Psalm 139 discusses the magnitude of God's investment in the human component of His creation. God purposed us as fearfully and wonderfully made. There is no place we can go to escape His existence for He is ever present. There is no place He is not. He is everywhere at the same time. God is high and low, above and beneath, visible and invisible, within and without. Knowing our place in Him prepares us for having faith in Him, and being obedient to and used by Him for His purpose.

What We Are

God designed us with a specific purpose in mind. God made the man and woman, the male and the female. He designed each of these with a specific role and place to fill. Both the male and the female have a ministry to complete. God was absolute and resolute when He created all things, especially when He formed these two beings. These two were designed to minister in a very specific way. Both of them were expected to love, honor and worship God freely. By their choosing, they would live in harmony with God's plan for their lives. In addition, these two were designed to minister to each other in a very specific way to create community. As a developed community, they were expected to live harmoniously with one another. Again by their choosing, they would live in a connected environment with mutual respect.

What Happened?

God's plan for mankind to live in harmony with Him was destroyed when humanity disobeyed Him and sinned. According to Genesis 3, the man and the woman fell into sin when Adam and Eve ate from the tree God instructed them from which not to eat. They ate the forbidden fruit from the Tree of Knowledge of Good and Evil and subsequently fell. This fall happened when one of them listened to the beguiling serpent which caused a breach in the fellowship with God to which God responded by removing the man and the woman from the precious Garden of Eden. While they were not functioning anymore within the same and original community God established between Him and them, they were still in community with each other. This all changed in Genesis 4 when Cain killed his brother Abel based on petty jealousy. This petty jealousy more than likely was caused by demonic influence. What happened in these two instances created a chasm that heretofore has been the reason healing and deliverance ministry is needed for all mankind.

The Story

The Bible declares that when the man and the woman were placed in the garden, they were innocent, naked and unashamed. They were instructed by God regarding how He expected them to live. All they had to do was follow His statutes and they could have lived harmoniously and eternally without incident. By the deception of the serpent on the woman, she disobeyed God. Not wanting to be alone in this new state, she caused the man to disobey as well. This is our first case of someone sinning and someone else being sinned against. Eve sinned, then she sinned against Adam and both of them sinned against God. What should have happened next could have prevented the catastrophe of Cain and Abel. Had Eve acknowledged that she had sinned, repented and renounced her sin to God and her husband, the story would have taken a different turn. While we may only conjecture the possibilities, what is certain is that Adam and God's fellowship would have remained in tact. Additionally, Eve would not have caused Adam to sin. The resultant demonic influence over them would have been thwarted, or minimized at the very least.

Dr. Leah Coulter in her book *Rediscovering the Power of Repentance and Forgiveness*, shares what happens when a person sins. She says, "When we sin against another or offend someone, we incur a moral debt and that moral debt obligates the offender to the offended.[23] Debt is defined as "something owed to another person such as goods, property, or money. In the Bible, righteous conduct is something one 'owes' to God; hence, in theology, sin is described figuratively as being 'in debt.'"[24] Debt is the "owing money or property of some kind to another person."[25] When we are in debt it means we owe somebody something. When we sin against an individual, we owe a debt to

[23] Leah Coulter, *Rediscovering the Power of Repentance – Finding Healing and Justice for Reconcilable and Irreconcilable Wrongs* (Atlanta: Ampelon Publishing, 2006), 21.

[24] W. A. Elwell and B. J. Beitzel, *Baker Encyclopedia of the Bible* (Grand Rapids: Baker Book House, 1988), 605.

[25] P. J. Achtemeier, *Harper's Bible Dictionary* – 1st ed. (San Francisco: Harper & Row, 1985), 215.

them. In like manner, whenever we sin against God, we owe a debt to Him. The only way to get out of debt is to have that debt paid in full. According to Dr. Coulter, the only way to move beyond this debt is to acknowledge that we sinned, repent for the sin, renounce whatever caused the sin, ask for forgiveness, and submit to the power of God to change our attitude so that we will choose to no longer do whatever we did that led to the sin in the first place.[26] This is referred to as the Choice/Bondage Continuum. Each of us who sins has a choice to make. When we choose to sin and willfully continue to sin, that sin becomes a habit. When we habitually sin, that habit leads to bondage because there is a compulsive behavior associated with that sin. This is an entry point where demonic influence or infestation can take place and lead to obsessive behavior. In this case, one needs deliverance which includes confession of sinful behavior, repentance of sin, renunciation of sin, and restitution of the cost

---

[26] Leah Coulter, *Rediscovering the Power of Repentance – Finding Healing and Justice for Reconcilable and Irreconcilable Wrongs* (Atlanta: Ampelon Publishing, 2006), 65.

of sin. After completing these steps, one is delivered and restored back to liberty and a right relationship with God. One learns to do as James 4:7 suggests, "Resist the devil and he will flee." This process is the same whenever we sin against someone else. There is still a debt incurred and someone has to pay the price. The debt is owed and it needs remuneration. There is another continuum.

When a person sins against another, this is referred to as the Sinned-Against/Bondage Continuum. This means that the sinned-against has no choice in the sin. The sinned against then responds to the trauma in various ways which include coping mechanisms. These coping mechanisms surface as Multiple Personality Disorders, Dissociative Identity Disorders, Schizophrenia, mental illness, and so much more. These psychological illnesses help a person deal with the trauma by burying it within the person's psyche. The sinned against person survives the ordeal because these psychological options are triggered to buffer and buffet the damaged person from further harm. The sinned-against often faces bondage which include holding on to the painful memories of the trauma. This becomes an entry point for demonic influence or infestation which leads to obsessive behavior. The sinned-against at this point needs deliverance which includes being rescued from their painful situation, revoking anger and revenge of the perpetrator, transferring the debt of that sin to God. This brings the sinned against back to liberation and freedom where they are now able to make better choices in their lives.[27] The Bible confirms, "He who the Son sets free is free indeed" (John 8:36). It is God's desire that each of us has free will so we will freely choose to serve and be in fellowship with Him. A bound person can't make the same choices an unbound person can make. Therefore freedom is necessary for our spiritual success.

Returning to Adam and Eve's sin, their debt to God was remunerated when they were removed from the garden. It was

---

[27] Ibid., 123.

sealed by the sacrifice of innocent blood so that their nakedness could be covered with its skin (fur/hide).

A different area of note regarding The Fall is the response of each perpetrator. When God questioned Adam why he sinned, Adam blamed Eve. When God asked Eve why she sinned, she blamed the deceiving serpent. When God questioned the serpent, he had no one to blame. When God asked Cain about Abel, he claimed he had no knowledge of his brother's whereabouts. These persons (and creature) and their response to God and each other address the fundamental issues that identify the need for healing and deliverance. Deception, guilt, shame and blame are all byproducts of Satan's tactics and are indicators of the presence in his pseudo-kingdom. The story of Adam and Eve, Cain and Abel prove that unless one is willing to have a right relationship with God and each other, there is no reason to expect we are going to lead healthy whole lives.

Chapter 4

Chapter Four – Learning about Healing and Deliverance

Healing and the Symptoms

Healing presupposes the existence of illness, sickness or disease. This means that there is something going on in a person's body that causes it not to function as God originally intended the body to function. As a car owner can attest, it doesn't take much to notice that a problem exists. When the car idles too high or too low, runs too hot or too cold, sputters or misfires, it usually means something is terribly wrong. Our bodies are similar. When our blood rate or sugar level is too high or too low, our body temperature is too hot or too cold, or when we sputter or misfire, something is obviously wrong. When our bodies do not function as designed, healing is necessary. John Wimber and Kevin Springer offer some guiding principles to assist us in dealing with healing the whole person. The guiding principles are: "God wants us to heal the sick today; corporate ministry is important; our trust in God is demonstrated by action; we are empowered by the Holy Spirit; loving relationships with our brothers and sisters is important; and God wants to heal the whole person today."[28] One does not get healed unless one is sick. Similarly, one does not get delivered unless one has been influenced or possessed by a demon. (We'll come back to this in a moment.) We are complex creatures. We are socio-pneuma-psycho-somatic creatures. We are social beings designed to live in community. We are spiritual creatures designed to live in communion with God. We are psychological creatures designed to think, feel, react and interact with animate and inanimate objects. We are physiological creatures designed with physical bodies that do tangible things. Whenever we are damaged in any area of our socio-pneuma-psycho-somatic being, we are sick and in need of healing or deliverance.

Charles Kraft offers another opinion to this ministry of healing and deliverance. Kraft says, "It is people, not miracles...that God is concerned about. We are, therefore, to

---

[28] John Wimber and Kevin Springer, *Power Healing* (New York: HarperCollins Publishers, 1987), 170-172.

learn to minister to people, not simply to pray for healing."[29]

True ministry addresses the need of the person. It is a real person who has issues, feelings, emotions, hurts, illness, sickness and disease. The focus should always be on the person.

Deliverance and the Symptoms

Whenever there is a form of illness, there is usually an underlying cause. What has happened is a virus or a strand of bacteria has lodged itself somewhere in the body and has begun attacking the health of the individual. The paralysis, muteness, blindness and other symptoms bespeak an invisible underlying culprit – the virus or bacteria. The only way to remedy this illness is to address that which is attacking the body. This is what healing the whole person aims to do. We aim to get at the root source of the problem. According to John Wimber and Kevin Springer, "Emotional and psychological hurts linger in the form of bad memories (thoughts of hurtful experiences from the past)

---

[29] Charles H. Kraft, Christianity with Power (Ann Arbor: Vine Books, 1989), 134.

and form barriers to personal growth. They may even lead us into various forms of sin, emotional problems and physical illnesses."[30] There is a reason why people are mean, sad, depressed, addicted, aloof, secluded, vulgar, guarded, alone, nervous, jittery, gluttonous, or lost. These are merely symptoms of something else that is going on within. That something is causing the pain that pushes these symptoms to the forefront. Larry Crabb offers a different perspective.

> "God doesn't fix us or pressure us. He does whatever it takes to reveal himself to us…God helps us become more like Christ by doing three things: First, he provides a taste of Christ delighting in us – the essence of connection; Second, he diligently searches within us for the good he has put there – an affirming exposure; and Third, he engagingly exposes what is bad and painful – a disruptive exposure."[31]

For Crabb then, healing happens when we connect the real us with the real God. We are undressed so that we are naked before Him and forced to deal with the ugly reality of our degenerated

---

[30] John Wimber and Kevin Springer, *Power Healing* (New York: HarperCollins Publishers, 1987), 79-80.

[31] Larry Crabb, *Connecting – Healing for Ourselves and Our Relationships* (Nashville: W. Publishing Group, 1997), 10-11.

nature. Peter Scazzerro similarly assesses this way, "In neglecting our intense emotions, we are false to ourselves and lose a wonderful opportunity to know God. We forget that change comes through brutal honesty and vulnerability before God."[32] Being truthful with ourselves is often found to be woefully unattractive. It is when we focus on the image staring back at us in the mirror where we discover the ugly side of our lives and from this ugliness we need real healing and deliverance. We must take inventory and recognize where we are as it relates to God's purpose. If we are in any way found lacking, healing and/or deliverance needs to come find us. Real healing can occur in our lives when we address the root cause of our trouble, and only God can help us with this.

When our symptoms are caused by a sinister agent, we are in a different environment altogether. According to Chris Hayward, "We can live in captivity, be held in bondage to the

---

[32] Peter Scazzero with Warren Bird, *The Emotionally Healthy Church – A Strategy for Discipleship that Actually Changes Lives* (Grand Rapids: Zondervan, 2003), 53.

enemy, and not even realize it."[33] It is therefore a bit more difficult for the individual to recognize the problem or the solution. The ailing person may attribute their condition as mere illness with which they have to live. As it relates to the issue of forgiveness, two biblical accounts bear this out. The man at the pool of Bethesda found in John 5:1-16 and the paralytic assisted by four friends found in Luke 5:17-26. In both stories, the men were paralyzed and had been in that condition for a period of time. When Jesus healed them, He made a reference to sin or forgiveness. To the man at the pool of Bethesda He said (John 5:14), "Behold, thou art made whole: sin no more lest a worse thing come to thee." To the man helped by four He said (Luke 5:20), "Man, thy sins are forgiven thee." Whatever caused their illness, forgiveness released them to wholeness.

While it is possible for a tormented person to be unaware of what caused their condition, sometimes they are aware.

---

[33] Chris Hayward, *God's Cleansing Stream* (Ventura: Regal Books, 2003), 33.

According to Francis McNutt, "The first and most common way we find out that a person needs deliverance is that he tells us. Affected people usually know not only that something is wrong, but that their problem might be caused by evil spirits."[34] Whatever the case whether that causes one to be bound by an evil spirit, deliverance is the solution. One additional note must be added, however. As it relates to those who belong to God, there is no such thing as demonic possession. According to Jack Hayford, "Whatever the dimension of bondage, the redeemed SPIRIT of a believer not only IS not but CANNOT be indwelt by an evil spirit."[35] Whatever is wrong with the individual, God does not lose control of what He owns. Jesus said in John 10:29, "My Father, who has given them to Me is greater than all, and no one is able to snatch them out of the Father's hand." When God possesses us, He protects us. When we sin against Him or one

---

[34] Francis McNutt, *Deliverance from Evil Spirits* (Grand Rapids: Chosen Books, 2009), 80.

[35] Jack W. Hayford, *The Finger of God* (Van Nuys: Living Way Ministries), 10.

another, there is a process that includes repentance and forgiveness that brings us back in a right relationship with God. If our sin is caused by demonic influence, there is still a process of deliverance through forgiveness. Let us review the steps to wholeness.

Chapter 5

Chapter Five – Following the Steps

Step One – Consult God

We cannot hope to discover anything significant outside of the self without first having a relationship with God. As the Creator of all things, God knows everything and everybody. He knows each person before they were formed in their mother's womb and even before the foundation of the world. He knows the number of hairs on each person's head and each name before they were conceived. He knows what's right and He knows what's wrong. There is nothing He does not know about His creation and there is nothing He cannot handle. Since He knows each of us better than we know ourselves, it stands to reason that talking with Him makes good sense. Consulting God not only strengthens our relationship with Him but it also gives insight on what to do. Our lives need to be governed by what God says and desires. The best way to make this happen is by talking to and contemplating on Him. According to Barry and Connolly, "The contemplative core of prayer and all Christian life is conscious relationship with God. The tasks are: First, helping the directee pay attention to God as he reveals himself; second, helping the directee recognize his reactions and decide on his responses to this God."[36] We cannot expect to do any meaningful service for God until we are intimately acquainted with Him and committed to His ways. It is in this form of fellowship that ministry begins.

When we are consistent in consulting God, then whenever one of our fellow brothers or sisters is not well, God can direct our attention to what is wrong. God knows. We cannot help an ailing brother or sister without the input of God. God's input moves past the smoke screens and gets right to the source of the problem. When a person has been sick or demonized because of sin, there are two ways to approach this condition. The first is to simply ask God to heal or deliver them. God does not require a person to believe in Him but He does require that a person accept His healing and deliverance. If the person in need

---

[36] William A. Barry & William J. Connolly, *The Practice of Spiritual Direction* (Minneapolis: HarperCollins Publishers, 1982), 46.

of a miracle of God, the main requirement is that they become willing participants. There will be more on this later.

The second way to approach the condition is by getting the sick or demonized person to reaffirm his/her relationship with God. Francis McNutt drives this point home by stating,

> "A person who seeks healing of any kind should be committed to the Healer, Jesus Christ…It is particularly important that the person you are praying for has made a commitment to Jesus, since he has wandered, directly or indirectly, into Satan's dominion. In order to get out, he needs to voice an explicit agreement to serve God and no one else – to transfer his allegiance to the Kingdom of God."[37]

This is just the beginning of deliverance for there are other components to bring a person to wholeness. According to McNutt, one must also repent of the sin and renounce all activities that led to the sin before one is able to be made whole. When God forgives the sin, one is made whole. Thus, the answer to this problem of sin lies in consulting God as the vessel being used to bring about deliverance and the one needing deliverance.

---

[37] Francis McNutt, *Deliverance from Evil Spirits* (Grand Rapids: Chosen Books, 2009), 217-218.

Step Two – Consult Scripture

God has provided us with a valuable resource tool in His Word. In His Word are stories of individuals who struggle with many of the issues we face today. There is nothing new that the Lord has not already seen or handled. God has breathed upon His Scriptures. God's Word has full authority and power. God's Word is inerrant and infallible. According to 2 Timothy 3:16-17, God's Word is given by inspiration and is "profitable for doctrine, reproof, correction, instruction in righteousness that we may be perfect, thoroughly furnished unto all good works." God's Word is complete enough to instruct us in handling anything and everything we will ever face. God's Word is a two-edged sword that is still a Lamp unto our feet and a Light unto our pathway. If we can become familiar with what His Word says, we will be more able to help an individual who is in need. There will be more on this later.

Step Three – Partnering with the Holy Spirit

When Jesus departed His earthly ministry, He stated that He would ask the Father to send the Comforter to abide with us. This Comforter is also our Advocate. As such, He guides us to all truth. Additionally, He gifts us according to His will and purpose for God's glory and the church's edification. God is glorified and the church is edified whenever His Spirit works in and through His people. The Bible is replete with examples of how the people of God were impacted by those upon whom the Spirit dwelled in order for blessing to flow. The testimony of Enoch was that he walked with God. The testimony of Noah was that he built for God. The testimony of Abraham was that he was faithful to God. The testimony of Jacob was that he was transformed by God. The testimony of Joseph was that he interpreted for God. The testimony of Moses was that he communed with God. The testimony of Joshua was that he functioned in God. The testimony of David was that he prayed to God. Elijah, Daniel, Ezekiel, Isaiah and the other prophets prophesied for God. Whenever the Spirit of God dwells on an individual, blessings will flow. Blessings flow to them and through them.

According to 1 Corinthians 12:1-11, God gifts us with the Word of Wisdom, the Word of Knowledge, Faith, Gifts of Healings, Working of Miracles, Prophecy, Discernment of Spirits, Speaking in Tongues and Interpretation of Tongues. According to Howard Ervin, "The gifts, ministries and workings are all manifestations of the Holy Spirit. They are not proprietary gifting bestowed upon gifted individuals."[38] These are God's gifts for God's purpose. Each of these gifts is for the benefit of the church and God's glory. Being led by the Spirit will allow us to call those things that be not as though they were; to walk by faith and not by sight; to become God-pleasers rather than man-pleasers; and will allow God to use us as His vessels for His purpose.

---

[38] Howard M. Ervin, *Healing – Sign of the Kingdom* (Peabody, Mass: Hendrickson Publishers, Inc., 2002), 27.

Chapter 6

Chapter Six – The Healing and Deliverance Process

The earthly ministry of Jesus featured preaching, teaching, exhorting, healing and delivering. His purpose was to do the works of His Father bringing the faithless to faith, the hopeless to hope, the sick to wholeness and the demonized to deliverance. Jesus is the perfect example for our discussion of the healing and deliverance process. Each time He responded to a person's need, He was moved with compassion. Compassion is best understood as an emotion where one is moved in the inward parts. It is a deep emotion that requires something from within. It is like taking pity on the individual in need and being moved into action.[39] Jesus did not operate out of necessity or out of obligation. He operated out of love and genuine concern for the well-being of the individual.

---

[39] R. L. Thomas, *New American Standard Hebrew-Aramaic and Greek Dictionaries: Updated Edition* (Anaheim: Foundation Publications, Inc., 1998), n. p.

Jesus always led with the message of God. He did not perform any miracle apart from the message. Ervin states, "The sign and the message complement each other. The sign confirms the message. The message authenticates the sign, for no miracle is self-authenticating."[40] A message without a sign loses drawing power. A sign with no message draws people for the wrong reasons. Jesus made sure that those who came to Him for help came for the right reasons. According to Howard Ervin, "the way Jesus healed can be found in three categories: (1) healing miracles that took place in response to Jesus' spoken word; (2) healing miracles that were communicated by a physical touch; and (3) the use of a material substance."[41] Depending on what was going on at the time when Jesus was preparing to heal an individual, one of these methods would be used in tandem with the message He was trying to convey. God's Word must always direct the healing or deliverance process. Kraft adds, "In the

---

[40] Ibid., 2.

[41] Ibid., 34.

encounter itself…whether we seek healing or deliverance – we take the authority we have been given and command the condition to be gone."[42] Jesus was often quoted saying, "I do what I see My Father doing and I say what I hear My Father saying." We must likewise be found faithful in doing and saying what God does and says. This guarantees we will be in His will when the time for ministry, healing and/or deliverance is right.

The Healing Stream

God wants each of us to enter His healing stream. To do so, there are some prerequisites. In order to be used by God, the first thing we need to do is become a part of God's redemptive order. We must be saved. In the third chapter of the Gospel according to John, Nicodemus came to Jesus by night and entered into a meaningful conversation. Nicodemus, a leader in the church, acknowledged that no one could do the things Jesus did unless God was with Him. The response Jesus gave to

---

[42] Charles H. Kraft, *Christianity with Power* (Ann Arbor: Vine Books, 1989), 149.

Nicodemus was that he must be born again. So should we. When a person is born from above, that means the person has acknowledged that they intend to be a part of God's purpose and plan for their personal life. When a person belongs to God, he/she has completed the first step in becoming a part of the healing stream. Let us pray that you become a part of the family of God. Please recite this simple prayer with me:

> *Dear Jesus, I ask You to come into my heart. I ask You to be my Savior and Lord. I ask You to forgive me of all my sins. I am sorry for all of the sins I committed before You. I thank You that You died on the cross for me. I praise God that You rose from the dead to break the hold of sin and death on my life. I know that You are seated at the right hand of the Father in heaven petitioning the Father on my behalf. I accept You as my personal Lord and Savior and will live according to the new life You have established for me. I intend to be baptized according to my confession this day. I need You to help me find a church where I can be baptized and grow in Your will. I thank You now for my salvation. Amen.*

The next step includes the sanctification process. The sanctification process means that the old nature is being purged out and the new nature is being taken on. The Apostle Paul shares in 2 Corinthians 5:17, "If any man be in Christ, he is a new creation. Old things are passed away and behold, all things are become new." This means that the things that used to drive the person (before salvation) in the past, no longer drive them. The things that drive them (after salvation) in the present and future are the things of God. The sanctification process means that a person seeks to satisfy the Spirit and deny the flesh. When a person takes an active role in reducing and removing the desires of the flesh and lifting the desires of the Spirit, they have completed the second step in becoming a part of the healing stream. Please pray with me:

> *Dear Jesus, I thank You for coming into my heart. I thank You for being my Savior and Lord. I thank You for forgiving me of all my sins. I am sorry for all of the sins I committed before You. I renounce every deed and habit that caused me to sin. I renounce every relationship that led me to sin. I renounce every behavior, thought, or activity that You are not pleased with. I renounce every association with every spirit that has bound me to sin. I call that spirit what it is. That spirit is a liar, a thief, a deceiver, a destroyer and an accuser of the faithful. I thank and praise You Jesus that You have the power over Satan and his demonic forces. You have defeated them and by Your power, so will I. I plead the Blood of Jesus to be poured upon me now for covering and protection. It is by Your power and Your grace that I will purge the old*

and embrace the new. This is my confession this day. I
thank You now for my sanctification. Amen.

A word of encouragement is warranted here. Sometimes
no matter how hard we try, we continue to fail God. We
occasionally stumble. Paul referred to this as the "war in his
members" in the seventh chapter of Romans. He said that there
were things he desired not to do that he found himself doing. He
also said that there were some things he desired to do that he
found himself not doing. This will always be an obstacle for
those desiring to flow in God's healing stream. We are born in
sin and from our mother's womb were shaped in iniquity. The
key for us is to keep dying daily and continue striving for the
things of God. If we do this, we will find that we are good
candidates for God's healing stream.

A word of warning is warranted here. The previous
paragraph offers no license to sin. We are not to abide in sin that
grace may abound. We must remember that the Bible says in 1
Corinthians 3:16-17 that "Our body is the temple of God in
which the Spirit of God dwells. If we defile the temple of God,

him God will destroy for the temple of God is holy." It is imperative that we remember that we belong to God and must behave accordingly. The Bible also says in 2 Corinthians 6:16-18,

> [16] And what agreement hath the temple of God with idols? for ye are the temple of the living God; as God hath said, I will dwell in them, and walk in *them*; and I will be their God, and they shall be my people.
> [17] Wherefore come out from among them, and be ye separate, saith the Lord, and touch not the unclean *thing*; and I will receive you, [18] And will be a Father unto you, and ye shall be my sons and daughters, saith the Lord Almighty.

If we truly desire to be a part of God's healing stream, we must be serious. We cannot enter into this ministry lightly without counting the cost. There is a price we will have to be willing to pay to be used by Him. This is not something we can simply turn on and off like a light switch. The seven sons of Sceva found in the book of Acts discovered that healing and deliverance ministry is nothing to be played with. We will discuss them later.

The third step in becoming a part of God's healing stream is to be filled by God's Spirit. There is no substitute. The

Holy Spirit must be a vital part of one's life and active in one's daily walk. Ministry is all around us and God is interested in ministry. Flowing in the Spirit of God allows one to hear God when He speaks and obey God at his command. God uses His healing stream for specific ministry. God ministers through ordinary people like you and me. God uses His vessels for His purpose. Every place where there is need for ministry, healing or deliverance, God usually sends a Word through one of His servants. This manual is designed to prepare you to be such a one if God has gifted and anointed you for this purpose. Completing these three steps will place you in a position to be used in God's healing stream. Please pray with me:

Holy Spirit, I pray that You fill and form me for Your usefulness. I have emptied myself that You may fill me this day. Let Your presence overpower me that I may be filled for Your glory. I want to be used by You for Your purpose. I accept each and every gift Your Spirit offers. I accept the Word of Wisdom. I accept the Word of Knowledge. I accept the Gift of Faith. I accept the Gifts of Healings. I accept the Working of Miracles. I accept the Gift of Prophecy. I accept the Discernment of Spirits. I accept the Gift of Speaking in Tongues. I accept the Gift of Interpretation of Tongues. I am open to Your filling me

with any and all of Your gifts to be used for Your glory. I
accept if You give me one or all of Your gifts. I know that
Your sovereignty will give me what is best for me. I am
aware that whatever gift(s) You give me is to be given
away that I may receive Your gift(s) anew. I thank You
now for filling me with Your Spirit. Amen.

Being a part of God's healing ministry is serious business. Be

thankful if God chooses you.

Chapter 7

Chapter Seven – Learning How to Connect

Larry Crabb addresses how we become effective in healing ministry by using a term called connecting. "Connecting begins when we enter into someone else's battle to experience God with the empathy of a fellow struggler and the faith to know it can happen. So much 'connecting' centers on our problems in the hope that someone can make them go away. True connecting centers on the spirit within us, that awakened capacity to experience God."[43] In order to help the hurting we must connect with them. Connecting establishes some basic rules of engagement. Wimber and Springer offer a systematic yet simple approach in five steps.

> "The first step in the healing prayer is the interview. *The interview answers the question, 'Where does it hurt?'* The second step in the diagnostic procedure is making a diagnostic decision, that is, identifying and clarifying the root of the person's problem. *The diagnostic decision answers the question, 'Why does this person have this condition?'* The third step of the healing procedure is

---

[43] Larry Crabb, *Connecting – Healing for Ourselves and Our Relationships* (Nashville: W. Publishing Group, 1997), 151.

prayer selection. *This step answers the question, 'What kind of prayer is needed to help this person?'* The fourth step of the healing procedure is prayer engagement. *This step answers the question, 'How effective are our prayers?'* The last step in the healing procedure is the post-prayer directions. *The post-prayer directions answer the questions, 'What should this person do to remain healed?' and 'What should this person do if he or she was not healed?'*[44]

The five steps of Wimber and Springer offer a simple strategy so as to not have the healing advocate enter the process presumptively. Kraft adds two steps to the model of Wimber and Springer on the front end of the process. Prior to the interview Kraft endorses, "One must invite the Spirit of God to come, to reveal His will, and to lead the time of ministry…the next step is usually to bless the person with peace. Often at this point the Holy Spirit makes His presence felt."[45] In a word, no glossed over or simplified cookie-cutter approach to healing and deliverance will work. Each person is different and needs to be handled differently in order for healing and deliverance to occur.

_____

[44] John Wimber and Kevin Springer, *Power Healing* (New York: HarperCollins Publishers, 1987), 199-235.

[45] Charles H. Kraft, *Christianity with Power* (Ann Arbor: Vine Books, 1989) 150-151.

When the need arises, the prayer has to be specific. If the Spirit of God leads us to pray for healing, that prayer has to be specific to that which is to be healed. If God leads us to pray for deliverance, then that prayer has to specifically address the area of deliverance. If we are led to pray for the sinned against, we must ask God to hold the abuser accountable for what he/she did to the abused, and for healing to occur and forgiveness to prevail. Healing needs specific prayers done with unwavering faith. No rushed cursory cookie-cutter prayer will do.

It is here that I must insert my traditional Baptist upbringing. Time and time again, I have heard my well-meaning brothers and sisters in Christ offer powerless prayers. They pray for someone's healing or deliverance and then tag the prayer with the phrase "If it be Your will." The Phrase, "If it be Your will" is a fear-based phrase. It is a phrase that guarantees the correctness and rightness of the one praying. Here is how it works. If the person prays for healing or deliverance, on the one hand, and God provides the miracle, it was His will. On the other hand, if the person prays for healing or deliverance and God does not provide the miracle, it was His will. This type of prayer is not a prayer of faith. This type of prayer does not put God's Word to the test. This type of prayer guarantees one thing: that the person praying will always be correct. God expects more from us than that.

At the time of this writing (February 2011), two events come to mind. One has to do with the weather. The other has to do with civil unrest in the Middle East. My Bible Study group at Calvary Baptist Church brought these two issues of concern while we were studying effective and effectual fervent prayer models. Concerning the first issue, the weather patterns were so bad in the Midwest that people were snowed-in and unable to go to work or school. I remember getting reports of between minus 10 and minus 30 degrees Fahrenheit. What makes this significant is that members of our church have friends and family in these parts of the country and they were concerned for the wellbeing of their friends and family. The second issue has to do will an

Egyptian president who had caused so much trouble for his country that the people revolted and wanted him out of office. He stated that he would never step down. The prayer group shared that we needed to pray for Egypt. With these two issues, I reminded the group that we needed to do three things: 1) Be specific in our prayer; 2) Pray as if no one in the world is praying for the same thing; and 3) Pray out loud. With this in mind, we offered our prayers effectively and fervently. For the first time, some prayed audibly and I could feel the presence of the Lord. When we finished, I sent everybody home and told them to go watch the news. It was not more than three days that the Lord answered our prayers. By Sunday the testimonies came flowing in. I was literally accosted while coming into the sanctuary by those exclaiming, "Have you seen the news?" The weather in the mid-west had changed from the minuses to plus 30-40 degrees Fahrenheit. The president of Egypt stepped down from office. In addition, the Swiss bank accounts he had accumulated were frozen by the Swiss who had determined to do the right thing and give the money back to Egypt. God showed us that He is willing to do what we ask Him to do as long as we are willing to do what He asks us to do. I am grateful God put our lesson to the test.

Praying for healing and deliverance is spiritual, therefore patience and being led by the Spirit of God is necessary. Being mindful of moderation (Phil. 4) and being orderly (1 Cor. 14:40) is needed. There is a process for healing prayer.

Chapter 8

Chapter Eight – A Series of Sermons and Lessons On What the Bible Says and What We Should Do

"A God Who Understands," Exodus 2:24-25; 3:14

Read the Word of the Lord – Exodus 2

[1] And there went a man of the house of Levi, and took *to wife* a daughter of Levi. [2] And the woman conceived, and bare a son: and when she saw him that he *was a* goodly *child*, she hid him three months. [3] And when she could not longer hide him, she took for him an ark of bulrushes, and daubed it with slime and with pitch, and put the child therein; and she laid *it* in the flags by the river's brink. [4] And his sister stood afar off, to wit what would be done to him.

[5] And the daughter of Pharaoh came down to wash *herself* at the river; and her maidens walked along by the river's side; and when she saw the ark among the flags, she sent her maid to fetch it. [6] And when she had opened *it*, she saw the child: and, behold, the babe wept. And she had compassion on him, and said, This *is one* of the Hebrews' children. [7] Then said his sister to Pharaoh's daughter, Shall I go and call to thee a nurse of the Hebrew women, that she may nurse the child for thee? [8] And Pharaoh's daughter said to her, Go. And the maid went and called the child's mother. [9] And Pharaoh's daughter said unto her, Take this child away, and nurse it for me, and I will give *thee* thy wages. And the woman took the child, and nursed it. [10] And the child grew, and she brought him unto Pharaoh's daughter, and he became her son. And she called his name Moses: and she said, Because I drew him out of the water.

¹¹ And it came to pass in those days, when Moses was grown, that he went out unto his brethren, and looked on their burdens: and he spied an Egyptian smiting an Hebrew, one of his brethren. ¹² And he looked this way and that way, and when he saw that *there was* no man, he slew the Egyptian, and hid him in the sand. ¹³ And when he went out the second day, behold, two men of the Hebrews strove together: and he said to him that did the wrong, Wherefore smitest thou thy fellow? ¹⁴ And he said, Who made thee a prince and a judge over us? intendest thou to kill me, as thou killedst the Egyptian? And Moses feared, and said, Surely this thing is known. ¹⁵ Now when Pharaoh heard this thing, he sought to slay Moses. But Moses fled from the face of Pharaoh, and dwelt in the land of Midian: and he sat down by a well.

¹⁶ Now the priest of Midian had seven daughters: and they came and drew *water*, and filled the troughs to water their father's flock. ¹⁷ And the shepherds came and drove them away: but Moses stood up and helped them, and watered their flock. ¹⁸ And when they came to Reuel their father, he said, How *is it that* ye are come so soon to day? ¹⁹ And they said, An Egyptian delivered us out of the hand of the shepherds, and also drew *water* enough for us, and watered the flock. ²⁰ And he said unto his daughters, And where *is* he? why *is* it *that* ye have left the man? call him, that he may eat bread. ²¹ And Moses was content to dwell with the man: and he gave Moses Zipporah his daughter. ²² And she bare *him* a son, and he called his name Gershom: for he said, I have been a stranger in a strange land.

²³ And it came to pass in process of time, that the king of Egypt died: and the children of Israel sighed by reason of the bondage, and they cried, and their cry came up unto God by reason of the bondage. ²⁴ And God heard their groaning, and God remembered his covenant with

Abraham, with Isaac, and with Jacob. [25] And God looked upon the children of Israel, and God had respect unto *them*.

Before spending time discussing this passage, I must digress to acknowledge that each of us desires truly in our heart to be accepted. We just want people to like, respect and value us. This leads to at least two frustrations.

We are frustrated when we are not understood.

We are always battling between who we are, and who and what others think we are. Not being understood has to do with people not understanding the way we think, the way we are, or what makes us tick. We call that the battle between character and reputation. Character is who and what we really are. Reputation is who and what people think we are. Character is what we are in private. Reputation is what we are in public. I may have a tattoo, braids or piercings but that doesn't make me a dope fiend, gang banger or metro-sexual. I am who and what I am. Beloved, it hurts when we are not understood. When people are unable to figure us out, it is a frustrating thing. Again, it is frustrating not being understood.

It is also frustrating to be misunderstood.

Not being understood and being misunderstood are similar but different. Not being understood means someone misappropriates how we think. Being misunderstood means someone misappropriates what we have said. Not being understood means someone misapplies our feelings. Being misunderstood means someone misapplies our deeds. Yes, these two are similar but different and I would like to hang out on the "word channel" for a while. Being misunderstood has more to do with our communication. Being misunderstood means there is a disconnection between what was said and what was comprehended.

One of the main problems of communication is when we misunderstand one another. We say one thing but they hear another. It is not so much what we say but what others understand we said. I said all that to say this – it is no fun being misunderstood nor is it any fun not being understood. How can we communicate then? How can we communicate that we are hurting and be sure that we are understood? How can we communicate that we are grieving and be sure that we are understood? How can we communicate that we are depressed and be sure that we are understood? How can we communicate that we are disappointed and be sure that we are understood? How can we communicate that we need help and be sure that someone is listening, that someone cares, that someone is concerned?

Position yourself with me under the shade tree in the hot Egyptian desert just off the Nile River. Grab a seat and get as comfortable as you can in this triple digit weather. It is here that we find the descendants of Abraham, Isaac and Jacob. This is the place where Joseph has moved his family to save them from the famine. This is the place where Joseph, Jacob and Rachel's son, received his prominence and notoriety. This is the place where Joseph, that interpreter of dreams, blessed captors and country.

This is the place where Joseph was given *Carte Blanche* because of the way God used him. Joseph's people multiplied, prospered and grew in this strange land.

At some point both Joseph, Potiphar and the pharaoh passed away. Now there is a new pharaoh who did not know Joseph or his people as did his predecessors and as a result began to misunderstand the people. This new pharaoh misunderstood their religion. He misunderstood their ways, rituals, intentions and God.

As a consequence, pharaoh falls into the familiar trap of seeking to destroy what one does not understand. He enslaves the people and intensifies their burden. He has killed a generation of their male children. He has intensified their labor and their pain to the point that they begin to cry unto the Lord. You will discover that the Scripture says they sighed and cried unto the Lord.

A simple Word Study will suffice. The word used for "sigh" signifies moaning individually. The word used for "cry" signifies weeping collectively. Both words are used in the imperfect tense which means that this moaning and weeping was continuous day in and day out.

They would moan in private and moan in public. They would weep individually and weep collectively. Their condition was so depressing that they could see no way out. Their situation was so down that they could see no way up. Their pain and misery was so severe that all they could do was cry, weep and moan all day. They'd cry, weep and moan when they rose in the morning and they'd cry, weep and moan when they went to bed at night.

In case you're going through a storm and can't see your way, pay close attention. You may not know when your storm will be passing over so that you can say, "Hallelujah." You've been waiting a long time for the Master of the sea to come by and say, "Peace, be still." You may be sick and tired of being sick and tired. You may have waited all the days of your appointed time plus some, seemingly too long and long enough, for your change to come. God's got a Word for you today.

Whatever you're going through, hold on. Whatever you're dealing with, stay tuned.

In case you're not going through a storm, you're going to need this message to prepare you for a storm. It may not be your storm but it may be someone else's storm that will need this lesson. There are churched, unchurched and unsaved people who will face storms in this life and this lesson will make all the difference. If you do not feel the need to learn this lesson for you, learn it for someone else. There are four things we see in this passage.

1. Their cry reached God.

God heard their weeping. God heard their groaning. God heard their moaning. When we cry, it is either out of extreme joy or extreme pain. We are emotional creatures. We are designed to show emotions and to be emotional. We are designed to show happiness when we are happy or sad. The Children of Israel were sad and depressed. God saw their tears and heard their cry. He is Omniscient and there is nothing that escapes Him. He knows everything there is to know. He knows all about it. The Children of Israel wept and groaned. God heard every tear that fell from their faces. There was not one tear that fell to the earth that He did not hear. I am sure to Him it sounded like thunder. It is good to know that our weeping and groaning is not in isolation. God knows and God hears. He is a God who understands.

2. Their condition reached God.

The Scripture says they cried by reason of the bondage they were under. Their condition was bondage. They were enslaved. The Israelites could not get themselves out of that condition. They could not walk away. They could not move away. They could not free themselves. Their condition was continuous and severe. There was no way out for them. There was no way of escape. There was no hope in sight.

It is a fact that there are times we are in conditions where there is no humanly possible way of escape. We become boxed in on all sides. We want to escape but we cannot. There are battered women who want to get out but their abusive mates will not let them. There are prostitutes who want to get out but their pimps will not let them. There are drug addicts who want to get out but their addiction will not let them. There are people who are boxed in financially. They are boxed in emotionally, relationally, physically and mentally. Their condition is hopeless and helpless. That's why the songwriter assessed it correctly.

> *In times like these we need a Savior. In times like these we need an anchor.*
> *Be very sure, be very sure; your anchor holds and grips the Solid Rock.*
> *That Rock is Jesus, He's the One.*

This lesson teaches that their cry and condition reached God.

3. Their covenant reminded God.

The Scripture says when God heard them weep, moan and cry; He remembered His covenant with Abraham, Isaac and Jacob. God remembered His covenant. I will make you a father of many nations. Your descendents will be as the grains of sand on the sea shore. They will be numbered as the stars in the sky. From your seed will all other nations be blessed.

God is one who knows and hears. He is a God who understands. He is a God who remembers. God remembered He told Abraham to leave his father's country. God remembered that Abraham followed His instructions. God remembered telling Abraham that he and Sarah would have a son. God remembered that Abraham and Sarah did eventually have a son called Isaac. God remembered testing Abraham with Isaac. God remembered Abraham was found faithful. God remembered Isaac would marry Rebecca. God remembered that there would be two nations warring in her womb. God remembered that the older would serve the younger. God remembered that Jacob would be the youngest who would carry the promise. God remembered that Jacob was twisted and needed a transformation and a name change. God remembered changing Jacob's ways and changing his name to Israel. God remembers His covenants. I'm so glad we serve a God who remembers.

God is so awesome that He remembers covenants He made with folks we have never met.

Many people have prayed for us years ago. There are slaves and former slaves who have prayed for the success of future generations. Many slaves and former slaves have prayed for the benefit, increase, inalienable rights and freedom of those they have never met. I am encouraged today because we have a God who understands. This lesson teaches that their cry and condition reached God. Their covenant reminded God.

4. Their call remained with God.

God had respect for them. He heard them. He listened to them. He inclined His ear to them. He focused on them. He paid attention to them. As a recipient of Abraham's blessing, I am glad God told Abraham and his descendants what He told them. Because of what He said to Abraham, Isaac and Jacob we are blessed today. Because of what He said to Abraham, Isaac and Jacob we don't have to worry today. Because of what He said to Abraham, Isaac and Jacob we can tap into those promises today. God remembered calling them a mighty nation, a holy and blessed people.

God took someone within and moved him without. The baby Moses was moved out of harm's way and certain death. Pharaoh's daughter raised Moses as her son. Then God took the one who was within but now without. Moses killed an Egyptian and ran to another country to escape punishment, likely the death penalty. God took the one who was within but now without and moved him back in. He sent Moses to Pharaoh and called for their release (See Exodus 3:14). So God took him who was within without and out and in to go back in and come back out. The Great I Am called for their release. The Great Provider called in a provision. The Sustainer of all things made a way of escape. The Bible confirms that the one within who went without, went back in and came back out with they that were in and now were out. (Please forgive the preacher in me. He strikes yet again.)

They that were in "defeated" went out victorious. They that were in "abased" went out lifted. They that were in "bound" went out free. I'm so glad that God took him who was within without and out and in to go back in and come back out with those who were in but now out.

There is another story about the within and the without. There was One who was up who came down. The One who was up went down to dwell within. The One who dwelled within went about. The One who dwelled within had something else within that shined without. The One who was up and went down to dwell within and went about who had something else within that shined without, called some outsiders inside to walk alongside. There were some outsiders who didn't want to come inside and walk alongside who decided to put the One that was up who came down back up. The outsiders who didn't want to come inside beat Him up, strung Him up, nailed Him up and hung Him up. The One who was up and came down was put up and brought back down. That same One who dwelled within went within. He went within and was covered without. He stayed there three long days. But early, One Sunday morning the One above moved that which was without and the One within came without. The One who was within came without with all power in His hands. The One who was within came without with all power in heaven above. The One who was within came without with all power in earth below. That's not how the story ends.

The story continues. The One who was up and came down to dwell within had something else within. The One who was put back up and placed back down by some outsiders didn't want to come inside and walk alongside the One; the same One who went within and came without with all power, went from down back up and is now seated alongside the One who sent Him down in the first place. That same One who dwelled within the One who dwelt within, dwells within the outsiders who came inside to walk alongside. That's why I can agree with the songwriter:

> *There's something within me that holds the reins.*
> *There's something within me that banishes pain.*
> *There's something within me that I can't explain.*
> *All I know is I thank God that there's something within me.*

Why don't you let the One who was up and came down, went down and back up dwell within? He is a God who understands. He hears. He listens. He sees. He knows. He is a burden bearer. He is a Heart-fixer, Mind-regulator, Friend to the friendless, Hope for the hopeless, and Help for the helpless.

"A God Who Heals"
Luke 4:14-22; Matthew 4:23-24; Isaiah 61; 53

It does not take a genius to discover that God desires the best for His children.

God has fundamental provisions.

These refer to the physical. Concerning the physical, He puts food on our tables, clothes on our backs, shoes on our feet, a roof over our head, and activity in our limbs. He grants us the mental capacity to function.

When we are born, we possess the capacity to learn and grow. We learn how to obey, think, read, and understand. When we develop and hit all our milestones, we begin to understand our purpose. Our purpose becomes our means for living. We earn our keep as we function within our purpose. Some of us are preachers, teachers, politicians, doctors, lawyers, electricians, business owners, fire fighters, social workers, and crime fighters. Yes, God desires the best for His children by making fundamental provisions.

God has fellowship provisions.

This refers to the relational. Concerning the relational, He wants us to relate to Him. We relate to Him by reading His Word, talking to Him daily, inviting Him into our presence. We relate to Him best by giving Him preference. God deserves to be first. We relate to Him by giving Him respect. God deserves our reverence and love. We relate to Him by giving Him honor. God desires that we live according to His will.

Not only does God want us to relate to Him but also to each other. We are to live peaceably together. This means I respect you and you respect me; I honor you and you honor me.

When we respect each other, we can harmoniously live together. Yes, God desires the best for His children by making fundamental and fellowship provisions.

He has favorable provisions.

This refers to the spiritual. Concerning the spiritual, when we live according to His will, He gives us favor. People will respond to us in unusual ways because of the favor of God. Joseph had a coat of many colors and David was a man after God's own heart. These are two examples of many that bear the record that God does give favor to individuals. When we have favor, people will give to us and not know why. They will encourage, honor, prefer, bless us and not even know why they are doing it. It does not matter what they know, what matters is what God knows.

If we live according to God's Word, standards, way, will, and direction, we will be blessed. The songwriter and psalmist's words will ring true:

We're blessed in the city, blessed in the fields;

Blessed when we come and when we go;
We'll cast down every stronghold; sickness and poverty
must cease;
The devil is defeated, we are blessed.
Yes, God desires the best for His children by making

fundamental, fellowship and favorable provisions. The Epistle of

3 John 2:2 says, "Beloved, I wish above all things that thou

mayest prosper and be in health, even as thy soul prospereth." If

this passage is true, how is it that sickness and disease come

upon us?

If we refer back to the creation story, we will discover

that God made good things. The effervescent illuminators that

ellipse their way around that shiny solar center piece were good.

That invisible element that provides life to the visible was good.

The wet and the dry land including all that is within, without and

upon were good. Everything God made, He called good. He did

not wait for somebody else's opinion. He called it good Himself.

The original question still persists, how does sickness and

disease come upon us?

The following few paragraphs can be found in the first three chapters of Genesis. I apologize in advance if the word-smithy phraseology seems out of place. I am what I am. Please indulge and forgive the preacher in me.

If the Creator creates the created and calls the created good, that means everything the Creator created is good. Since the Creator created the created and called the created good, the Creator also created another creature and called that creature very good. Since the Creator created that other creature and called it very good, all that other creature was supposed to do was live a certain way – in obedience to the will of God.

The Creator created a place for that creature to live comfortably. If the creature living within creation lived according to the Creator's command, that creature's comfort would not be limited but always good. It was the Creator's plan all along for the creature to live comfortably within creation only knowing good. Here comes the answer to the question.

The creature created by the Creator whom He called very good chose a path diametrically opposed to the plan. The created was captivated by a conundrum caused by the calamity in his consciousness thus choosing another way that challenged the Creator's commandment and created a chasm in the cosmos. By choosing another way sickness, disease and death became our reality. The original plan of living eternally in direct fellowship with the Father surrounded by all good was transmuted to living temporally in distant fellowship with the Father surrounded by good and bad. The taintless became tainted when the taintless made the tainted choice. So here we are living with sickness, disease and death all around us. I hear other questions forming: How do we rid ourselves of the result of sin? Rephrased: How do we rid ourselves of sickness, disease and death? Luke 4 which borrows from Isaiah 61 shares how the Reconciler and Redeemer remedies.

- **The Reconciler**

The sin caused by man separated man from God. Since humanity could not find his way back to divinity, Divinity had to make His way to humanity. The Word was made flesh and dwelled among us. God was in Christ reconciling the world unto Himself. Jesus Christ is the Reconciler. He is the only Bridge over our troubled waters. He has the only Name given among men whereby all must be saved. He is the only Name under the heavens that causes knees to bow and tongues to confess. Luke 4 which borrows from Isaiah 61 shares how the Reconciler and Redeemer remedies.

- **The Redeemer**

Redemption would come through Jesus' work on the cross. Jesus was born to die that we might live. The Redeemer's death would pay the ransom for all the sin of the world. The Redeemer's death and burial would take with it that which causes sickness, disease and death. The Redeemer's death, burial and resurrection would grant power over sin, sickness, disease and death. Luke 4 which borrows from Isaiah 61 shares how the Reconciler and Redeemer remedies.

- **The Remedy**

The remedy is realized by reading what is written concerning the Reconciler and Redeemer. The writer wrote about the remedy that comes only through the Royal Reconciler and Redeemer. Luke 4 which borrows from Isaiah 61 shares the remedy that comes through the Reconciler and Redeemer's willingness to commit Himself to the words on the page. As we review Luke 4 (a New Testament passage) and Isaiah 61 (an Old Testament passage) we discover that what was Jesus Christ concealed (O.T.) becomes Jesus Christ revealed (N.T.). In so doing, there are three discoveries we find in the remedy.

1. The remedy is Scriptural.

Luke 4:14-17 says,

> "And Jesus returned in the power of the Spirit into Galilee: and there went out a fame of him through all the region round about. [15] And he taught in their synagogues, being glorified of all. [16] And he came to Nazareth, where he had been brought up: and, as his custom was, he went

115

into the synagogue on the Sabbath day, and stood up for to read. [17] And there was delivered unto him the book of the prophet Esaias. And when he had opened the book, he found the place where it was written."

Jesus reads from Isaiah 61. Jesus knows that in order to get beyond sin, sickness, disease and death requires understanding Scripture. Beloved, if we truly desire to get beyond the troubles of this world, we must find time to read the Word of God. God's Word is a Lamp unto our feet and a Light to our pathway. God's Word ought to be hidden in our hearts that we might not sin against Him. Proverbs 3:5-6 says, "Trust in the Lord with all your heart, lean not to your own understanding; in all your ways acknowledge Him and He shall direct your path." 2 Chronicles 7:14 says, "If My people who are called by My Name would humble themselves and pray, and seek My face and turn from their wicked ways; then will I hear from heaven and will forgive their sin and heal their land." Isaiah 40:31 says, "But they that wait upon the Lord shall renew their strength. They shall mount up with wings as eagles; they shall run and not be weary; they shall walk and not faint." Yes, all the answers to life's problems are found in Scripture and we would do well to read it. Reading the Word of God is important but there is more. We are admonished by James to be not hearers only but also doers of the Word. Our remedy is Scriptural.

2. The remedy is Spiritual.

Luke 4:18a says, "The Spirit of the Lord *is* upon me." It is important to note that all remedies come from God. Remedies begin and end with God's Spirit. There is no solution to sin, sickness, disease and death without God's Spirit. God's Spirit must be upon the vessel God is going use for His purpose. God's Spirit cannot be purchased, coerced, coaxed, concocted, or counterfeited. God's Spirit must fall afresh upon His vessel. The Spirit of God must be real in the life of His vessel. A story in Acts tells what happens whenever we fake, front and floss.

Acts 19:13-20

> "Then certain of the vagabond Jews, exorcists, took upon them to call over them which had evil spirits the name of the Lord Jesus, saying, We adjure you by Jesus whom Paul preacheth. [14] And there were seven sons of *one* Sceva, a Jew, *and* chief of the priests, which did so. [15]

117

And the evil spirit answered and said, Jesus I know, and Paul I know; but who are ye? [16] And the man in whom the evil spirit was leaped on them, and overcame them, and prevailed against them, so that they fled out of that house naked and wounded. [17] And this was known to all the Jews and Greeks also dwelling at Ephesus; and fear fell on them all, and the name of the Lord Jesus was magnified. [18] And many that believed came, and confessed, and shewed their deeds. [19] Many of them also which used curious arts brought their books together, and burned them before all *men*: and they counted the price of them, and found *it* fifty thousand *pieces* of silver. [20] So mightily grew the word of God and prevailed."

Whenever we fake, front and floss, we are in dangerous territory.

It is not good to go into the devil's territory unarmed. We will quickly become trapped and the devil will take advantage of us. The story above remind us that this is spiritual warfare and it is not to be played with. Spiritual warfare requires being covered by the Blood of Jesus and moving in the anointing and power of God. Jesus had that anointing whenever He ministered.

Jesus understood His readiness to minister. He said, "The Spirit of the Lord is upon Me," which means that Jesus was ready to remedy. That the Spirit of the Lord was upon Him allowed Jesus to do God's work. The remedy of God was to bring His Kingdom to earth through righteous living so that the

world may know what a true witness looks and acts like. The

whole covenant with Abraham was to secure a peculiar people

who would live according to God's standard. The failure of

Abraham and the victory of Jesus prove that the remedy is both

spiritual and scriptural.

3. The remedy is systematic.

Luke 4:18-21 says,

> "The Spirit of the Lord *is* upon me because he hath
> anointed me to preach the gospel to the poor; he hath sent
> me to heal the brokenhearted, to preach deliverance to the
> captives, and recovering of sight to the blind, to set at
> liberty them that are bruised, [19] To preach the acceptable
> year of the Lord. [20] And he closed the book, and he gave
> *it* again to the minister, and sat down. And the eyes of all
> them that were in the synagogue were fastened on him. [21]
> And he began to say unto them, This day is this scripture
> fulfilled in your ears."

God's Spirit anointed Jesus to preach the Gospel, heal the broken

hearted, set the captives free, give sight to the blind, and minister

to the bruised. God's remedy begins with the preached Word.

The preached Word systematically sets the stage for the healed

heart, the liberated soul, the return of vision and ministry to the hurting. The preached Word helps and heals. The systematic remedy acknowledges a God who heals and delivers. There are particular attributes to God's healing of which we ought to be aware.

God's healing includes cleansing.

The Bible is clear that God does cleanse. Naaman, Miriam and the ten lepers are all witnesses that God's healing includes cleansing. Naaman was cleansed from leprosy when he dipped in the Jordan River seven times. Miriam was cleansed from leprosy after she repented to the Lord and Moses interceded on her behalf. Jesus cleansed the ten lepers after they begged for His mercy. God's healing includes cleansing.

God's healing includes wholeness.

The Bible is clear that God does make one whole. Sarah, Rachel, Hannah and the woman with the issue of blood are just a few witnesses that God's healing includes making someone whole. Sarah (Abraham's wife), Rachel (Jacob's wife), and Hannah (Samuel's mother) each were made whole from their barrenness after each of them prayed to God. The woman with the issue of blood was made whole when she touched the hem of Jesus' garment. God's healing includes wholeness.

God's healing includes restoration.

The Bible is clear that God does restore. The original intent for the body was to function for our benefit. Eyes were made to see, ears were made to hear, the mouth was made to speak, the mind was made to think, legs were made to walk, and so forth. Jesus restored functionality to hand of the man with the withered hand. Jesus straightened out the woman who was bent over. Jesus caused the blind to see, the lame to walk, the dumb to speak, the deaf to hear. God's healing includes restoration.

God's healing includes deliverance.

The Bible is clear that God does deliver. Jesus delivered the Syro-Phoenecian woman's daughter from demon possession. Jesus delivered the paralytic boy who fell into fire and foamed at the mouth from demon possession. Jesus delivered the man living in the tombs with a Legion of demonic spirits from demon possession. God's healing includes deliverance.

God's healing includes raising the dead.

The Bible is clear that God does raise the dead. Elijah raised the son of the widow woman of Zarephath from the dead. Jesus raised the son of the widow woman of Nain from the dead. Jesus raised Jairus' daughter from the dead. Jesus raised Lazarus from the Dead. God raised Jesus from the dead. All I'm trying to say is God's healing includes cleansing, wholeness, restoration, deliverance and raising the dead.

That's why **Matthew 4:23-24** is so significant.

> "And Jesus went about all Galilee, teaching in their synagogues, and preaching the gospel of the kingdom, and healing all manner of sickness and all manner of disease among the people. [24] And his fame went throughout all Syria: and they brought unto him all sick people that were taken with divers diseases and torments, and those which were possessed with devils, and those which were lunatick, and those that had the palsy; and he healed them."

Jesus said to His disciples, "Greater things than these you shall do in My name." The work of Jesus and the Passion of the cross is the foundation upon which the healing of God rests.

Isaiah 53:1-6

> "Who hath believed our report ? and to whom is the arm of the LORD revealed? [2] For he shall grow up before him as a tender plant, and as a root out of a dry ground: he hath no form nor comeliness; and when we shall see him, *there is* no beauty that we should desire him. [3] He is despised and rejected of men; a man of sorrows, and acquainted with grief: and we hid as it were *our* faces from him; he was despised, and we esteemed him not. [4] Surely he hath borne our griefs, and carried our sorrows: yet we did esteem him stricken, smitten of God, and afflicted. [5] But he *was* wounded for our transgressions, *he was* bruised for our iniquities: the chastisement of our peace *was* upon him; and with his stripes we are healed. [6] All we like sheep have gone astray; we have turned every one to his own way; and the LORD hath laid on him the iniquity of us all."

The work, death, resurrection and ascension of Jesus all set the stage for healing and deliverance ministry. After Jesus was raised from the dead, He gave the Great Commission.

Mark 16:15-18 says:

"Go ye into all the world, and preach the gospel to every creature. [16] He that believeth and is baptized shall be saved; but he that believeth not shall be damned. [17] And these signs shall follow them that believe; In my name shall they cast out devils; they shall speak with new tongues; [18] They shall take up serpents; and if they drink any deadly thing, it shall not hurt them; they shall lay hands on the sick, and they shall recover."

The Great Commission is a call to serve. Serving includes preaching, teaching, baptizing, healing and delivering. It is true then that if we desire to serve God that our decision includes serving a God who heals and delivers. We live in the twenty-first century. Some are of the opinion that God does not heal or deliver today. I am not sure where they get their theology from because the Word of God is clear. The plan of God was as clear then as it is now. The service of God affects the then and now. What God said then is what God says now. If God healed then, God heals now. If God delivered then, God delivers now. If God cleansed then, God cleanses now. If God made whole then, God makes whole now. God heals the insider and the outsider; the Jew and the Gentile; the dark skinned and the light skinned;

the straight hair and the corn row; the rich and the poor; the big and the small; the Republican and the Democrat; the college graduate and the high school drop-out. God is capable of healing and delivering us all.

The primary rule of engagement for any healing environment to occur is based on two precepts: God gets the glory and the Church gets edified. If either of these is missing healing and deliverance will probably not be on the agenda. The secondary rule of engagement is linked to the primary. This means we can have the primary without the secondary but we cannot have the secondary without the primary.

The secondary rule of engagement for any healing environment to occur is based on two concepts: There must be faith and there should be testimony of the saints. Somebody in the process has to have faith. Hebrews 11:1 and 6 says, "Now faith is the substance of things hoped for and the evidence of things not seen...Without faith it is impossible to please God." Either the one who needs the healing has to have faith or the one

125

who is praying (as God's vessel) has to have faith. Faith is the key that unlocks the door to healing and deliverance. Once miracles occur, somebody has to tell somebody else about the miracle. If no one tells what happened then people will not know what happened. If no one knows what happened, God does not get the glory nor does the church get edified. If no one tells about how God healed or delivered them, then the unbelievers and the unchurched will not know the power of God. They will see a form of godliness without the power of God. The healing/deliverance environment is available as long as the primary and secondary rules of engagement are met.

A final note on how God performs His miracles. There are times God performs His miracles by touch. There are times God performs His miracles by spoken word. There are times God performs His miracles by prayer. There are times God performs His miracles by command. Whichever way He does it, God expects the vessel to follow Him. God says what He says and do what He does. Not all healing and deliverance ministry will result in people fainting. Not too long ago, I remember a Spirit-filled person told me he was going to pray for me. I had confidence in him because he was truly a vessel God used for His glory. He had signs and wonders following him day by day. I do know why he wanted to pray for me. It was because he wanted to give me what he had which was the anointing of God. Before he prayed, he told me two things would happen. First, he said that I would feel some heat. Secondly, he said that I would faint under the anointing. When he prayed, I felt neither heat nor the inclination to faint. After several moments of uncomfortable petitions, he stopped. We discussed in private why I felt no heat or an inclination to faint. Later we discovered that it was neither he nor I at fault. The reality was that God will not hold Himself to cookie-cutter environments. He is always doing great things and He often does it in unique and fresh ways. We would do well to stay unique and fresh with Him.

There is just another parenthetical point to ponder before moving on. We must be aware that there are certain conditions that must be met before healing can occur. Many a servant has prayed effectual fervent prayers over the sick to no avail and often wondered why the dismal result. Among the reasons many are not healed are these: there is either unrepentant sin, or sins they do not want to give up. When we pray for God to perform a miracle on someone else's behalf, we must make sure they are willing to participate in everything God reveals to us concerning their condition. Failing to get a commitment that one's healing may require a change in behavior may just be the reason no miracle has occurred. While the sovereignty of God can overrule and override any situation, it is always best to get commitments when and where God calls for them. The best protection for this is to listen to what God is saying and to watch what God is doing, then follow what we see Him doing and hear Him saying. This makes us true disciples of God. Whatever instructions God gave to His disciples, He gives to us.

James 5:13-16 says,

"Is any among you afflicted? let him pray. Is any merry? let him sing psalms. [14] Is any sick among you? let him call for the elders of the church; and let them pray over him, anointing him with oil in the name of the Lord: [15] And the prayer of faith shall save the sick, and the Lord shall raise him up; and if he have committed sins, they shall be forgiven him. [16] Confess *your* faults one to another, and pray one for another, that ye may be healed. The effectual fervent prayer of a righteous man availeth much."

The Inquisitive Child Strikes Again

I shared earlier about how inquisitive I was as a child. At age eight or ten I took my teacher at her word, "All you need is faith, faith like Jesus and Peter and you can walk on water" and sank in the family pool. Now I am nineteen or twenty and am new in the ministry. I remember as vividly now as if it were yesterday a lesson from John 11. Here is the lesson where Jesus raised Lazarus from the dead. I heard the Lord tell me that He was going to use me to do wonderful works. He said, "I'm going to gift you to do great things. In My Name, you will pray over the sick and they shall recover. In My name, you will cast out demons. In My name, you will raise the dead." God should have known better than to tell someone like me something like this. I am a firm believer in the Word of God. I always have been. From an early age, I have believed every word in the Holy Bible.

Well, I had to go prove God's words. I got in my car and drove over to a local mortuary. One of our members had recently died, so I had an excuse to go. I went to the parlor where she lay. There were a few familiar faces that I greeted. I prayed silently at the casket, comforted the family and left. I was on a mission for the Lord. I stepped over to another room where there was a regal-looking woman. She was probably in her sixties or seventies and looked as if she was a deaconess, pastor's wife or a mother's board member. She had a tinge of gray in her hair and appeared stately. I was haunted by the Father. God said, "I'm going to gift you to do great things. In My Name, you will pray over the sick and they shall recover. In My name, you will cast out demons. In My name, you will raise the dead." There I was standing near a recently deceased stately woman. I was looking at her but she wasn't looking at me. I was thinking about her but she wasn't thinking about me. God's words loomed in my mind. As I drew closer to the casket, I kept hearing, "I'm going to gift you to do great things. In My Name, you will pray over the sick and they shall recover. In My name, you will cast out demons. In My name, you will raise the dead." I was now perched against the casket and nervously, I took my left hand and placed it on that stately woman's forehead and began to pray. "In the name of Jesus get up! I loose you from the bonds of death. I command you by the blood of Jesus to come forth!" I prayed until my sweat was like drops of blood. She never moved. I expected her to sit up but she just lay there. Now her hair was askew. Unfortunately I was so moved in the "spirit" that I shifted her wig. I moved it back in place and quickly made my exit.

As I got in my car and drove away, I remember pondering why God would tell me such a thing if He had no intention of making it come to pass? I pondered what I saw as a child, the angel of death. I pondered God's own statement, "I'm going to gift you to do great things. In My Name, you will pray over the sick and they shall recover. In My name, you will cast out demons. In My name, you will raise the dead." I knew one day all of this would come together. I never once doubted God at His Word. Whatever He was going to do had to come at His timing.

"A God Who Delivers," Exodus 6:6-8
Read the Word of the Lord – Exodus 6

¹ Then the LORD said unto Moses, Now shalt thou see what I will do to Pharaoh: for with a strong hand shall he let them go, and with a strong hand shall he drive them out of his land. ² And God spake unto Moses, and said unto him, I *am* the LORD: ³ And I appeared unto Abraham, unto Isaac, and unto Jacob, by *the name of* God Almighty, but by my name JEHOVAH was I not known to them. ⁴ And I have also established my covenant with them, to give them the land of Canaan, the land of their pilgrimage, wherein they were strangers. ⁵ And I have also heard the groaning of the children of Israel, whom the Egyptians keep in bondage; and I have remembered my covenant. ⁶ Wherefore say unto the children of Israel, I *am* the LORD, and I will bring you out from under the burdens of the Egyptians, and I will rid you out of their bondage, and I will redeem you with a stretched out arm, and with great judgments: ⁷ And I will take you to me for a people, and I will be to you a God: and ye shall know that I *am* the LORD your God, which bringeth you out from under the burdens of the Egyptians. ⁸ And I will bring you in unto the land, concerning the which I did swear to give it to Abraham, to Isaac, and to Jacob; and I will give it you for an

heritage: I *am* the LORD. ⁹ And Moses spake so unto the children of Israel: but they hearkened not unto Moses for anguish of spirit, and for cruel bondage.

¹⁰ And the LORD spake unto Moses, saying, ¹¹ Go in, speak unto Pharaoh king of Egypt, that he let the children of Israel go out of his land. ¹² And Moses spake before the LORD, saying, Behold, the children of Israel have not hearkened unto me; how then shall Pharaoh hear me, who *am* of uncircumcised lips? ¹³ And the LORD spake unto Moses and unto Aaron, and gave them a charge unto the children of Israel, and unto Pharaoh king of Egypt, to bring the children of Israel out of the land of Egypt.

¹⁴ These *be* the heads of their fathers' houses: The sons of Reuben the firstborn of Israel; Hanoch, and Pallu, Hezron, and Carmi: these *be* the families of Reuben. ¹⁵ And the sons of Simeon; Jemuel, and Jamin, and Ohad, and Jachin, and Zohar, and Shaul the son of a Canaanitish woman: these *are* the families of Simeon. ¹⁶ And these *are* the names of the sons of Levi according to their generations; Gershon, and Kohath, and Merari: and the years of the life of Levi *were* an hundred thirty and seven years. ¹⁷ The sons of Gershon; Libni, and Shimi, according to their families. ¹⁸ And the sons of Kohath; Amram, and Izhar, and Hebron, and Uzziel: and the years of the life of Kohath *were* an hundred thirty and three years. ¹⁹ And the sons of Merari; Mahali and Mushi: these *are* the families of Levi according to their generations. ²⁰ And Amram took him Jochebed his father's sister to wife; and she bare him Aaron and Moses: and the years of the life of Amram *were* an hundred and thirty and seven years. ²¹ And the sons of Izhar; Korah, and Nepheg, and Zichri. ²² And the sons of Uzziel; Mishael, and Elzaphan, and Zithri. ²³ And Aaron took him Elisheba, daughter of Amminadab, sister of

Naashon, to wife; and she bare him Nadab, and Abihu, Eleazar, and Ithamar. [24] And the sons of Korah; Assir, and Elkanah, and Abiasaph: these *are* the families of the Korhites. [25] And Eleazar Aaron's son took him *one* of the daughters of Putiel to wife; and she bare him Phinehas: these *are* the heads of the fathers of the Levites according to their families. [26] These *are* that Aaron and Moses, to whom the LORD said, Bring out the children of Israel from the land of Egypt according to their armies. [27] These *are* they which spake to Pharaoh king of Egypt, to bring out the children of Israel from Egypt: these *are* that Moses and Aaron. [28] And it came to pass on the day *when* the LORD spake unto Moses in the land of Egypt, [29] That the LORD spake unto Moses, saying, I *am* the LORD: speak thou unto Pharaoh king of Egypt all that I say unto thee. [30] And Moses said before the LORD, Behold, I *am* of uncircumcised lips, and how shall Pharaoh hearken unto me?

It is quite obvious to me that anyone who has spent at least a day in bondage needs to get out. They need to be free. They need to be freed. They need their freedom. If they are not freed immediately, they will develop a mentality that they cannot or will not ever be free. They will begin to think that they deserve to be where they are. They will begin to think that there is no hope for them and that there is no help on the way. If you are reading this book and know someone who is bound by someone or something, be encouraged because there is a God who delivers.

Sail with me down the Mediterranean Sea. We will land on the shores of the Egypt.

Remove your deck shoes and lace up your sandals. We will perch ourselves in Goshen and peek over the fence at the people who need to know about a God who delivers. We already know that the Israelites are in bondage and are in need of someone outside of themselves to come and deliver them. God finds Moses on the backside of Midian and sends him back to Egypt to give them His message. God's message is broken into three parts.

God makes a prophetic pronouncement.

When God shared what He knew of their past, He told them something about Himself and something about themselves.

- ***God addressed His ancestral appearance.***

He said, "I appeared to Abraham, Isaac and Jacob." In other words, He revealed Himself to them. God name-dropped some familiar people that the people might identify with Him.

- ***He addressed their ancestral acquaintance.***

He said, "When I appeared to them, I was known by the name of God Almighty." I was known as El Shaddai. They knew me as the God of Power. They understood My Omnipotence. My power moved Abraham out of his comfort zone. My power reached into Sarah's barren womb.

My power tested Abraham's trust in Me. My power set a ram in the bush. My power set two warring nations in Rebecca's womb. My power set the youngest over the eldest. My power straightens out the crooked, smoothes out the rough, lifts up the down, and brings down the exalted. My power changes names. When I appeared before your ancestors, they knew me as the God of Power. I was not known as Jehovah or Yahweh as you will know Me.

In our passage, God uses the phrase: "I am the Lord" three times. He says it in verse 6, verse 7 and in verse 8. In the entire sixth chapter, He says it in verse 2 and verse 29. In fact, "Lord" is used 13 times in this chapter.

The study continues. Please take notice that their names – past and present – are mentioned in this chapter. What this means is this: God knows them by name and they are going to know Him by name. I was not known by My name, "Yahweh." Your ancestors knew Me by My attribute. They knew Me by what I do. It was good for them to know Me by what I do because that's all I revealed to them. You will know Me by My name because that's what I will reveal to you. They knew Me powerfully, you will know Me personally. My name is Yahweh. Yahweh means Existing One. Stay with me.

As we read, we get a glimpse in Exodus 3:14 as God calls Himself "I AM." In other words, I AM the Existing One. That means I am one who always exists. Before existence began existing, I exist. In other words, I always AM. There is never a

137

time when I was not. In the beginning, I AM. From the beginning, I AM. Through the ages I AM. God made a prophetic pronouncement by addressing His ancestral appearance and their ancestral acquaintance.

God mentions a prophetic promise.

I established a covenant with your ancestors. I set in motion a binding agreement between Me and them. What I promised them, I intend to finish. I intend to complete what I started. I intend on fulfilling My plans for them. God is not a man that He should lie. If He said He will do it, He will do it. God made Abraham the Father of the Faithful, the Father of Many Nations.

God told Abraham, Isaac and Jacob that He would give them the Land of Canaan – a land overflowing with milk and honey. Their descendants would be numbered as the stars in the sky and the sand on the sea shore. God said, "I remember a past promise I made with your ancestors and I will keep it." What God promised Abraham, Isaac and Jacob, He was going to give to Moses and the Children of Israel.

When one thinks about what God said to Moses, one must remember this: God's past promise preempts one's present predicament. Stay with me. If you're in a bad situation, God has you covered. If you're in a bad relationship, God has you covered. If you're in a bad shape, God has you covered. If your money is funny and your change is strange, God has you covered. If your body is wrecked with pain, God has you covered. Don't worry about your job, your home, your food or your needs because God's past promise preempts your present predicament. The Bible says, "I once was young but now I'm old, I have never seen the righteous forsaken nor its seed begging bread." It says, "But my God shall supply all my need according to His riches in glory." It says, "Greater is He that's within me than he that's in the world." It infers, "If God be for me, He's more than the world against me." No one can steal my blessing or my joy. No matter what I'm going through, all I need to remember is: God's past promise preempts my present predicament.

God makes a prophetic proclamation.

We already know that the Children of Israel were weeping, moaning, groaning and crying. They were moaning, groaning and crying privately, by themselves. They were moaning, groaning and crying publicly, as a group. We already know that their moaning, groaning and crying was continuous and consistent. We already know that God heard them and responded. Their situation was so desperate that they could not see their way out. They needed someone outside of themselves to come deliver them. If you are bound and can't wiggle yourself free, you need to understand that there is a God who delivers. If someone or something has you tied down, take notice of God's prophetic proclamation. In our text, God makes six declarations. God says, I will release, remove, redeem, reclaim, remind and reward you.

1. I will release you.

I will bring you out from under the burdens of the Egyptians. I will release you from your current condition.

2. I will remove you.

I will take you out of their bondage. I will remove you from your cold captivity.

3. I will redeem you.

I will come and get you Myself and judge those who bothered you. I will redeem you and cause calamity for your captors.

4. I will reclaim you.

I will bring you to me to be my people and be to you your God. I will reclaim you as covenant constituents.

5. I will remind you.

You will know that I brought you out of your predicament. I will remind you of your Courageous Comforting Creator.

6. I will reward you.

I will take you to the land I promised to your forefathers. I will reward you with Canaan's completeness.

God's prophetic proclamation included their release, removal, redemption, reclamation, reminder and reward.

What happens next is probably the most frustrating part of the story. It says that they hearkened not unto Moses. There are two reasons for their hard hearts. Their anguish and their bondage were too great. They were down for so long and so hard that they could not receive an encouraging word. Their condition was so bad that they could not understand the Word of the Lord. Their situation was so futile and complete that they could not process the prophetic proclamation. Saints, there are some people out there that are so indoctrinated with bad news that they cannot process good news. They have fallen and cannot get up. Their heads have been down so long that they do not even know how to lift their heads up again.

I am certain that there is at least one unchurched or unsaved person who needs this message today. If you don't have a right relationship with God or a church, stay tuned. Jesus lived, taught, preached, performed miracles, was crucified, died, was buried, and rose again for you. If you don't know Jesus as your Lord and Savior, I have just one testimony for you. Before I testify, you do know that the story did not end with their heads down in disbelief? God did deliver them. God caused Pharaoh to let His people go and the Children of Israel did eventually get to the land God promised them. They reached the Land of Canaan – a land overflowing with milk and honey. Whether you want to believe it or not, God has a Land of Canaan for you. He wants you to reach a land overflowing with milk and honey. He wants to deliver you from poverty to plenty, from drought to drench, from nothing to something, from less to more, from down to up. If you want your deliverance, listen to this testimony.

"In Times Like These"

(Verse 1)
In times like these you need a Savior.
In times like these you need an Anchor.
(Verse 2)
In times like these you need the Bible.
In times like these oh be not idle.
(Chorus)
Be very sure (2x) your anchor holds and grips the Solid Rock.

This Rock is Jesus! Yes, He's the One.
This Rock is Jesus! The Only One.
Be very sure (2x) your anchor holds and grips the Solid
Rock.

(Verse 3)
In times like these I have a Savior.
In times like these I have an Anchor.
I'm very sure (2x) my anchor holds and grips the Solid
Rock.

This Rock is Jesus! Yes, He's the One.
This Rock is Jesus! The Only One.
I'm very sure (2x) my anchor holds and grips the Solid
Rock.

"The Healing and Deliverance Agenda,"
Ex. 17:1-7; Num. 20:1-13; John 10:1-18; Acts 19:13-20

One of the more important things we will recognize in healing and deliverance prayer ministry is the fact that people will be faced with illness, sickness, disease and demonization. There are reasons for this. There are three main reasons why humanity needs the Finger of God.

Bad Background

People come from various backgrounds. Their family lineage may have engaged in the occult, witchcraft or any number of things. While we can pick our friends, we cannot pick our family. Whatever house we are born in comes with either blessings or baggage. If this is you, do not lose heart because God can help you overcome your issues with a bad background.

Bad Behavior

A second area that affects people is bad behavior. It is true that while some are born into houses where any number of issues may reside, at some point the individual has to take ownership of their own behavior. Addictions, unforgiveness, living in sin all speak to the area where we may have behavior problems. If this is you, do not lose heart because God can help you overcome your issues with bad behavior.

Bad Beliefs

A third area that affects people is bad beliefs. A person who is a hypochondriac, engages in pagan worship, is superstitious or is full of phobias is a prime candidate for being tricked by the enemy. The postmodern philosophy of relativism pushes this subject to its limit by suggesting that there is no absolute truth. While I do address this subject in another area of this book, I will make at least one statement here. Truth has no association with relativism. There is nothing relative about truth. There is only One line of Truth and the Holy Spirit guides us to all Truth. If this is you, do not lose heart because God can help you overcome your issues with bad beliefs.

Because of problems in people's background, behavior or beliefs, healing and deliverance ministry becomes necessary. People need to be made whole and God wants to make them whole. All He needs is a willing vessel that is Spirit-formed and Spirit-filled so that His Spirit can flow. God aims to flow His miraculous touch to those in need. To do this ministry there are six things we need to know.

The Who

God is always the Who. He is always the One performing the miracles.

The What

The what is always the miracle. Healing and deliverance are just two aspects of the miraculous power of God.

The When

The when is something we may never fully and completely know. Every miracle depends on God's timing. God will do whatever He wants to *when* He wants to because He's Sovereign.

The Where

The where is someplace we may never fully and completely know. Every miracle depends on God's sovereignty. God will do whatever He wants to *where* He wants to because He's Sovereign.

The Why

The why is something we always know. God loves us. God cares for us. God has compassion on us.

The How

The how is something we may never fully and completely know. Every miracle depends on God's sovereignty. God will do whatever He wants to *how* He wants to because He's Sovereign.

This six-point information guideline provides the data needed to move forward in the healing, deliverance and prayer ministry. God's sovereignty makes it impossible to assume a cookie-cutter approach. The lesson Moses learned about God bringing water from rocks prove that a willing and obedient vessel is all God is looking for to do what He aims to do.

Read the Word of the Lord – Exodus 17:1-7

> And all the congregation of the children of Israel journeyed from the wilderness of Sin, after their journeys, according to the commandment of the LORD, and pitched in Rephidim: and *there was* no water for the people to drink. [2] Wherefore the people did chide with Moses, and said, Give us water that we may drink. And Moses said unto them, Why chide ye with me? wherefore do ye tempt the LORD? [3] And the people thirsted there for water; and the people murmured against Moses, and said, Wherefore *is* this *that* thou hast brought us up out of Egypt, to kill us and our children and our cattle with thirst? [4] And Moses cried unto the LORD, saying, What shall I do unto this people? they be almost ready to stone me. [5] And the LORD said unto Moses, Go on before the people, and take with thee of the elders of Israel; and thy

rod, wherewith thou smotest the river, take in thine hand, and go. ⁶ Behold, I will stand before thee there upon the rock in Horeb; and thou shalt smite the rock, and there shall come water out of it, that the people may drink. And Moses did so in the sight of the elders of Israel. ⁷ And he called the name of the place Massah, and Meribah, because of the chiding of the children of Israel, and because they tempted the LORD, saying, Is the LORD among us, or not?

Read the Word of the Lord – Numbers 20:1-13

Then came the children of Israel, *even* the whole congregation, into the desert of Zin in the first month: and the people abode in Kadesh; and Miriam died there, and was buried there. ² And there was no water for the congregation: and they gathered themselves together against Moses and against Aaron. ³ And the people chode with Moses, and spake, saying, Would God that we had died when our brethren died before the LORD! ⁴ And why have ye brought up the congregation of the LORD into this wilderness, that we and our cattle should die there? ⁵ And wherefore have ye made us to come up out of Egypt, to bring us in unto this evil place? it *is* no place of seed, or of figs, or of vines, or of pomegranates; neither *is* there any water to drink. ⁶ And Moses and Aaron went from the presence of the assembly unto the door of the tabernacle of the congregation, and they fell upon their faces: and the glory of the LORD appeared unto them. ⁷ And the LORD spake unto Moses, saying, ⁸ Take the rod, and gather thou the assembly together, thou, and Aaron thy brother, and speak ye unto the rock before their eyes; and it shall give forth his water, and thou shalt bring forth to them water out of the rock: so thou shalt give the congregation and their beasts drink. ⁹ And Moses took the rod from before the LORD, as he commanded him. [10] And Moses and Aaron gathered the congregation together before the rock, and he said unto them, Hear now, ye rebels; must we fetch you water out of this rock? [11] And Moses lifted up his hand, and with his rod he smote the rock twice: and the water came out abundantly, and the congregation drank, and their beasts *also*. [12] And the LORD spake unto Moses and Aaron, Because ye believed me not, to sanctify me in the eyes of the children of Israel, therefore ye shall not bring this congregation into the land which I have given them. [13] This *is* the water of Meribah; because the children of Israel strove with the LORD, and he was sanctified in them.

Let us review the texts.

In these two texts, Moses was chided by the Children of Israel for lack of water in the desert. He went to God to see how God intended to handle their request. God answered their request two different ways. In the first passage (Exodus 17), God instructed Moses to smite the rock (verse 6). In the second passage (Numbers 20), God instructed Moses to speak to the rock (verse 8). In both stories, God sent water but God was not pleased in both cases. When Moses followed God's instructions in the Exodus passage and smote the rock as God commanded him, God was pleased, sent the miracle and gave them water. In

150

the second passage, Moses did not please God. He was instructed to speak to the rock but in his anger, smote the rock twice (verse 11). Theologians vary here why God gave the miracle. The best answer we can suggest here is that sometimes God will honor a disobedient request in public and punish the offender in private. We must be reminded of the sovereignty of God who desires to do things His way, not ours. If we are going to do healing and deliverance prayer ministry and look for signs and wonders, we must allow God to do things His way. His way does not offer a cookie-cutter mentality. He does not do the same thing the same way. The lesson on leprosy (Chapter 9) verifies this. If we would just listen to God and let Him speak and lead, we will find more success than failure. As we are led, there are three main questions that we must ask ourselves before we do anything.

- What is God doing or saying?
- What am I doing in response to what God is doing or saying?

- How can I cooperate (or co-operate) with what God is doing or saying?

If we don't answer these questions, we have no right to advance. Each of these questions must be followed in succession. We must get an answer from the first question before moving to the second, and from the second before moving to the third. We cannot skip steps and expect a miracle. God has His own way and perfect timing. We must follow His flow by listening to His voice. Effective ministers of healing and deliverance must listen to God.

Read the Word of the Lord – John 10:1-18 concerning the Good Shepherd and the Door

Verily, verily, I say unto you, He that entereth not by the door into the sheepfold, but climbeth up some other way, the same is a thief and a robber. [2] But he that entereth in by the door is the shepherd of the sheep. [3] To him the porter openeth; and the sheep hear his voice: and he calleth his own sheep by name, and leadeth them out. [4] And when he putteth forth his own sheep, he goeth before them, and the sheep follow him: for they know his voice. [5] And a stranger will they not follow, but will flee from him: for they know not the voice of strangers. [6] This parable spake Jesus unto them: but they understood not what things they were which he spake unto them.

[7] Then said Jesus unto them again, Verily, verily, I say unto you, I am the door of the sheep. [8] All that ever came before me are thieves and robbers: but the sheep did not hear them. [9] I am the door: by me if any man enter in, he shall be saved, and shall go in and out, and find pasture. [10] The thief cometh not, but for to steal, and to kill, and to destroy: I am come that they might have life, and that they might have *it* more abundantly. [11] I am the good shepherd: the good shepherd giveth his life for the sheep. [12] But he that is an hireling, and not the shepherd, whose own the sheep are not, seeth the wolf coming, and leaveth the sheep, and fleeth: and the wolf catcheth them, and scattereth the sheep. [13] The hireling fleeth, because he is an hireling, and careth not for the sheep. [14] I am the good shepherd, and know my *sheep*, and am known of mine. [15] As the Father knoweth me, even so know I the Father: and I lay down my life for the sheep. [16] And other sheep I have, which are not of this fold: them also I must bring, and they shall hear my voice; and there shall be one fold, *and* one shepherd. [17] Therefore doth my Father love me, because I lay down my life, that I might take it again. [18] No man taketh it from me, but I lay it down of myself. I have power to lay it down, and I have power to take it again. This commandment have I received of my Father.

As God's sheep, we are expected to listen to His voice. To do good ministry, we are expected to follow God's voice because He knows what He's doing, where He is going to do it, how He's going to do it and when He is going to do it. God always knows where He is going. It is we that don't know where we are going.

This is why it is so important to listen to God. He is both the Good Shepherd and the Door.

Read the Word of the Lord in Acts 19 concerning the Seven Sons of Sceva

[13] Then certain of the vagabond Jews, exorcists, took upon them to call over them which had evil spirits the name of the Lord Jesus, saying, We adjure you by Jesus whom Paul preacheth. [14] And there were seven sons of *one* Sceva, a Jew, *and* chief of the priests, which did so. [15] And the evil spirit answered and said, Jesus I know, and Paul I know; but who are ye? [16] And the man in whom the evil spirit was leaped on them, and overcame them, and prevailed against them, so that they fled out of that house naked and wounded. [17] And this was known to all the Jews and Greeks also dwelling at Ephesus; and fear fell on them all, and the name of the Lord Jesus was magnified. [18] And many that believed came, and confessed, and shewed their deeds. [19] Many of them also which used curious arts brought their books together, and burned them before all *men*: and they counted the price of them, and found *it* fifty thousand *pieces* of silver. [20] So mightily grew the word of God and prevailed.

Healing and deliverance prayer ministry is no play thing. It is serious business. If you have no intention of listening to God, you are better off staying out of the game. What happened to these seven sons proved once and for all that God's voice and God's agenda are the only driving forces that will make this ministry effective.

"Healing and Deliverance Explained,"
Matthew 4:23-25; Mark 1:32-39; Luke 6:17-19; 7:19-23

One of the more intriguing subjects in our church experience seems to be that of healing and deliverance.

The discussion of healing and deliverance is based on a presupposition.

Healing presupposes illness, sickness or disease. Healing is a way of dealing with illness, sickness or disease. One has to have been sick before one can receive healing. Deliverance presupposes demonic influence or oppression. Deliverance is a way of dealing with demonic influence or oppression. One has to have been affected by demons before one can receive deliverance. The discussion of healing and deliverance is based on a presupposition.

The discussion of healing and deliverance leads to postulation.

Whenever healing and deliverance are discussed, they often come with a bunch of questions like these: Is healing and deliverance ministry of God? Is healing and deliverance real? If healing and deliverance are real, why doesn't every church offer ministries in these two areas? Is healing and deliverance for me? How do I know if I need healing or deliverance? What is healing and deliverance? The discussion of healing and deliverance leads to postulation.

The discussion of healing and deliverance leads to prognostication.

Cessation theorists and dispensation gurus say that miracles are no more. They contend that miracles ceased when the church was born. For them, miracles were necessary when the church was being formed and established but are not available now. They contend that miracles, healing and deliverance were necessary to get the people to believe and have faith in the first century or two to help get the church off the ground but they are inappropriate and unnecessary for today. The discussion of healing and deliverance leads to prognostication.

The discussion of healing and deliverance leads to propagation.

Propagators suggest that healing and deliverance ministries are a sham. They suggest that healing and deliverance ministries use a bunch of smoke and mirrors, and hocus pocus. They imply that all healing and deliverance ministers do is bring healthy people into different cities, put on an act for the people, and then take their money. They say, "Show me a faith healer and I'll show you a con artist." One of the more intriguing subjects in our church experience seems to be that of healing and deliverance. The discussion of healing and deliverance leads to presupposition, postulation, prognostication and propagation.

Here is an obvious question. If healing and deliverance ministries today are shams, how do we account for the miracles that are happening today? There are too many eyewitness accounts and personal testimonies from reliable resources that prove without a doubt that something supernatural is going on. One can only presuppose, postulate, prognosticate and propagate so long. Sooner or later sickness, disease or demonic influence is going to reach your doorstep and you are going to need some help. When sickness, disease and demonic influence are happening to someone else, we can discount it all we want. We can say "liar, liar, pants on fire" and laugh others to scorn. But nobody's laughing when sickness, disease and demonic influence begin to knock on our door. Nobody's laughing when the door creaks open and these three come in and take a seat. Nobody's laughing when our Lazy Boy Lounge Chair is being used by an uninvited guest. Our best option is not to postulate, prognosticate and propagate but to understand what is really going on.

We have enemies we cannot see. These are the invisible troublemakers whose effects are visible. They can make robust shrink down to nothing. They can make the articulate unable to speak. They can make the marathon runner unable to take a single step. They can make the sane insane. We have enemies we cannot see whose job is to reduce us to dust. This is the Palestine that Jesus finds when He begins His ministry.

1. The Acknowledgment

There were all sorts of problems. The fall of man created a whole set of problems. Man's sin caused a separation between himself and God. Man's sin passed to Satan the keys to earth. Because of man's sin, trouble became our daily companion. Sickness, disease, jealousy, finger-pointing, backbiting, backstabbing, lying, cheating, drinking, fornicating, stealing, killing, destroying, mistreating, misusing, abusing, using, losing, choosing, cursing, degrading, demanding, hating, laziness, slothfulness, excuse-making, habit-forming, lust, wearing too little, showing too much, looking too much, talking too much, sleeping too much, begging too much, poverty, homelessness, hunger, demon possession, demonic influence, demonization are all because of man's sin. Jesus made an acknowledgment. Sickness, disease and demonic influence were all over the land. Jesus understood the invisible as well as the visible. He saw the visible corruption of power, prestige and people. He saw the invisible corruption of other forces at work. Jesus did acknowledge what was going on.

2. The Authority

There is something we need to know about authority. Whenever someone is in authority it means he/she is in control. We don't answer to things, things answer to us. Jesus took authority and command over everything within His reach. This is why sickness, disease, demonic influence and oppression responded to His voice. Jesus did teach and preach but He also healed and delivered. Jesus validated the first real healing and deliverance ministry of the New Testament. I would be remiss if I didn't tell you that there were pseudo-faith healers in Jesus' day. There were those who claimed to have the power. They used magic, divination, soothsaying, charms and other tools to "help" the oppressed. This so called help was nothing more than switching demons around. Someone would lose their cough but pick up a limp. They would lose their limp but pick up the shakes. These so called healers were big business. They would go from town to town claiming to heal and exorcise but they were all in cahoots with the devil. They could get rid of one thing but they would also leave you with something else that would bring you back to them. The healing was not real healing – just temporary relief. The "plop-plop, fizz-fizz; oh, what a relief it is" was just a temporary thing.

Jesus came into the strong man's house and bound him up. Jesus came into Satan's backyard and ruined the barbeque. This puts to rest the argument of fakes in the present because there were fakes in Jesus' day as well. Jesus had a real healing and deliverance ministry. Jesus took authority over illness, sickness and disease. He healed the sick by speaking to the sickness. By speaking to it, He would command sickness to leave and it would leave. Jesus took authority over demonic influence and oppression. He delivered the oppressed by speaking to the demons. By speaking to the demon/demons, He would command them to leave and they would leave. Jesus maintained authority.

3. The Answer

No matter how bad things got, there is always an answer. No matter the problem, there is always an answer. The ways of God are higher than the ways of man. His thoughts are higher than man's thoughts. No matter the test, God has the Answer. The Answer left glory and came to earth. The Answer became flesh and dwelt among us. The Answer came to preach, teach, heal and deliver. There is something you need to know about the answer. Whenever people have a problem, they will seek the answer. Scriptural review:

Matthew 4:23-25

> "And Jesus went about all Galilee, teaching in their synagogues, and preaching the gospel of the kingdom, and healing all manner of sickness and all manner of disease among the people. [24] And his fame went throughout all Syria: and they brought unto him all sick people that were taken with divers diseases and torments, and those which were possessed with devils, and those which were lunatick, and those that had the palsy; and he healed them. [25] And there followed him great multitudes

of people from Galilee, and *from* Decapolis, and *from* Jerusalem, and *from* Judaea, and *from* beyond Jordan."

In other words, Jesus is the Answer and wise men still seek Jesus. Let us keep reviewing.

Mark 1:32-39

"And at even, when the sun did set, they brought unto him all that were diseased, and them that were possessed with devils. [33] And all the city was gathered together at the door. [34] And he healed many that were sick of divers diseases, and cast out many devils; and suffered not the devils to speak, because they knew him. [35] And in the morning, rising up a great while before day, he went out, and departed into a solitary place, and there prayed. [36] And Simon and they that were with him followed after him. [37] And when they had found him, they said unto him, All *men* seek for thee. [38] And he said unto them, Let us go into the next towns, that I may preach there also: for therefore came I forth. [39] And he preached in their synagogues throughout all Galilee, and cast out devils."

In other words, Jesus is the Answer and wise men still seek Jesus. Keep reviewing.

Luke 6:17-19

"And he came down with them, and stood in the plain, and the company of his disciples, and a great multitude of people out of all Judaea and Jerusalem, and from the sea coast of Tyre and Sidon, which came to hear him, and to be healed of their diseases; [18] And they that were vexed with unclean spirits: and they were healed. [19] And the whole multitude sought to touch him: for there went virtue out of him, and healed *them* all."

In other words, Jesus is the Answer and wise men still seek Jesus. Keep reviewing.

Luke 7:19-23

> "And John calling *unto him* two of his disciples sent *them* to Jesus, saying, Art thou he that should come? or look we for another? [20] When the men were come unto him, they said, John Baptist hath sent us unto thee, saying, Art thou he that should come? or look we for another? [21] And in that same hour he cured many of *their* infirmities and plagues, and of evil spirits; and unto many *that were* blind he gave sight. [22] Then Jesus answering said unto them, Go your way, and tell John what things ye have seen and heard; how that the blind see, the lame walk, the lepers are cleansed, the deaf hear, the dead are raised, to the poor the gospel is preached. [23] And blessed is *he*, whosoever shall not be offended in me."

Stated again for the effect, Jesus is the Answer and wise men still seek Jesus. Jesus is the Answer to all of our problems, issues, sickness, and diseases. Jesus is the Answer to all of Satan's traps. He answered Satan's lie with the Truth. He answered Satan's calamity with peace. He answered Satan's charges with silence. He answered Satan's slap with the other cheek. He answered Satan's crucifixion with acceptance. He answered Satan's nails with His hands. He answered Satan's spikes with His feet. He answered Satan's spear with His water and blood. He answered Satan's tool of death with resurrection.

Jesus is the Answer to all of Satan's tricks and all of Satan's

traps. For this reason there is power in the name of Jesus.

Mark 16:15-20
> "And he said unto them, Go ye into all the world, and preach the gospel to every creature. [16] He that believeth and is baptized shall be saved; but he that believeth not shall be damned. [17] And these signs shall follow them that believe; In my name shall they cast out devils; they shall speak with new tongues; [18] They shall take up serpents; and if they drink any deadly thing, it shall not hurt them; they shall lay hands on the sick, and they shall recover. [19] So then after the Lord had spoken unto them, he was received up into heaven, and sat on the right hand of God. [20] And they went forth, and preached every where, the Lord working with *them*, and confirming the word with signs following. Amen."

"The Healing and Deliverance Environment,"
Mark 3:1-6; Luke 4:31-37*; 13:10-17; Acts 3

One of the things we may never truly understand is why

people come to church.

Some come for the Word.

The Word refers to the Word of God. We receive the ministry of the Word through teaching, preaching, speaking and Bible discussion. The ministry of the Word includes biblical instruction.

Ephesians 4:11-16 says:

> [11] And he gave some, apostles; and some, prophets; and some, evangelists; and some, pastors and teachers; [12] For the perfecting of the saints, for the work of the ministry, for the edifying of the body of Christ: [13] Till we all come in the unity of the faith, and of the knowledge of the Son of God, unto a perfect man, unto the measure of the stature of the fulness of Christ: [14] That we *henceforth* be no more children, tossed to and fro, and carried about with every wind of doctrine, by the sleight of men, *and* cunning craftiness, whereby they lie in wait to deceive; [15] But speaking the truth in love, may grow up into him in all things, which is the head, *even* Christ: [16] From whom the whole body fitly joined together and compacted by that which every joint supplieth, according to the effectual working in the measure of every part, maketh increase of the body unto the edifying of itself in love.

It is a good thing that some people come to church for the Word of God.

Some come for the worship.

There is worship of God. Worship includes singing to God, praising God, and thanking God. There are those who also shout and dance in their praise. There are those who lift up holy hands. There are those who clap their hands. There are those who wave their hands. There are those who weep, cry and moan.

Psalm 34:1-3 says:
"I will bless the LORD at all times: his praise *shall* continually *be* in my mouth. [2] My soul shall make her boast in the LORD: the humble shall hear *thereof,* and be glad. [3] O magnify the LORD with me, and let us exalt his name together."

Psalms 100 says:
"Make a joyful noise unto the LORD, all ye lands. [2] Serve the LORD with gladness: come before his presence with singing. [3] Know ye that the LORD he *is* God: *it is* he *that* hath made us, and not we ourselves; *we are* his people, and the sheep of his pasture. [4] Enter into his gates with thanksgiving, *and* into his courts with praise: be thankful unto him, *and* bless his name. [5] For the LORD *is* good; his mercy *is* everlasting; and his truth *endureth* to all generations."

Psalms 150 says:
"Praise ye the LORD. Praise God in his sanctuary: praise him in the firmament of his power. [2] Praise him for his mighty acts: praise him according to his excellent greatness. [3] Praise him with the sound of the trumpet: praise him with the psaltery and harp. [4] Praise him with the timbrel and dance: praise him with stringed instruments and organs. [5] Praise him upon the loud cymbals: praise him upon the high sounding cymbals. [6]

Let every thing that hath breath praise the LORD. Praise
ye the LORD."
We tell Him:

> *Because of who You are I give You glory.*
> *Because of who You are I give You praise.*
> *Because of who You I will lift Your name and say;*
> *Lord I worship because of who you are.*

It is a good thing that some people come to church for the

Worship of God.

Some come for the witness.

There is witnessing to and witnessing for God. When we

witness to God we usually do that in prayer. Prayer is often done

in private. It means we are acknowledging Him for who He is.

When we pray we encourage others to come, worship, bow

down and kneel before the LORD our maker. When we witness

for God it usually means we testify about Him. Testimony is

usually done in public. When we testify, we tell others what God

has done. We tell them how He did what He did when He did

what He did and where He did what He did to us and for us. We

tell them how we felt before He did what He did and how we felt after He did what He did. That's why our testimony agrees with the songwriter's testimony:

> *I was sinking deep in sin far from the peaceful shore;*
> *Very deeply stained within, sinking to rise no more;*
> *But the Master of the sea heard my despairing cry;*
> *From the water lifted me, now safe am I.*

Another testified

> *I came to Jesus just as I was – weary, worn and sad.*
> *I found in Him a resting place and He has made me glad.*

It is good to hear the testimony of the saints. It is by the testimony of the saints that we are able to taste and see that the Lord is good. It is a good thing that some people come to church for the Word, worship and witness of God.

It is a sad fact that some people come to church for the wrong.

They come offering nothing but their smug scrutiny. They come for posts, positions, pedistalization and presidentialism. They come to see just enough, hear just enough, and read just enough so they can go back and discount, discredit and disrespect those with whom they should be working to build the Kingdom of God. These are they who have ears but do not hear. They have eyes but do not see. They have hearts that do not feel. They have hands that do not help. Yes, while there are those who come for the Word, worship and witness, there are others who come for the wrong.

In our lesson today, we find three stories that claim our attention. I'm going to feature the two that are the most similar.

Read the Word of the Lord – Mark 3:1-6

"And he entered again into the synagogue; and there was a man there which had a withered hand. [2] And they watched him, whether he would heal him on the sabbath day; that they might accuse him. [3] And he saith unto the man which had the withered hand, Stand forth. [4] And he saith unto them, Is it lawful to do good on the sabbath days, or to do evil? to save life, or to kill? But they held their peace. [5] And when he had looked round about on them with anger, being grieved for the hardness of their hearts, he saith unto the man, Stretch forth thine hand. And he stretched *it* out: and his hand was restored whole as the other. [6] And the Pharisees went forth, and straightway took counsel with the Herodians against him, how they might destroy him."

Read the Word of the Lord – Luke 13:10-17

"And he was teaching in one of the synagogues on the sabbath. [11] And, behold, there was a woman which had a spirit of infirmity eighteen years, and was bowed together, and could in no wise lift up *herself.* [12] And when Jesus saw her, he called *her to him*, and said unto her, Woman, thou art loosed from thine infirmity. [13] And he laid *his* hands on her: and immediately she was made straight, and glorified God. [14] And the ruler of the synagogue answered with indignation, because that Jesus had healed on the sabbath day, and said unto the people, There are six days in which men ought to work: in them therefore come and be healed, and not on the sabbath day. [15] The Lord then answered him, and said, *Thou* hypocrite, doth not each one of you on the sabbath loose his ox or *his* ass from the stall, and lead *him* away to watering? [16] And ought not this woman, being a daughter of Abraham, whom Satan hath bound, lo, these eighteen years, be loosed from this bond on the sabbath day? [17] And when he had said these things, all his adversaries were ashamed: and all the people rejoiced for all the glorious things that were done by him."

Read the Word of the Lord – Acts 3:1-11

"Now Peter and John went up together into the temple at the hour of prayer, *being* the ninth *hour.* [2] And a certain man lame from his mother's womb was carried, whom they laid daily at the gate of the temple which is called Beautiful, to ask alms of them that entered into the temple; [3] Who seeing Peter and John about to go into the temple asked an alms. [4] And Peter, fastening his eyes upon him with John, said, Look on us. [5] And he gave heed unto them, expecting to receive something of them. [6] Then Peter said, Silver and gold have I none; but such as I have give I thee: In the name of Jesus Christ of Nazareth rise up and walk. [7] And he took him by the right hand, and lifted *him* up: and immediately his feet and ankle bones received strength. [8] And he leaping up stood, and walked, and entered with them into the temple, walking, and leaping, and praising God. [9] And all the people saw him walking and praising God: [10] And they knew that it was he which sat for alms at the Beautiful gate of the temple: and they were filled with wonder and amazement at that which had happened unto him. [11] And as the lame man which was healed held Peter and John, all the people ran together unto them in the porch that is called Solomon's, greatly wondering."

The passages in Mark, Luke and Acts pull and tug at us. All three stories tell about miracles that were performed on church property. Mark 3 and Luke 13 present a telling account about church and the people in church. Acts 3 presents a telling account about the church and the people outside the church. These three stories are similar but different. Mark and Luke mention that Jesus enters the synagogue on the Sabbath Day. Acts mentions that Peter and John were on their way to the temple to pray. Mark and Luke mention that Jesus saw someone in church who had a need. Acts mentions that Peter and John saw someone on the outside of the church in need. Mark and Luke mention that Jesus did something about the need in while in the church. Acts mentions that Peter and John did something about the need outside the church. Mark and Luke mention that the Jewish leaders had a problem with what Jesus did inside the church. Acts mentions that the Jewish leaders had a problem with what Peter and John did outside the church.

Let me explain what was going on. There were three types of people who came to church – the hurting, the helper and the harassers. The hurting are those with a problem. The helpers are those with a solution. The harassers are those who hinder the helpers. The hurting are those who are broken. The helpers are those with the fix. The harassers are those who frustrate the fixers.

The hurting are those who are reduced. The helpers are those who redeem. The harassers are those who restrict the redeemers. The stories are similar but different.

- **There is the description.**

Mark mentions a man; Luke mentions a woman. Acts mentions a man. It is not likely that the men and the woman

173

belonged to the same church although it is a possibility. The men and the woman have a particular condition. One man had a withered hand. The other man was lame and could not walk. The woman was bowed completely forward. One man could stand up straight. The other man could not stand at all. The woman could not stand up straight. Both men may have been born in the condition they were in but the woman was not born in the condition she was in. There was no time table but the men probably had their condition since birth whereas the woman had her condition for eighteen years. The men may never have known what it felt like to have a completely healthy life whereas the woman would have known. The men had a health issue whereas the woman had a demon issue. The men needed healing but the woman needed deliverance. All three stories are similar but different.

- **There is the disposition.**

We can surmise that the man and the woman (in Mark and Luke) came to church with the right purpose and for the right reason. We can surmise that the man who came to the church gates came for the right reason. He came for help. If there is any place where the needy ought to come for help, it ought to be the church. It would have been easy for either of them to stay home. Think about it. Each time either of them would come to church they would have to deal with people who would rather look at their frailty than their face. Each time they would come they would have to deal with being shunned rather than embraced. I am sure they heard more whispering than worship. I'm sure they experienced more pointing than praise. It would have been easy to stay home. Think about it for a moment. At home we do not have to worry about people laughing at us. At home we do not have to worry about people talking, joking, making fun of or pitying us. I am certain it would have been easier to stay home but each of them came to church. The fact that they were there had to be because they had the right disposition. Each of them I'm sure felt this sentiment:

I'm pressing on the upward way. New heights I'm gaining every day.

Still praying as I onward bound, Lord plant my feet on higher ground.

Lord, lift me up and I shall stand by faith on heaven's table land.

I higher plane than I have found Lord, plant my feet on higher ground.

The three stories are similar but different. There is the

description and the disposition.

- **There is the divine.**

Beloved, whenever you come to church for the right

reason and purpose, you will meet God more than you will miss

God. I submit today that no matter how rough life gets, your best

place to be is in the church or around the church. The road might

be rough, the going might be tough and the hills hard to climb. I

started out a long time ago and there is no doubt in my mind.

I've decided to make Jesus my choice. I know that God doe so't

only heal in the church but I declare the church house is a good

place to get your healing. The church is known as the House of

Prayer. The church is the House of God. It is a good thing to get

oneself in the church and hang around the church. There is

another story about the church and Sabbath day that does not

quite fit.

**Read the Word of the Lord – Luke 4:31-37 (This story
doesn't quite fit.)**

"And came down to Capernaum, a city of Galilee, and
taught them on the Sabbath days. [32] And they were
astonished at his doctrine: for his word was with power.
[33] And in the synagogue there was a man, which had a
spirit of an unclean devil, and cried out with a loud voice,
[34] Saying, Let *us* alone; what have we to do with thee,
thou Jesus of Nazareth? art thou come to destroy us? I
know thee who thou art; the Holy One of God. [35] And
Jesus rebuked him, saying, Hold thy peace, and come out
of him. And when the devil had thrown him in the midst,
he came out of him, and hurt him not. [36] And they were
all amazed, and spake among themselves, saying, What a
word *is* this! for with authority and power he
commandeth the unclean spirits, and they come out. [37]
And the fame of him went out into every place of the
country round about."

As I explore this lesson, I am personally omitting Luke 4:31-37

because the events go in a direction that does not fit this lesson. I

will say that in Luke 4, there was a man in church with a need –

he had an unclean spirit. Jesus did come to church that day – and

He met the man's need and cast out the demon. The crowd was

amazed at what happened. This is all the similarity this story has with the other three. We will pick this story up however at another time.

Praying to God for His Power Provides Enablement

There are some presuppositions to the healing and deliverance environment. The healing and deliverance environment includes the Power of God. The power of God is ushered in by prayer. When we pray we ask for God's enablement. We already know that prayer changes things. Prayer changes environments, hearts, and conditions. There is no power like prayer power. We've heard it said over and over: "No prayer, no power. Little prayer, little power. Much prayer, much power." There is no other power like the power of God. If we want to function in healing and deliverance ministry, we have to be enabled. There will be no real healing or deliverance without the power of God.

Praising God for His Presence Prepares the Environment

Not only is prayer important, but we also must offer God praise. The healing and deliverance environment includes the

Presence of God. Psalms 22:3 declares that God inhabits the praise of His people therefore if we want God's presence all we have to do is praise Him. Our praise must be authentic. Authentic praise gets God's attention. There is no presence like the presence of God. If we want to function in healing and deliverance ministry, we have to be enabled and in the right environment. There will be no real healing or deliverance without the power or presence of God.

Partnership with God Produces Employment

Once God's power and presence have been established, we have to be partner with God so that He may employ our services. When we partner with God, He will be able to use us for His glory. God usually blessed His partners with favor and fruitfulness. If we want to function in healing and deliverance ministry, we have to be enabled, in the right environment and employed by God. There will be no real healing or deliverance without the power, presence or partnership of God.

Potential for Godly Usefulness

Once God's power, presence and partnership are upon us, we will possess the potential for God's usefulness. Within this potential are three requirements. The first two are interconnected. Unless we have the first two, the third becomes somewhat moot. We must be *Spirit-formed* and *Spirit-filled*. Being Spirit-formed and Spirit-filled means that we are saved, sanctified and indwelt by God's Spirit. This means that the gifts of the Spirit and the fruit of the Spirit are vibrant in our lives. These two allow for the third requirement which is having a *Spirit-flow*. When we are prepared by God, He will be able to flow through us. When God's Spirit flows through us, we will maintain *observation*, *operation* and *obedience* to Him. As observers, we hear what He says and see what He does. As operators we learn to do what He does and say what He says. As obedient vessels, we learn to move when He moves. Being filled and led by God's Spirit allows God to work through us, heal through us, speak through us, and perform miracles through us.

There will be no healing or deliverance without our first being filled and led by God's Spirit.

Speaking in Authority

The healing and deliverance environment includes standing and speaking in authority. Beloved, the only authority we have is the *Name of Jesus*. When we use the *Name of Jesus*, we have access to the only authority that matters. The *Name of Jesus* is literally "the phrase that pays." It might sound cliché but it is true nonetheless. The *Name of Jesus* causes demons to flee, the dead to rise, lepers to be cleansed and sickness to leave. The *Name of Jesus* makes the blind to see, the lame to walk, the dumb to speak, and the deaf to hear. The *Name of Jesus* puts under our authority everything that is under His authority. When we use the *Name of Jesus*, we can't be wishy-washy, mealy-mouthed, jelly-legged, flip-flopping, talking out of both sides of our mouths, faithful and faithless, carefree and careless, timid, afraid, scardy-cat, ducking and hiding, or all over the map. We have to be sure. We have to be sure that God gave us a Word.

Not long ago I visited a hospital where one of my members had undergone back surgery. She had been on her bed of affliction for a few weeks unable to move. She did not lack faith and I did not lack faith. While her condition appeared as though she had several weeks of therapy to go, I began to ask the Lord if this was her day to get a miracle. Well, not only did He answer but she confirmed it. She told me, "I have been waiting on you to bring me God's miracle." Beloved, we are merely servers bringing the orders from the kitchen. The Chef has already prepared their order. All we have to do is bring it to Him. Today was my day to serve what God was cooking. Her order came with a course of events.

I watched as she positioned herself for prayer. I held her by the hands as she sat on the edge of her bed. We began the prayer and I asked for God's power to get enablement. As soon as I felt God's power over me, we began to praise God for His presence to get in the right environment. When I felt His anointing I began to participate in what God is doing and saying.

I began cooperating with God which allowed for my employment. He hired me to bring her the miracle. I called for her healing by using the *Name of Jesus.* I can't explain what happened next any better than this. I felt something leaving my hands and entering her hands and she started straightening up. She received strength she did not have prior to that day. When we finished prayer she told me to stand back and watch. I watched her stand for the first time on her own without assistance. Then she said, "Hold my hand, we're about to take a walk." At that point, not only did she walk but she high-stepped as if she were marching for Grambling University in the Southern Classic.

Speaking Accurately

I would be remiss if I did not tell you why my sister was able to get up and walk that day. It is because I learned to speak accurately. One of the keys to healing and deliverance ministry is learning to stand and speak accurately. Whenever there is a miracle in the room, we have to be specific. Yes I have read the passage that says, God knows what we have need of before we ask it. I am aware that God will provide all my needs according to His riches in glory. But I am also aware that we are encouraged to ask. Ask and it shall be given. Seek and we shall find. Knock and it shall be opened unto us. Speaking accurately means speaking specifically.

I remember visiting another member of my church. She was on her bed of affliction. She had been missing from our worship services for a few weeks and my deacons advised me that they did not feel as though she had long to go. Our deacons and deaconesses are my eyes and ears. Whenever they visit the sick, they give me the report. If things look grave, they get to me right away. This was the case for this lady.

When I arrived at the hospital, she was in despair. There were tubes plugged into her body all over the place. She looked as if she had resigned herself to accept this condition. She had a large tumor growing in her midsection and she was nearing the point of death. Let me share with you that this was a woman who did not lack faith. She was a prayer warrior like no other I had seen in out Baptist church. She could get a prayer through. That she was on her bed of affliction was not because she lacked faith. You need to know this before I share what happened next.

As I stood near her bed and called her name, her eyes lit up. It was as if Jesus had entered the room. (Keep that thought.) I told her that the Lord sent me to bring her the order she was waiting for. I sensed the Lord impressing upon me to anoint my hands with oil. I do not always pray with oil. I usually keep it in a sealed plastic bag in my briefcase or on my desk at church. This time as I got out of my car, I put it in my pocket. When I took the oil from my pocket, I told her what I was doing to which she responded by agreeing with me by her eyes.

Before going further, I have two side notes. It is never good to use oil on those who are not familiar with it. This could be the barrier to their miracle. In addition, any person in the intensive care unit or critical care unit needs not to be touched by unclean and unsterile hands. Most of the time when I am praying for a person in this condition I make sure I don't touch them unless I am specifically sure the Lord tells me to do so. God does not need us to touch anybody to do what He does. When I do not get a sense that God wants me to touch the person directly, I touch them indirectly. I touch what touches them. This can be the bed, the blanket, the mattress, whatever.

As I stood by my sister's bed, I anointed my hands with oil, touched her blanket and began to pray. Much like the person mentioned before, I asked for God's power to get enablement. As soon as I felt God's power over me, I began to praise God for His presence to get in the right environment. When I felt His anointing I began to participate in what God is doing and saying. I began cooperating with God which allowed for my employment. He hired me to bring her the miracle. I called for her healing by using the *Name of Jesus.* In particular, I sensed God telling me to call that tumor by name and instruct it to shrink. I did exactly what God told me to do and I tarried. What seemed to be an eternity were really several minutes. I took authority and commanded the tumor to shrink. After a while, I called the angels of healing into the room to minister to her. In addition, I spoke to the covers and bed to effectively soak her with healing. I know that sometimes healing takes more than a few seconds. Soaking a person in healing prayer is appropriate and good for them. When I left I felt sure God heard me and was going to complete that miracle.

After a couple of days, I got the call that she passed away. I was devastated. The reason I was devastated is because I knew what God said to me. I did not get the sense that He did not hear me. I did not get the sense that He was not going to heal her. I was preparing to hear her testimony in church. The news of her death flattened me. Often, I have a saying, "Wait for the other shoe to fall." It comes from a story where a family who has a cabin in the woods went to spend a weekend at their cabin. Upon entry, they found a shoe in the fireplace. Thinking it odd, they simply removed the shoe and thought nothing of it. They enjoyed their time that weekend without incident and returned home when it was over. After several months had passed, they found another break in their busy schedule and decided to take another trip to their weekend hideaway. Upon entry, they again found a shoe sitting in the fireplace. Now intrigued, the husband grabs a flashlight and looked up the fireplace. There he found a corpse stuck in the chimney. Apparently, the person was trying to break in and rob the place, got stuck and died there. What brought this ordeal to their attention was waiting until the other show fell. Much like this story, I found myself waiting until the other shoe fell.

The funeral was over, we had completed the repast and I was just sick. Just before the family was about to leave the church I went over to say my good byes to the family when the daughter asked me if her husband spoke to me. I responded that he hadn't. She told me, he had something to tell me. I sat down prepared to hear, "Your charlatan prayer killed my mother in law." She went to get her husband. He came and sat down next to me. As I sat there, I saw tears well up in his eyes. As he began to form his words, I remember thinking "here it comes. Boy am I about to get it now." He shared this story with me.

"That afternoon after you left the hospital something happened. I knew you had been there because they called me to come. My mother in law was sitting up and talking. She had not been able to do that in weeks. She was pulling out the plugs telling people that she was healed. The doctors thought she was hysterical and called me to come calm her down. I sat with her and she told me how you came and prayed for her. She told me how she felt the power of God overshadow her. She told me how she felt the tumor shrinking in her body. She told me she was ready to go home. For precautionary measures, we kept her overnight until the doctor could come and discharge her in the morning. When we woke up in the morning preparing to go bring her home, we received a call. She had passed away. We were shocked because we were sure that she was healed. Healing was all over her and the joy of the Lord strengthened her. We later found out that during the night somebody came in and probably overly sedated her to her demise. We can't prove it and the hospital is not cooperating but for all practical purposes, that is what happened."

While this was not good news to me, it was news nonetheless. The other shoe had fallen and I was now at peace. I was at peace because I was sure God gave me a Word for my dearly departed sister. Beloved, we have to be sure that God gave us a Word for this person or that person. We have to be sure that God gave us a Word for this one or that one right now. We have to be sure that God gave us a Word of healing or deliverance for them right now. Beloved, I'd be remiss if I didn't give you this word of warning. People get damaged by well-meaning persons all the time. They don't mean any harm but they say things God didn't tell them to say. God does not commit Himself to the words we say. He commits Himself to the words He says. If we don't say what we hear Him saying or do what we see Him doing, we're going to look foolish. There is the description, the disposition and the divine. God employs us to speak with authority, speak accurately and secure an assessment.

Secure an Assessment

One of the surest signs that they have received their order from the Lord is having the ability to do what they were unable to do before the order. This is securing an assessment. That the woman who had back surgery was able to stand up and walk was my secured assessment. That my dearly departed member had received her healing notwithstanding the medicinal failure was my securing an assessment. Securing an assessment is biblical my friends. The man with the withered hand was able to stretch out his hand unlike any time prior. The woman who was bent over was able to stand up straight unlike she was able to do before. The man at the Gate called Beautiful was able to stand and walk unlike he was able to do before. The man at the Pool of Bethesda was able to arise and take up his bed and walk unlike he was able to do before. There are just too many examples of this reality. Before departing anyone's bedside, I plead the phrase that stays, the *Blood of Jesus*. The *Blood of Jesus* is the seal. The *Blood of Jesus* makes sure they keep whatever healing they received. The *Blood of Jesus* makes sure they keep whatever deliverance they received. The *Blood of Jesus* makes sure they keep whatever miracle they received. The *Name of Jesus* gets them there and the *Blood of Jesus* keeps them there.

Mark and Luke represent a pre-cross, pre-resurrection miracle. Acts represents a post-cross, post-resurrection miracle. In Mark and Luke, God uses Jesus to perform the miracle. In Acts, God uses Peter and John to perform the miracle. These stories are similar but different. Mark's Gospel says Jesus entered in. Luke's Gospel says Jesus was teaching. In Acts Peter and John were on their way to prayer meeting. In other words, they went to church for the right reason. They went to worship God in Spirit and in Truth. When they got to church, God showed them somebody that needed a blessing. These stories are similar but different. Mark presents a man with a withered hand. Luke presents a woman who was bent over. Acts presents a man who was lame. These stories are similar but different. All three present miracles happening on the church property. Mark and Luke present miracles happening in the sanctuary. Acts presents a miracle happening at the gate. These stories are similar but different. The two men needed healing; the woman needed deliverance. Mark and Luke do not record either of them asking God for anything. The Acts story records that the lame man did ask for something. In any event, they just came just as they were and got something they did not expect – a miracle. The fact that they came after all they had been through got God's attention. These stories are similar but different.

I have a bit of encouraging news. If you are reading this book and have a good attitude and a right spirit stay tuned. If you don't have a habit of complaining or have scrutiny in your heart, your blessing is closer than you think. The secret is found in your attendance in worship service. Sometimes we come to church prepared to worship God in Spirit and in Truth. Sometimes we slip in and slip out seemingly unnoticed. Please be aware that God notices. Nothing escapes Him. Please do not underestimate the benefit of simply coming to church. Mark and Luke do not record the man or the woman asking anybody for anything. Acts records that the lame man was asking anybody for anything. Whether you are one who asks or not, God sees and understands. God hears the audible and the inaudible whisper of this hope:

> *I'm looking for a miracle. I expect the impossible.*
> *I feel the intangible. I see the invisible.*
> *The sky is the limit to what I can have.*
> *Just believe and receive it – God will perform it today.*

It's time to tie this thing up. The healing and deliverance environment was set. I'm glad that when God showed Jesus who needed a blessing, Jesus followed God's lead. In Mark's Gospel, Jesus told the man with the withered hand to stand up. It was here where the man had a choice to make. Will I remain sitting or stand as I have been told? I must share this with you. The man with the withered hand had his healing held in the balance. His healing depended on his obedience. Had the man not stood, the story would not be what the story is. The man stood in obedience. Once the man stood Jesus told the man, "Stretch forth your hand." It was here where the man had a second choice to make. Will I keep my hand down and out of sight or stretch it forth as I have been told? The man's healing held in the balance. His healing depended on his obedience. Had the man not stretched forth his hand, the story would not be what the story is. The man stretched forth his hand in obedience and my Bible says that his hand was restored whole as the other hand. When the healing or deliverance environment is upon us, we have to learn to be obedient. Beloved, many of us do not get our blessing or breakthrough because we are unwilling to follow instructions. We want God to do the miracle but we want Him to do it our way. God doesn't work that way. Obedience has everything to do with whether or not we get our blessing. When God is preparing to bless us, we need to follow instructions. I'm glad that when God showed Jesus who needed a blessing, He followed God's lead and the people were healed and delivered.

In Acts, Peter and John Peter and John walked up to him at the gate. They said, "Silver and gold we do not have. But such as we have, we give it to thee. In the name of Jesus of Nazareth, arise, take up your bed and walk." It was here that this lame man had a decision to make. Do I obey Peter's voice and get up or do I remain here just as I am? His healing held in the balance. What happens next is Peter took him by the hand, lifted and him up. Sometimes we have to learn how to help people up. We have to help them get their healing, deliverance, breakthrough or miracle. We must help them as if our lives depend on it. If we are willing to take this attitude, we will see God move with signs and wonders. Peter helped the man up and my Bible says his feet and ankles received strength so that he was able to leap up on his feet.

In Luke's Gospel, Jesus did something different. Instead of telling the woman who was bent over to stand up, He said, "Woman, thou art loosed from thine infirmity." These stories are similar but different. In a healing environment, Jesus spoke to the illness and it went away based on the man's obedience and participation. In the woman's case, Jesus spoke to the demonic spirit and loosed her from the spirit that caused the condition. Where the men had a choice to make, woman didn't. Not only did Jesus speak to the demonic spirit but Jesus also went over to her, laid His hands on her and immediately she was made straight. The healing of the men came as a result of their obedience. The woman's healing came as a result of Jesus casting out a demon. These stories are similar but different.

Concerning the miracle that each experienced, we have some intriguing data to share. Mark does not record the man's response to his healing. Luke and Acts do record a response. Luke says that the delivered woman began to praise God. Acts says the healed man began praising God. They looked at their hands and they looked new. They looked at their feet and they did too. I suspect that each of them were thankful. Whenever we get our healing or deliverance, it is a good thing to give God some praise. This is the same as sounding the alarm. We have to tell somebody about the goodness of God. We have to testify about His great and mighty works. These stories are similar but different.

All three stories record a response in the crowd. There were some who were amazed and excited and there were some filled with righteous indignation. In Mark and Luke, Jesus rebukes those who had a problem with Him. In Acts, Peter began to preach to the people who had a problem with John and himself. These problem people were the same type as who conspired against Jesus. The same type who arrested Him at night. The same type who led Him from judgment hall to judgment hall. The same type who called for His crucifixion. The same type who led Him up a hill called Calvary. The same type who nailed His hands and His feet. The same type who watched Him hang His head and die. When He died, they placed Him in a borrowed tomb. He stayed there for three long days. Early on the third day, He got up with all power in His hands.

God sent His Son and they called Him Jesus.

He came to love, heal and forgive.
He came to die to buy my pardon.
An empty grave is there to prove my Savior lives.

A Deliverer Needing Deliverance

I was in my early teens when I heard the Lord's voice. His voice was as clear as a digital mobile phone right next to the cell site. He said to me, "I am calling you to preach." At first I was not interested. Preachers did not make the money I wanted to make. Preachers could not do what I wanted to do. I knew then that if I was going to preach His Word, I'd have to be willing to pay the price. My life would have to resemble one who has been converted by God. Preaching was no play thing for me.

After a few weeks of deliberation, I heard God's voice again. The day was just as clear and His message was the same as before but He added an addendum. "In My name you will heal the sick. In My name you will raise the dead. In My name you will cast out devils. In My name you will perform miracles." My

response was a resounding, "Yes. I am going to cast out devils!"
I went immediately looking for a devil to cast out. I searched
high and low but to no avail. I searched throughout my
neighborhood, nothing. I walked up and down the street,
nothing. There was no devil to be found that day.

I went home frustrated. At some point I found myself
looking in a mirror and to my surprise, there he was staring back
at me. The devil I went looking for on the outside was really on
the inside. Those sinister eyes. That horrendous smile. It was
him. I began doing exactly what I saw those televangelists do,
cast that demon out. I placed my hand on my forehead and began
my televangelistic tirade. "Satan, you foul demon. Come out in
the name of Jesus!" I tarried until I felt a breakthrough. From
that point on I was ready for ministry. Keep in mind, I was in my
early teens. I said all that to say this. Beloved, we cannot get the
devil out of anybody else until we first get the devil out of
ourselves. Matthew 7:3 declares that we must get the beam out
of our own eye before we can remove the splinter out of

someone else's eye. Charity starts at home. It is imperative that we receive ministry before we aim to minister to others.

Fast forward. I have been preaching the Gospel for over twenty years now. I received a call from a member of our church. I also considered her a friend. Occasionally, I would call her mother just to say hello. Additionally, I would call her and see how she was doing. Her job required her to travel a great deal so I did not see her in church very often. Be that as it may, when she called me, it was not out of the ordinary but her request was. She told me her sister was in town and that she wanted me to come speak with her. She told me that her sister felt she has a demon and she wanted me to pray that it would leave her alone. I set up the appointment and went to her home.

When I got there, I was a bit apprehensive. I sat in the car for a few moments and gathered myself. I prayed the God would direct me and give me the words to say. When I finished, I went to the door, pushed the intercom and she buzzed me in. When I got to her door she welcomed me. There sat mom, her sister and she in the living room. She offered and brought me a glass of water. I remember looking around to find an appropriate place to sit the glass. Her home was so well manicured, I was afraid to put the cup down. She really did have a nice place.

After a bit of small talk, I began to interview her sister. She told me her story. As she spoke, I looked for some demonic presence. One thing I know about demons is this, when they see the power and presence of God, they will often manifest. People have experienced cursing, convulsing and all sorts of manifestations. As she spoke, there was no visible manifestation that I could see. Another thing I learned about people who say they have a demon is that often they don't. They may have guilt, shame or indigestion but not a demon. I have never told people that they did not have what they say they had. I have learned to trust them because they know themselves better than anyone else.

Over the years I have learned that demons affect us in two ways. When we have accepted Jesus Christ as Lord and

Savior, we can only be influenced by demons. When we have not accepted Jesus Christ as Lord and Savior, we can be influenced and/or possessed. Often the manifestations appear the same but one is from the outside-in and the other is from the inside-out.

After listening and observing until she finished, I agreed to pray. I asked that we get in a circle and close our eyes. As I began I asked the *Blood of Jesus* to cover everybody in the room so that whatever was bothering our sister would not leave her and jump on someone else. I asked God to give me the words to say so that from this day forward she would no longer be bothered by whatever this was. I used the *Name of Jesus* to break every chain that the enemy had placed on her life. And I let the Holy Spirit give me all the rest of the words to say. I remember hitting all the major points. I **Spoke in Authority** by called the demon out. I **Spoke Accurately** by telling the demon to leave. I **Secured an Assessment** for when I finished praying, I asked her how she felt. She told me she felt different, free. After a few additional moments of small talk, I left. I made a few calls later to check on my friend's sister. She said there were no further symptoms.

In reflection, I realize I made some blunders. Now, I would never go to pray over a person who says they have a demon without a team. A team will have people praying in agreement and observing as they prayed. A team would have one take the lead with others prepared to switch places when the lead gets tired. Demons are unpredictable and can often be in groups. Once you get one out, you may have a second, third or any number still in there. We can ill afford to begin an exorcism without counting the cost. It may take several hours to finish the job. Once we get finished, we have to give the person we are praying for some instructions so as to not have any additional manifestations affect them. Praise God for His blundering servant. He protected me against my naiveté.

"The Healing and Deliverance Experience"
Mark 6; Luke 10; John 14; 1 Corinthians 12

Probably the most understated portion of church history is that of the healing and deliverance experience.

God is in charge of healing and deliverance. There is no place we can go other than Him. Soothsayers and charm wearers cannot out-perform Him. Palm readers and card holders cannot outthink Him. Crystal ball gazers and incense burners cannot out maneuver Him. God is in a class all by Himself and is in charge of healing and deliverance.

God is in control of healing and deliverance. He knows who needs it and to whom He will give it. He cannot be bought, outfoxed, finagled, coaxed, coerced, or blackmailed. Healing and deliverance are at His choosing and in His sovereign hand. God is in a class all by Himself and is in control of healing and deliverance.

God is capable of healing and deliverance. Nothing is too hard for Him. There is no sickness He cannot eradicate; no disease He cannot fix; no demonic presence He cannot eliminate. He is neither weak-kneed nor jelly-legged. The Lord, our God is strong and mighty. God is in a class all by Himself and is capable of healing and deliverance.

As we consider the healing and deliverance experience we must remember that healing and deliverance ministry is real. Sickness is real and the demonic realm is real. People really do get sick and people really do get oppressed by demons. People who are sick or oppressed need real ministry.

As we consider the healing and deliverance experience we must remember that healing and deliverance ministry is right. It is always the wrong choice if we ignore the sick or oppressed. It is always the wrong choice if we leave the sick or oppressed to themselves. It is always the wrong choice if we leave the sick or oppressed in the hands of doctors and psychologists alone. They need right ministry and right ministry comes to their aid. Right ministry is unafraid to touch them where they are hurting, to teach them why they are hurting and to transform them from their hurting.

As we consider the healing and deliverance experience we must remember that healing and deliverance ministry is rewarding. There is no joy like that of the one whom God has healed or delivered. There is no peace or testimony like that of those who have been healed or delivered. And there is no satisfaction like that of those whom God has used to bring the blessing to those in need of it. This is where our story begins.

Jesus had spent much time teaching His disciples and followers about the Kingdom of God. He had done enough show and tell. They had seen enough ministry and heard enough explanation that they could finish sentences He would start. They had seen and heard enough so that when He felt led to go here or there, not to overly question His motives. They had seen and heard enough to know that when God presses upon us to do something, we have to do it.

Jesus did a great deal of teaching and the disciples did a great deal of learning. An important part of ministry is to sit and learn. We all need to sit and learn. Sitting and learning is critical to our spiritual development. Jesus embraced teaching and His followers embraced learning.

Jesus was not just an instructor, He was also one who performed ministry. Another critical part of ministry is to go and do. We are not expected to learn and sit only. Sitting and learning are precursors to going and doing. We are expected to sit and learn so we can go and do. These passages of Scripture are before us so that we may understand why we have sat and learned so we can go and do. We must learn to say what the Father says and do what the Father does. Jesus presents the reach, the reality, the revelation, the request, the reward, and the redundancy as important components of healing and deliverance ministry.

Read the Word of the Lord – Mark 6

[1] And he went out from thence, and came into his own country; and his disciples follow him. [2] And when the sabbath day was come, he began to teach in the synagogue: and many hearing *him* were astonished, saying, From whence hath this *man* these things? and what wisdom *is* this which is given unto him, that even such mighty works are wrought by his hands? [3] Is not this the carpenter, the son of Mary, the brother of James, and

Joses, and of Juda, and Simon? and are not his sisters here with us? And they were offended at him. ⁴ But Jesus said unto them, A prophet is not without honour, but in his own country, and among his own kin, and in his own house. ⁵ And he could there do no mighty work, save that he laid his hands upon a few sick folk, and healed *them.* ⁶ And he marvelled because of their unbelief. And he went round about the villages, teaching.

⁷ And he called *unto him* the twelve, and began to send them forth by two and two; and gave them power over unclean spirits; ⁸ And commanded them that they should take nothing for *their* journey, save a staff only; no scrip, no bread, no money in *their* purse: ⁹ But *be* shod with sandals; and not put on two coats. ¹⁰ And he said unto them, In what place soever ye enter into an house, there abide till ye depart from that place. ¹¹ And whosoever shall not receive you, nor hear you, when ye depart thence, shake off the dust under your feet for a testimony against them. Verily I say unto you, It shall be more tolerable for Sodom and Gomorrha in the day of judgment, than for that city. ¹² And they went out, and preached that men should repent. ¹³ And they cast out many devils, and anointed with oil many that were sick, and healed *them.*

¹⁴ And king Herod heard *of him;* (for his name was spread abroad:) and he said, That John the Baptist was risen from the dead, and therefore mighty works do shew forth themselves in him. ¹⁵ Others said, That it is Elias. And others said, That it is a prophet, or as one of the prophets. ¹⁶ But when Herod heard *thereof,* he said, It is John, whom I beheaded: he is risen from the dead. ¹⁷ For Herod himself had sent forth and laid hold upon John, and bound him in prison for Herodias' sake, his brother Philip's wife: for he had married her. ¹⁸ For John had said unto Herod, It is not lawful for thee to have thy

brother's wife. [19] Therefore Herodias had a quarrel against him, and would have killed him; but she could not: [20] For Herod feared John, knowing that he was a just man and an holy, and observed him; and when he heard him, he did many things, and heard him gladly. [21] And when a convenient day was come, that Herod on his birthday made a supper to his lords, high captains, and chief *estates* of Galilee; [22] And when the daughter of the said Herodias came in, and danced, and pleased Herod and them that sat with him, the king said unto the damsel, Ask of me whatsoever thou wilt, and I will give *it* thee. [23] And he sware unto her, Whatsoever thou shalt ask of me, I will give *it* thee, unto the half of my kingdom. [24] And she went forth, and said unto her mother, What shall I ask? And she said, The head of John the Baptist. [25] And she came in straightway with haste unto the king, and asked, saying, I will that thou give me by and by in a charger the head of John the Baptist. [26] And the king was exceeding sorry; *yet* for his oath's sake, and for their sakes which sat with him, he would not reject her. [27] And immediately the king sent an executioner, and commanded his head to be brought: and he went and beheaded him in the prison, [28] And brought his head in a charger, and gave it to the damsel: and the damsel gave it to her mother. [29] And when his disciples heard *of it*, they came and took up his corpse, and laid it in a tomb.

[30] And the apostles gathered themselves together unto Jesus, and told him all things, both what they had done, and what they had taught. [31] And he said unto them, Come ye yourselves apart into a desert place, and rest a while: for there were many coming and going, and they had no leisure so much as to eat. [32] And they departed into a desert place by ship privately. [33] And the people saw them departing, and many knew him, and ran afoot thither out of all cities, and outwent them, and came

together unto him. ³⁴ And Jesus, when he came out, saw much people, and was moved with compassion toward them, because they were as sheep not having a shepherd: and he began to teach them many things. ³⁵ And when the day was now far spent, his disciples came unto him, and said, This is a desert place, and now the time *is* far passed: ³⁶ Send them away, that they may go into the country round about, and into the villages, and buy themselves bread: for they have nothing to eat. ³⁷ He answered and said unto them, Give ye them to eat. And they say unto him, Shall we go and buy two hundred pennyworth of bread, and give them to eat? ³⁸ He saith unto them, How many loaves have ye? go and see. And when they knew, they say, Five, and two fishes. ³⁹ And he commanded them to make all sit down by companies upon the green grass. ⁴⁰ And they sat down in ranks, by hundreds, and by fifties. ⁴¹ And when he had taken the five loaves and the two fishes, he looked up to heaven, and blessed, and brake the loaves, and gave *them* to his disciples to set before them; and the two fishes divided he among them all. ⁴² And they did all eat, and were filled. ⁴³ And they took up twelve baskets full of the fragments, and of the fishes. ⁴⁴ And they that did eat of the loaves were about five thousand men.

⁴⁵ And straightway he constrained his disciples to get into the ship, and to go to the other side before unto Bethsaida, while he sent away the people. ⁴⁶ And when he had sent them away, he departed into a mountain to pray. ⁴⁷ And when even was come, the ship was in the midst of the sea, and he alone on the land. ⁴⁸ And he saw them toiling in rowing; for the wind was contrary unto them: and about the fourth watch of the night he cometh unto them, walking upon the sea, and would have passed by them. ⁴⁹ But when they saw him walking upon the sea, they supposed it had been a spirit, and cried out: ⁵⁰ For

they all saw him, and were troubled. And immediately he talked with them, and saith unto them, Be of good cheer: it is I; be not afraid. [51] And he went up unto them into the ship; and the wind ceased: and they were sore amazed in themselves beyond measure, and wondered. [52] For they considered not *the miracle* of the loaves: for their heart was hardened. [53] And when they had passed over, they came into the land of Gennesaret, and drew to the shore. [54] And when they were come out of the ship, straightway they knew him, [55] And ran through that whole region round about, and began to carry about in beds those that were sick, where they heard he was. [56] And whithersoever he entered, into villages, or cities, or country, they laid the sick in the streets, and besought him that they might touch if it were but the border of his garment: and as many as touched him were made whole.

1. The Reach

In Mark's Gospel, the ministry of Jesus is frustrated by the familiar. His ministry is rejected at home. I don't know what it is about home but it is a shame that outsiders tend to accept our ministries better than insiders. Home is where the heart is. If any place should benefit from the ministry of a child trained up, it is home. The sad reality is there are some people God will be able to reach through you and there are some people God will not be able to reach through you. There are some people who will accept what God is doing through your ministry and there are some who will not accept what God is doing through your ministry. There are those who have purposed it in their hearts that if their healing has to come through you, they'd prefer to stay sick. There are those who have purposed it in their hearts that if their deliverance has to come through you, they'd prefer to stay demonized. Some people will miss their breakthrough because they are looking for God to send it through anybody but you. Some people will miss their blessing because they are committed to getting it from any vessel God uses other than you. Those who think this way are sad individuals.

I'd like to encourage somebody right here. Just because some people reject your ministry does not mean God rejects your ministry. In fact, just because some may reject you does not mean everybody else will reject you. People's opinion of you does not invalidate God's purpose for you. Just hold on and trust in God. Whoever God calls, He qualifies. Whomever God selects, He prepares. Do not worry about what people think, say or do – just do the work of Him that sent you. Be very sure that your gifts will make room for you. As we look at the Gospel of Mark, healing and deliverance ministry begins with the reach.

Let us read the Word of the Lord – Luke 10

[1] After these things the Lord appointed other seventy also, and sent them two and two before his face into every city and place, whither he himself would come. [2] Therefore said he unto them, The harvest truly *is* great, but the labourers *are* few: pray ye therefore the Lord of the harvest, that he would send forth labourers into his harvest. [3] Go your ways: behold, I send you forth as lambs among wolves. [4] Carry neither purse, nor scrip, nor shoes: and salute no man by the way. [5] And into whatsoever house ye enter, first say, Peace *be* to this house. [6] And if the son of peace be there, your peace shall rest upon it: if not, it shall turn to you again. [7] And in the same house remain, eating and drinking such things as they give: for the labourer is worthy of his hire. Go not from house to house. [8] And into whatsoever city ye enter, and they receive you, eat such things as are set before you: [9] And heal the sick that are therein, and say unto them, The kingdom of God is come nigh unto you. [10] But into whatsoever city ye enter, and they receive you not, go your ways out into the streets of the same, and say, [11] Even the very dust of your city, which cleaveth on us, we do wipe off against you: notwithstanding be ye sure of this, that the kingdom of God is come nigh unto you. [12] But I say unto you, that it shall be more tolerable in that day for Sodom, than for that city. [13] Woe unto thee, Chorazin! woe unto thee, Bethsaida! for if the mighty works had been done in Tyre and Sidon, which have been done in you, they had a great while ago repented, sitting

in sackcloth and ashes. ^{14} But it shall be more tolerable for Tyre and Sidon at the judgment, than for you. ^{15} And thou, Capernaum, which art exalted to heaven, shalt be thrust down to hell. ^{16} He that heareth you heareth me; and he that despiseth you despiseth me; and he that despiseth me despiseth him that sent me.

^{17} And the seventy returned again with joy, saying, Lord, even the devils are subject unto us through thy name. ^{18} And he said unto them, I beheld Satan as lightning fall from heaven. ^{19} Behold, I give unto you power to tread on serpents and scorpions, and over all the power of the enemy: and nothing shall by any means hurt you. ^{20} Notwithstanding in this rejoice not, that the spirits are subject unto you; but rather rejoice, because your names are written in heaven. ^{21} In that hour Jesus rejoiced in spirit, and said, I thank thee, O Father, Lord of heaven and earth, that thou hast hid these things from the wise and prudent, and hast revealed them unto babes: even so, Father; for so it seemed good in thy sight. ^{22} All things are delivered to me of my Father: and no man knoweth who the Son is, but the Father; and who the Father is, but the Son, and *he* to whom the Son will reveal *him*. ^{23} And he turned him unto *his* disciples, and said privately, Blessed *are* the eyes which see the things that ye see: ^{24} For I tell you, that many prophets and kings have desired to see those things which ye see, and have not seen *them*; and to hear those things which ye hear, and have not heard *them*.

^{25} And, behold, a certain lawyer stood up, and tempted him, saying, Master, what shall I do to inherit eternal life? ^{26} He said unto him, What is written in the law? how readest thou? ^{27} And he answering said, Thou shalt love the Lord thy God with all thy heart, and with all thy soul, and with all thy strength, and with all thy mind; and thy neighbour as thyself. ^{28} And he said unto him, Thou hast answered right: this do, and thou shalt live. [29] But he, willing to justify himself, said unto Jesus, And who is my neighbour? [30] And Jesus answering said, A certain *man* went down from Jerusalem to Jericho, and fell among thieves, which stripped him of his raiment, and wounded *him*, and departed, leaving *him* half dead. [31] And by chance there came down a certain priest that way: and when he saw him, he passed by on the other side. [32] And likewise a Levite, when he was at the place, came and looked *on him*, and passed by on the other side. [33] But a certain Samaritan, as he journeyed, came where he was: and when he saw him, he had compassion *on him*, [34] And went to *him*, and bound up his wounds, pouring in oil and wine, and set him on his own beast, and brought him to an inn, and took care of him. [35] And on the morrow when he departed, he took out two pence, and gave *them* to the host, and said unto him, Take care of him; and whatsoever thou spendest more, when I come again, I will repay thee. [36] Which now of these three, thinkest thou, was neighbour unto him that fell among the thieves? [37] And he said, He that shewed mercy on him. Then said Jesus unto him, Go, and do thou likewise.

[38] Now it came to pass, as they went, that he entered into a certain village: and a certain woman named Martha received him into her house. [39] And she had a sister called Mary, which also sat at Jesus' feet, and heard his word. [40] But Martha was cumbered about much serving, and came to him, and said, Lord, dost thou not care that my sister hath left me to serve alone? bid her therefore that she help me. [41] And Jesus answered and said unto her, Martha, Martha, thou art careful and troubled about many things: [42] But one thing is needful: and Mary hath chosen that good part, which shall not be taken away from her.

2. The Reality

As we look at what both Mark and Luke wrote, Jesus prepared and sent His followers to heal the sick and deliver the demonized. He empowered them with authority over whatever they would encounter. He mandated that they go depending solely on God's direction and trust in God's provision. They were not to take any extra anything but go solely and depending on God. Saints, if you don't learn anything at all, please know that healing and deliverance depends solely on God. Healing and deliverance ministry is not done in a vacuum. God has a system to healing and deliverance ministry and that system is to depend completely on Him.

Jesus sent His followers to do ministry. The reason He sent them was based on a definite reality. The reality is there are sick and demonized people out there. Disease and the demonic have damaged the dust. All of us are damaged dust in one way or another. People who would otherwise be healthy are withering away. People who would otherwise be sane are behaving in ways that are outside their character. It is because the ruler of darkness has clouded our sunny day with doom and despair. He has reduced our capacity to think beyond what we can see. Instead of being faith experts, we have become fate experts with a "woe is me" mentality. If God wanted to heal me, He would heal me. I am sick because this is how God designed me. My flaws, my ailments, my way of thinking are all by God's design. If He wanted me healthy, He would make me healthy. Beloved, if this sounds like you or somebody you know, please understand that this kind of thinking is nothing but a trick of the enemy. God designed us to live happy, healthy and holy lives.

Some of us have resolved that health and wellness will not be our good fortune. We have been carried about by every wind of doctrine and cunningly devised fables. We believe the war is in doubt when the war is already won. Jesus already paid it all and all to Him we owe. He has already defeated Satan. If we belong to Him, we already have the victory. We have victory over death, sickness, disease and the demonic. Healing and deliverance ministry includes the reality.

3. The Revelation

As we look at these two gospel accounts, the revelation is implied. Jesus sent the Twelve Disciples (according to Mark) or the additional seventy (according to Luke) to go and minister. The ministry of Jesus includes preaching, teaching, healing and deliverance. Preaching and teaching address the *information* concerning the Kingdom of God. Healing and deliverance address the *inspiration* concerning the Kingdom of God. It is one thing to *tell* who God is, it is another thing altogether to *show* who God is. God's Kingdom is not powerless and He supports "show and tell." Show them what I do and tell them who I am. The reason revelation is implied here, is because Jesus tells them what they are going to face in advance.

His instructions here are prior to the coming of the Comforter. Jesus said in John 14 that Comforter would not come until He has gone away and been glorified at the right hand of the Father. Only after He had been positioned at the Power End of the Throne, would the Comforter be sent to fill the disciples with His presence and His gifts. Jesus' instructions here came before the disciples were officially filled with the Holy Spirit, according to 1 Corinthians 12. In the post-resurrection experience, the only way they would know what they would face would come through revelation. Three such revelations are the Word of Knowledge, the Word of Wisdom and the Gift of Prophecy.

There are nine gifts of the Spirit. Two such gifts are Word gifts. The Word of Knowledge and the Word of Wisdom are the Word gifts that reveal things only God can know. These gifts can reveal who is sick, who is demonized, how they got that way, and how long they've been that way.

Prophecy is another revelatory gift. God does not necessarily send all the data but He sends the answer. Prophetic gifts only share what is coming. Prophecy is fore-telling, forth-telling or forward-telling. Fore-telling is a way of predicting, prognosticating or forecasting.[46] Forth-telling is a way of sharing what God will do in a more immediate time frame. It is as if God is doing the miracle within moments of or during the moment of sharing the information.[47] Fore-telling causes one to anticipate that what was shared is coming in the future. Forward-telling aims at making a thorough and complete declaration of coming events.[48] Fore-telling, forth-telling and forward-telling each address speaking about something coming in the future. Prophecy, the Word of Knowledge and the Word of Wisdom come to us today by the Gifts of the Spirit as set forth by God Himself.

Read the Word of the Lord found in 1 Corinthians 12
[1] Now concerning spiritual *gifts*, brethren, I would not have you ignorant. [2] Ye know that ye were Gentiles, carried away unto these dumb idols, even as ye were led.

---

[46] *Merriam-Webster's Collegiate Dictionary – 10th ed.* (Springfield, Mass., U.S.A., 1996), n. p.

[47] K. H. Easley, *Holman Quick Source Guide to Understanding the Bible* (Nashville: Holman Bible Publishers, 2002), 236.

[48] S. Zodhiates, *The Complete Word Study Dictionary: New Testament – Electronic Edition* (Chattanooga: AMG Publishers, 2000), n. p.

[3] Wherefore I give you to understand, that no man speaking by the Spirit of God calleth Jesus accursed: and *that* no man can say that Jesus is the Lord, but by the Holy Ghost. [4] Now there are diversities of gifts, but the same Spirit. [5] And there are differences of administrations, but the same Lord. [6] And there are diversities of operations, but it is the same God which worketh all in all. [7] But the manifestation of the Spirit is given to every man to profit withal. [8] For to one is given by the Spirit the word of wisdom; to another the word of knowledge by the same Spirit; [9] To another faith by the same Spirit; to another the gifts of healing by the same Spirit; [10] To another the working of miracles; to another prophecy; to another discerning of spirits; to another *divers* kinds of tongues; to another the interpretation of tongues: [11] But all these worketh that one and the selfsame Spirit, dividing to every man severally as he will.

[12] For as the body is one, and hath many members, and all the members of that one body, being many, are one body: so also *is* Christ. [13] For by one Spirit are we all baptized into one body, whether *we be* Jews or Gentiles, whether *we be* bond or free; and have been all made to drink into one Spirit. [14] For the body is not one member, but many. [15] If the foot shall say, Because I am not the hand, I am not of the body; is it therefore not of the body? [16] And if the ear shall say, Because I am not the eye, I am not of the body; is it therefore not of the body? [17] If the whole body *were* an eye, where *were* the hearing? If the whole *were* hearing, where *were* the smelling? [18] But now hath God set the members every one of them in the body, as it hath pleased him. [19] And if they were all one member, where *were* the body? [20] But now *are they* many members, yet but one body. [21] And the eye cannot say unto the hand, I have no need of thee:

nor again the head to the feet, I have no need of you. [22] Nay, much more those members of the body, which seem to be more feeble, are necessary: [23] And those *members* of the body, which we think to be less honourable, upon these we bestow more abundant honour; and our uncomely *parts* have more abundant comeliness. [24] For our comely *parts* have no need: but God hath tempered the body together, having given more abundant honour to that *part* which lacked: [25] That there should be no schism in the body; but *that* the members should have the same care one for another. [26] And whether one member suffer, all the members suffer with it; or one member be honoured, all the members rejoice with it.

[27] Now ye are the body of Christ, and members in particular. [28] And God hath set some in the church, first apostles, secondarily prophets, thirdly teachers, after that miracles, then gifts of healings, helps, governments, diversities of tongues. [29] *Are* all apostles? *are* all prophets? *are* all teachers? *are* all workers of miracles? [30] Have all the gifts of healing? do all speak with tongues? do all interpret? [31] But covet earnestly the best gifts: and yet shew I unto you a more excellent way.

The only way to get the Gifts of the Spirit is to be filled by the Spirit. The fact that these gifts were sent to heal and deliver means that Jesus pre-endowed the disciples with some of the Gifts of the Spirit. Healing and deliverance ministry includes revelation.

4. The Request

Whenever there is someone who is diseased or demonized, God generally uses a willing and Spirit-filled vessel. Jesus trained His followers in how to deal with sick, diseased and demonized people. He gave them authority over sickness, disease and the demonic. It was His joy to provide relief for those in trouble. The problem with His provision was that everybody would not receive His gift. He acknowledged with His disciples that some people would reject what He had to offer.

It is a strange thing to consider that some people would actually reject the Word of God, His miracles. I had to ask God to help me understand how anyone could reject the Word of God, the healing of God or the deliverance of God. It seems to me that any person in need ought to be willing to accept help anyplace they can get it. The fact of the matter is some people are so committed to what they know that they are unable or unwilling to know anything else. Others are so committed to their condition that they are unable or unwilling to know another condition. Some have learned to live with their sickness and it is okay with them. As odd as it seems, it appears as though they are okay with their demons, okay with their limited understanding and okay with their lifestyle. It is as if they are unable or unwilling to know or learn anything else. I have discovered that whenever a person is unable or unwilling to learn anything new it usually means they have deified their humanity. Their opinion is bigger than the opinion of God. They have deified their humanity so that their word, way, wisdom and direction seems better than what God has to offer. And instead of living in the fullness of God, they live on the fragments – fragments of blessings, fragments of faith, fragments of love, fragments of hope, fragments of patience, fragments of healing, fragments of deliverance. Beloved, God wants us to enjoy the fullness of His blessings. God wants us to make the request. Even though He knows what we have need of, He still wants us to ask. The Bible confirms in Philippians 4:6: "Be careful for nothing; but in every thing by prayer and supplication with thanksgiving let your requests be made known unto God." Matthew 7:1 adds, "Ask and it shall be given, seek and ye shall find, knock and it shall be open unto you." God wants us to make the request, whether for our self or someone else.

God expects self-less petitioners. Before going further, God does not mind when we petition Him for what we need. He is faithful to provide for us. God understands that His children have needs and He honors our request. Being a self-less petitioner does not mean we never have an opportunity to ask for ourselves. When I speak of self-less, I am referring to what the Oxford Dictionary suggests as one "concerned more with the needs and wishes of others than with one's own."[49] Simply put, we are putting someone ahead of ourselves. As God's chosen vessels, we are expected to request a blessing on someone else's behalf. Jesus sent His followers to be a blessing. Jesus warned them that if anyone rejects what they had to offer, not to get

_____

[49] C. Soanes and A. Stevenson, *Concise Oxford English Dictionary – 11th ed.* (Oxford: Oxford University Press, 2004), n. p.

angry or frustrated. People who reject the minister of God are not really rejecting the minister, but God Himself. Jesus said if people don't want what you have to offer, just shake the dust off your feet. Don't even leave a shoe print of blessings on a place that rejects God's Kingdom. The dust of that place is not even worthy to rest on the bottom of our sandals. All I can say to that is, "WOW!"

I'd like to encourage somebody. Just in case you have tried to bless somebody and they have rejected you, you have to learn to smile and shake the dust off your feet. If you do not learn to shake the dust off early, you will have to shake the devil off later. Whenever we face rejection and we let that fester, what happens is our feelings get involved. Sooner or later we get a bad attitude. We begin talking too much and thinking too much about why we have been rejected. In addition, we begin to tell this person and that person about our ordeal. Before we know it, instead of focusing on ministry, we begin plotting an eye for an eye; a tooth for a tooth; revenge; a comeback; a bounce-back; a playback; a payback. We assent, "They did it to me, I'm going to do it to them." Jesus warned of fighting fire with fire. He said bless them or shake the dust. If we don't learn how to shake dust early, we'll have to learn to shake demons later. Somebody just slept through that statement. We must remember that it is never about us. It is always about God. Whether we are accepted or rejected, healing and deliverance is always about God. Ministry is always about what God is doing and saying. Healing and deliverance includes the request.

5. The Reward

Jesus sent His followers out to represent the Kingdom of God. He gave them the authority to discern their surroundings. He gave them authority to bless the houses wherein they would enter. He gave them authority to heal the sick and diseased and cast out demons. He sent them trusting and depending on God. He did not allow them to take any extra money or clothes. Everything they would receive would come by way of their ministering to the people. The minister of God needs to know how to depend on God. Those who ask of God need to know how He will respond. Hebrews 11:6 confirms, "But without faith *it is* impossible to please *him*: for he that cometh to God must believe that he is, and *that* he is a rewarder of them that diligently seek him." God does not provide a stone to His children who ask for bread. He does not give a serpent to those asking for a drink. When we have faith in God and petition Him, He will reward our efforts.

The Gospels of Mark and Luke share a powerful result. Both Gospels confirm that the followers came back rejoicing. They rejoiced that they could heal the sick and cast out demons. I'm sure some of the psalmist's words left their lips. "Oh, taste and see that the Lord is good." "Bless the Lord oh my soul and all that's within me, bless His Holy Name." "Oh magnify the Lord with me; let us exalt His name together." Let us praise together via Psalm 100.

> [1] Make a joyful noise unto the LORD, all ye lands. [2] Serve the LORD with gladness: come before his presence with singing. [3] Know ye that the LORD he is God: it is

he that hath made us, and not we ourselves; we are his people, and the sheep of his pasture. [4] Enter into his gates with thanksgiving, and into his courts with praise: be thankful unto him, and bless his name. [5] For the LORD is good; his mercy is everlasting; and his truth endureth to all generations.

Healing and deliverance ministry includes the reward.

6. The Redundancy

Jesus then finalizes His assessment of their mission. Whenever there is healing and deliverance, there is always a need to come back and assess the results. A person who has been healed or delivered needs as much counseling after the experience as they received before the experience. If they don't get adequate counseling after being healed or delivered, it is possible that they will get sick or demonized again. This is called the redundancy. Assessment is also necessary for the minister. If the minister is not counseled after he/she has been successful in healing and deliverance ministry, he/she might become arrogant. They might think it's all about them rather than about God. Jesus handles the redundancy specifically with His followers. In the passage of Luke, Jesus makes a glaring statement. Don't get too excited that you were able to do these wonderful things. Be excited that your name is written down in My Father's Kingdom. Blessed are the eyes that see what you see. Blessed are the hearts that feel what you feel. You are blessed because you know the Son of God.

I am same Son who saw Satan rise up against my Father. I am the same Son who saw Satan fall from heaven. I am the same Son who came through 42 generations. I am the same Son who left glory above for earth below. I am the same Son who was born to die that ye might live.

One of My own will betray me. They will lead Me from judgment hall to judgment hall. They will lead Me up a hill called Calvary. They will nail me to an old rugged cross. I will hang My head and die. They will place Me in a borrowed tomb. I will stay there three long days. But they do not know there would be another part of the story. Greater love hath no man than this that a man lay down his life for his friends. No man can take My life but I will give My life. I will be dead for three days.

When I give My life, Do not lose hope. When I give My life, do not lose faith. When I give My life, just believe. Yes, I will be dead for three days but keep on trusting because the story does not end at My death. Hallelujah!

Jesus presents the reach, the reality, the revelation, the request, the reward, and the redundancy as important components of healing and deliverance ministry. There is a final component.

7. The Resurrection

The reason we can shout is because Jesus makes this statement, "I can lay down My life but I can pick it up again." Someone dozed right there and missed the hallelujah point. God specializes in making things that were dead, come alive again. Healing and deliverance ministry is all about taking that which was dead and making it rise again. Let me spell this out. Sometimes when we are sick or oppressed our smile dies and our joy fades. It is hard to smile when the pep in our step is dead. It is hard to smile when the full activity of our limbs is dead. It is hard to smile when our doctors have given up on us. The key to the healing and deliverance experience is resurrection. God specializes in resurrection. He specializes in resurrecting organs that have died. The blind see; the dumb, speak; the lame, walk; the deaf, hear; the leper, cleansed; the demonized, delivered; and the dead, raised-up. That which was dead will rise again. Jesus specializes in rising again. Yes, I will be dead for three long days but early on the third day I'll rise again. I'll rise again – death can't keep me in the ground. I'll rise again – can't nobody keep me down. I'll rise again – this is something Satan cannot stand. I'll rise again with all power in My hand. I'll rise again – folks will believe it and they will receive it. I'll rise again – folks will know it and God will show it. I'll rise again – I can bear it and you will share it.

Be encouraged by the Word of the Lord – John 14
[1] Let not your heart be troubled: ye believe in God, believe also in me. [2] In my Father's house are many mansions: if *it were* not *so*, I would have told you. I go to prepare a place for you. [3] And if I go and prepare a place for you, I will come again, and receive you unto myself; that where I am, *there* ye may be also.

[4] And whither I go ye know, and the way ye know. [5] Thomas saith unto him, Lord, we know not whither thou goest; and how can we know the way? [6] Jesus saith unto him, I am the way, the truth, and the life: no man cometh unto the Father, but by me. [7] If ye had known me, ye should have known my Father also: and from henceforth ye know him, and have seen him. [8] Philip saith unto him, Lord, shew us the Father, and it sufficeth us. [9] Jesus saith unto him, Have I been so long time with you, and yet hast thou not known me, Philip? he that hath seen me hath seen the Father; and how sayest thou *then*, Shew us the Father? [10] Believest thou not that I am in the Father, and the Father in me? the words that I speak unto you I speak not of myself: but the Father that dwelleth in me, he doeth the works. [11] Believe me that I *am* in the Father, and the Father in me: or else believe me for the very works' sake.

[12] Verily, verily, I say unto you, He that believeth on me, the works that I do shall he do also; and greater *works* than these shall he do; because I go unto my Father. [13] And whatsoever ye shall ask in my name, that will I do, that the Father may be glorified in the Son. [14] If ye shall ask any thing in my name, I will do *it*.

[15] If ye love me, keep my commandments. [16] And I will pray the Father, and he shall give you another Comforter, that he may abide with you forever; [17] *Even* the Spirit of truth; whom the world cannot receive, because it seeth him not, neither knoweth him: but ye know him; for he dwelleth with you, and shall be in you.

[18] I will not leave you comfortless: I will come to you. [19] Yet a little while, and the world seeth me no more; but ye see me: because I live, ye shall live also. [20] At that day ye shall know that I *am* in my Father, and ye in me, and I in you. [21] He that hath my commandments, and keepeth them, he it is that loveth me: and he that

loveth me shall be loved of my Father, and I will love him, and will manifest myself to him. [22] Judas saith unto him, not Iscariot, Lord, how is it that thou wilt manifest thyself unto us, and not unto the world? [23] Jesus answered and said unto him, If a man love me, he will keep my words: and my Father will love him, and we will come unto him, and make our abode with him. [24] He that loveth me not keepeth not my sayings: and the word which ye hear is not mine, but the Father's which sent me.

[25] These things have I spoken unto you, being *yet* present with you. [26] But the Comforter, *which is* the Holy Ghost, whom the Father will send in my name, he shall teach you all things, and bring all things to your remembrance, whatsoever I have said unto you. [27] Peace I leave with you, my peace I give unto you: not as the world giveth, give I unto you. Let not your heart be troubled, neither let it be afraid.

[28] Ye have heard how I said unto you, I go away, and come *again* unto you. If ye loved me, ye would rejoice, because I said, I go unto the Father: for my Father is greater than I. [29] And now I have told you before it come to pass, that, when it is come to pass, ye might believe. [30] Hereafter I will not talk much with you: for the prince of this world cometh, and hath nothing in me. [31] But that the world may know that I love the Father; and as the Father gave me commandment, even so I do. Arise, let us go hence.

"Why God Heals and Delivers"
Luke 4:14-22; Isaiah 61; 53; Matthew 4:23-24

If there is anything obvious to me, it is the fact that humanity is in trouble. Death, destruction and disease are all around us.

Death

Death is that which is dead and decaying. Death is the product of something that was once alive. That which was living is now dead. The dead and decaying often come with a stench. More times than not, you can smell that which is dead and decaying before you see it.

Destruction

Destruction is that which breaks down that which is functioning. It takes the usable and makes it unusable. It takes the wanted and makes it unwanted. It takes the desirable and makes it undesirable. Destruction normally leaves rubble in its wake. There are fragment footnotes of what once was.

Disease

Disease is that which affects the living. It sends malfunction to the functioning. Its byproducts are symptoms that scream a cause beneath the effect. Pain, discomfort, incapacity are just a few effects behind the cause. If there is anything obvious to me, it is the fact that humanity is in trouble. Death, destruction and disease are all around us.

We do not have to search too far or too long to find these three troublemakers. If we turn on our television, we will find them. If we step outside our front door, we will find them. We will find them at school, work, the grocery store, barber shop, beauty shop, nail salon, everywhere. Death, destruction and disease are all around us.

I believe this is why people stay home. Beloved, you can stay home but I declare that death, destruction and disease are undaunted. Death, destruction and disease all say, "If you won't come outside and play with us, we'll come inside and play with you." That's not a petition – it's a promise! They don't ask permission to come – they just come. Some people have the feeling that they are automatically protected in the house of God. People say, "That's why I go to church. In church I'm protected." I hate to be the bearer of bad news but these three bunk-mates are often sitting in the pew right next to us.

Here comes the inquiry. How do death, destruction and disease find their way into the church? How do they get in there? These three are not on our invite list. We did not evangelize them. This place is no place for them because this is the house of God. Well, I'm not so sure of the above assessment. Death, destruction and disease are all around us. The unsaved and the unchurched are saturated with these three. Most of the time they are unaware because they don't realize how these three impact their existence. Whatever baggage they have, they carry it without knowing they can put it down. The unchurched and the unsaved that are aware, have learned to cope with them and if they come to church, they'll bring death, destruction and disease with them. Before you start looking around at unfamiliar faces, I declare to you that there is yet another sad reality.

The church folk are not as immune as you may think. Some people are so messed up at home that they have learned how to live with death, destruction and disease. They allow death, destruction and disease to co-habitate. They become running partners. They even bring these three with them to church – as invited guests! Don't look at the visitor's roster because they don't sign in. This makes us think twice about those on our right and our left. Some people make it obvious. They come to church with a foul attitude. They hardly speak to the people in the sanctuary. They come in with their negative spirits seemingly always ready to present their negative commentary. They are accusers of the bretheren. Whatever auxiliary they happen to be a part of, seems to be rife with trouble.

We all have either been members or visitors of churches like this. We know what it is to worship alongside a negative person in church. The church has its share of mean-spirited, jealous, gossiping, rude, cussing, fussing, ill-mannered people. I have traveled to and visited congregations in several parts of this country and much to my surprise, people do bring death, destruction and disease with them to church. Folks come to church like "Schleprock" (a la Flintstones) with a cloud of doom circling overhead. That's why sometimes when we say, "Church was bad today" we need to take inventory to see who was there. In a similar sense, we need to do the same when we say, "Church was good today" to see who was missing from service. I hear somebody asking the obvious, "Why can't we just get rid of them?" My answer is this, "How can you remove a sick person out of the hospital?" People who need healing and deliverance need to come where healing and deliverance is expected – and that is the House of Prayer. It is in the House of Prayer where we find hope for the hopeless and help for the helpless. It is in the House of Prayer where we find a God who heals and delivers.

We need to realize that death, destruction and disease are all symptoms of a greater problem. Ephesians 6:12 explains it this way: "We wrestle not against flesh and blood, but against principalities, against powers, against the rulers of the darkness of this world, against spiritual wickedness in high *places*." There is a spiritual dimension that explains why death, destruction and disease exist. Everything centers on the Fall of Man.

When man first sinned in the Garden of Eden, death, destruction and disease became our pilgrim partners. Everywhere we went, death, destruction and disease followed us. Isaiah 53:6 captures our incarceration. "All we like sheep have gone astray; we have turned every one to his own way." This is why the Ephesian statement is so important. Principalities, powers, rulers of the darkness of this world and spiritual wickedness in high places are behind the death, destruction and disease we face every day. We are suppressed, oppressed and depressed by a damaging dimension outside of ourselves. This is why God heals and delivers. We are unable to (on our own) heal and deliver ourselves from that which causes death, destruction and disease. We need a healer and a deliverer.

Yes, **Isaiah 53:6 says**, "All we like sheep have gone astray; we have turned every one to his own way." But that passage continues.

And the LORD hath laid on him the iniquity of us all. [7] He was oppressed, and he was afflicted, yet he opened not his mouth: he is brought as a lamb to the slaughter, and as a sheep before her shearers is dumb, so he openeth not his mouth. [8] He was taken from prison and from judgment: and who shall declare his generation? for he was cut off out of the land of the living: for the transgression of my people was he stricken. [9] And he made his grave with the wicked, and with the rich in his death; because he had done no violence, neither *was any* deceit in his mouth.

[10] Yet it pleased the LORD to bruise him; he hath put *him* to grief: when thou shalt make his soul an offering for sin, he shall see *his* seed, he shall prolong *his* days, and the pleasure of the LORD shall prosper in his hand. [11] He shall see of the travail of his soul, *and* shall be satisfied: by his knowledge shall my righteous servant justify many; for he shall bear their iniquities. [12] Therefore will I divide him *a portion* with the great, and he shall divide the spoil with the strong; because he hath poured out his soul unto death: and he was numbered with the transgressors; and he bare the sin of many, and made intercession for the transgressors.

God is our Healer and Deliverer. He heals and delivers through

His Son Jesus Christ. **Luke's passage (4:18-21),** quoted from

Isaiah 61 now makes sense.

[18] The Spirit of the Lord *is* upon me, because he hath anointed me to preach the gospel to the poor; he hath sent me to heal the brokenhearted, to preach deliverance to the captives, and recovering of sight to the blind, to set at liberty them that are bruised, [19] To preach the acceptable year of the Lord. [20] And he closed the

book, and he gave *it* again to the minister, and sat down. And the eyes of all them that were in the synagogue were fastened on him. [21] And he began to say unto them, This day is this scripture fulfilled in your ears.

Jesus is our Healer and our Deliverer. The preached Word is substance for the poor; mending for the torn asunder; fixing for the broken-hearted; deliverance for the captive; sight for the blind; and liberation for the bruised. The preached Word is acceptable here and now.

When Jesus departs from Isaiah's text and places His own footnote in verse 21, God's validation was with Him. "This day is this Scripture fulfilled in your ears," was His addendum which meant that the One whom we seek outside of ourselves for healing and deliverance is now present – Emmanuel, God with us. The One who can do something about our problem is here.

Sometimes when we have an answer to a problem, we deny the answer to that problem. In other words, when we accept a condition with our own assessment or the assessment of others, we tend to stop looking for *the answer*. An example of this is the homosexual community. Before going further, please know that

I am not homophobic. I have a few friends who are gay and others whom I suspect are gay as well. I relate to the homosexuals pretty much as I relate to heterosexuals. They are people who need the same love and attention as anybody else. Whenever I hear a discussion on why they are gay, I hear statements like these: "God made me this way;" "I was born this way;" or "I am really a person whose gender was placed in the wrong body." This is an answer but not *the answer*. *The answer* is found in Genesis 3:17-19.

> And unto Adam he said, "Because thou hast hearkened unto the voice of thy wife, and hast eaten of the tree, of which I commanded thee, saying, Thou shalt not eat of it: cursed *is* the ground for thy sake; in sorrow shalt thou eat *of* it all the days of thy life; [18] Thorns also and thistles shall it bring forth to thee; and thou shalt eat the herb of the field; [19] In the sweat of thy face shalt thou eat bread, till thou return unto the ground; for out of it wast thou taken: for dust thou *art*, and unto dust shalt thou return."

The answer is found in the statement, "cursed is the ground." When the ground was cursed, it meant that anything that resided on and ate that which came from the ground would be considered living with and consuming death. The cursed ground would affect all the inhabitants of earth. For this reason, people are born with conditions many of us question as to whether or not there is a generational issue involved. Persons are born with all sorts of diseases and we do not think twice about the cause. Birth defects abound and we have learned to accept them without question. When a person says they were born gay, we lift our hands in disdain. Yes, I have read Psalm 139:14 which states, "I will praise thee; for I am fearfully *and* wonderfully made: marvellous *are* thy works; and *that* my soul knoweth right well." I have read Psalm 51:5 which states, "Behold, I was shapen in iniquity; And in sin did my mother conceive me." I have also read Jeremiah 1:5 which states, "Before I formed thee in the belly I knew thee; and before thou camest forth out of the womb I sanctified thee, *and* I ordained thee a prophet unto the nations." The two Psalm passages speak of the conditions of birth. However we come into the world, God knows all about it. The often misquoted Jeremiah passage speaks of what God ordains.

People have used this Scripture as a way of proving God's acceptance. This passage really speaks of God's encouragement to one who feels unequipped to preach and prophesy for God. That God encourages Jeremiah this way by using these words will help him preach and prophesy to hard-headed and hard-hearted people. He is not licensing Jeremiah to live a life of sin. He is licensing Jeremiah to preach His Word.

To close this argument we must address *the answer* versus an answer. *The answer* for why people say they were born as homosexual is not because God made them what way but because the ground is cursed. Many homosexuals have taken *the answer* and replaced it with their answer. By trusting their answer, they in effect are rejecting *the answer*. I would be remiss if I did not get insight from **Leviticus 18:22-30.**

Leviticus 18:22-30
> [22] Thou shalt not lie with mankind, as with womankind: it *is* abomination. [23] Neither shalt thou lie with any beast to defile thyself therewith: neither shall any woman stand before a beast to lie down thereto: it *is* confusion.
> [24] Defile not ye yourselves in any of these things: for in

all these the nations are defiled which I cast out before you: ²⁵ And the land is defiled: therefore I do visit the iniquity thereof upon it, and the land itself vomiteth out her inhabitants. ²⁶ Ye shall therefore keep my statutes and my judgments, and shall not commit *any* of these abominations; *neither* any of your own nation, nor any stranger that sojourneth among you: ²⁷ (For all these abominations have the men of the land done, which *were* before you, and the land is defiled;) ²⁸ That the land spue not you out also, when ye defile it, as it spued out the nations that *were* before you. ²⁹ For whosoever shall commit any of these abominations, even the souls that commit *them* shall be cut off from among their people. ³⁰ Therefore shall ye keep mine ordinance, that *ye* commit not *any one* of these abominable customs, which were committed before you, and that ye defile not yourselves therein: I *am* the LORD your God.

Leviticus 22:10-27

¹⁰ And the man that committeth adultery with *another* man's wife, *even he* that committeth adultery with his neighbour's wife, the adulterer and the adulteress shall surely be put to death. ¹¹ And the man that lieth with his father's wife hath uncovered his father's nakedness: both of them shall surely be put to death; their blood *shall be* upon them. ¹² And if a man lie with his daughter in law, both of them shall surely be put to death: they have wrought confusion; their blood *shall be* upon them. ¹³ If a man also lie with mankind, as he lieth with a woman, both of them have committed an abomination: they shall surely be put to death; their blood *shall be* upon them. ¹⁴ And if a man take a wife and her mother, it *is* wickedness: they shall be burnt with fire, both he and they; that there be no wickedness among you. ¹⁵ And if a man lie with a beast, he shall surely be put to death: and ye shall slay the beast. ¹⁶ And if a woman approach unto

any beast, and lie down thereto, thou shalt kill the woman, and the beast: they shall surely be put to death; their blood *shall be* upon them. [17] And if a man shall take his sister, his father's daughter, or his mother's daughter, and see her nakedness, and she see his nakedness; it *is* a wicked thing; and they shall be cut off in the sight of their people: he hath uncovered his sister's nakedness; he shall bear his iniquity. [18] And if a man shall lie with a woman having her sickness, and shall uncover her nakedness; he hath discovered her fountain, and she hath uncovered the fountain of her blood: and both of them shall be cut off from among their people. [19] And thou shalt not uncover the nakedness of thy mother's sister, nor of thy father's sister: for he uncovereth his near kin: they shall bear their iniquity. [20] And if a man shall lie with his uncle's wife, he hath uncovered his uncle's nakedness: they shall bear their sin; they shall die childless. [21] And if a man shall take his brother's wife, it *is* an unclean thing: he hath uncovered his brother's nakedness; they shall be childless.

[22] Ye shall therefore keep all my statutes, and all my judgments, and do them: that the land, whither I bring you to dwell therein, spue you not out. [23] And ye shall not walk in the manners of the nation, which I cast out before you: for they committed all these things, and therefore I abhorred them. [24] But I have said unto you, Ye shall inherit their land, and I will give it unto you to possess it, a land that floweth with milk and honey: I *am* the LORD your God, which have separated you from *other* people. [25] Ye shall therefore put difference between clean beasts and unclean, and between unclean fowls and clean: and ye shall not make your souls abominable by beast, or by fowl, or by any manner of living thing that creepeth on the ground, which I have separated from you as unclean. [26] And ye shall be holy unto me: for I the

LORD *am* holy, and have severed you from *other* people, that ye should be mine. [27] A man also or woman that hath a familiar spirit, or that is a wizard, shall surely be put to death: they shall stone them with stones: their blood *shall be* upon them.

This passage addresses sexual behavior and spells it out completely. I do not feel compelled to say much more on this subject because it is not what this book is attempting to address. What I am merely pointing out is the fact that we often accept an answer over and above *the answer*. The Truth is not invalidated because we choose not to believe it. The Truth is the Truth in spite of our convictions. Regardless to what and how we were born, there is no condition that God is incapable of fixing. God can fix whoever wants to be fixed. He makes the crooked straight and the rough places plain. God is still the Heart-fixer and the Mind-regulator and He is the only One capable of healing and delivering us. Matthew 4:23-24 verifies that Jesus is our Healer and Deliverer.

[23] And Jesus went about all Galilee, teaching in their synagogues, and preaching the gospel of the kingdom,

249

and healing all manner of sickness and all manner of disease among the people. [24] And his fame went throughout all Syria: and they brought unto him all sick people that were taken with divers diseases and torments, and those which were possessed with devils, and those which were lunatick, and those that had the palsy; and he healed them.

There is only one reason why God heals and delivers. It is because He loves us. 2 Peter 3:9 says: "The Lord is not slack concerning his promise, as some men count slackness; but is longsuffering to us-ward, not willing that any should perish, but that all should come to repentance." Romans 5:8 says: "But God commendeth his love toward us, in that, while we were yet sinners, Christ died for us." John 3:16 says: "For God so loved the world that He gave His Only Begotten Son, that whosoever believeth on Him should not perish but have eternal life."

The reason why God heals and delivers is because He loves us. We don't have to live with death, destruction and disease any longer because Jesus is our Healer and Deliverer. It's time to evict the squatters from our residence. It's time to kick the non-rent payers out of our house. It's time to remove the problem and rely on the solution.

Not only should death, destruction and disease be removed from our *home* but we have the power to remove them from our *life*. He that has Jesus has eternal life. In Jesus there is no more death, no more sickness, and no more disease. In Jesus we take off the mortal and put on immortality; in Him, we take off corruption and put on incorruption; in Him, we take off death and put on life. There is only one reason why God heals and delivers. It is because He loves us.

Since we have been healed and delivered, we must remove death, destruction and disease from our hearing. Psalm 1 says:
[1] Blessed *is* the man that walketh not in the counsel of the ungodly, nor standeth in the way of sinners, nor sitteth in the seat of the scornful. [2] But his delight *is* in the law of the LORD; and in his law doth he meditate day and night. [3] And he shall be like a tree planted by the rivers of water, that bringeth forth his fruit in his season; his leaf also shall not wither; and whatsoever he doeth shall prosper.
[4] The ungodly *are* not so: but *are* like the chaff which the wind driveth away. [5] Therefore the ungodly shall not stand in the judgment, nor sinners in the congregation of the righteous. [6] For the LORD knoweth the way of the righteous: but the way of the ungodly shall perish.

Removing death, destruction and disease from our hearing is done purposefully through faith. Faith comes by hearing and hearing by the Word of God. The Word of God is a Lamp unto our feet and a Light unto our pathway. We must hide His Word in our hearts that we might not sin against Him. God's Word brings healing and deliverance. A familiar nursery rhyme refrains "Be careful little eyes what you see; be careful little ears what you hear and be careful little heart what you feel." There is so much truth in these simple words. To remedy our problem, we must see, hear and feel healing and deliverance.

Since we have been healed and delivered, we must remove death, destruction and disease from our thinking.

Norman Vincent Peale had an interesting assessment of the human mind. He said, "As a man thinketh in his heart, so is he." I do know there is much truth in this statement. I know people who think negatively and there is negative all around them. In the same sense, I know people who think positively and there is positive all around them. If we want to be free, we must elevate our thinking. Isaiah 26:3 says, "Thou will keep him in perfect peace all whose mind is stayed on Thee, because he

trusteth in Thee." Philippians 4:7-9

> [7] And the peace of God, which passeth all understanding,
> shall keep your hearts and minds through Christ Jesus. [8]
> Finally, brethren, whatsoever things are true, whatsoever
> things *are* honest, whatsoever things *are* just, whatsoever
> things *are* pure, whatsoever things *are* lovely,
> whatsoever things *are* of good report; if *there be* any
> virtue, and if *there be* any praise, think on these things.
> [9] Those things, which ye have both learned, and received,
> and heard, and seen in me, do: and the God of peace shall
> be with you.

If we want peace, we must think on the things of God. The

things of God bring healing, deliverance and peace. Be careful

little mind what you think. To remedy our problem, we must

think healing and deliverance.

***Since we have been healed and delivered, we must remove
death, destruction and disease from our speaking.***
Speaking is a form of communication that features

primarily the mouth. Notwithstanding gestures and body

language, the bulk of our communication comes by way of the

tongue. There are well over one hundred Bible entries related to

the tongue. Solomon is attributed to having had the most to say on the subject of the tongue. He should know since he had seven hundred wives and three hundred concubines. A man with that many women around him has to have learned what to say and when to say it. Knowing when and when not to speak has to have been a special gift to a man with a thousand women around.

In particular, the book of Proverbs has a great deal to say about the tongue. Proverbs 18:21 says, "there is life and death in the power of the **tongue**." Proverbs 10:31 says, "The mouth of the righteous brings forth wisdom, but the perverse **tongue** will be cut off." Proverbs 15:2 says, "The **tongue** of the wise commends knowledge, but the mouths of fools pour out folly." Learning what to say and when to say it is indeed a gift. For the believer, the best gift is learning how to speak with faith. Hebrews 11:1 says, "Now faith is the substance of things hoped for and the evidence of things not seen." It goes on to say in verse 6, "Without faith, it is impossible to please God." We need to learn to speak with mountain-moving faith trusting that God will do it. Speaking folly or foolishly keeps wrong things in our environment. Speaking spiritually or faithfully keeps right things in our environment. It is all up to us and how we use our tongues. Be careful little mouth what you speak. To remedy our problem of sickness, disease and demonization, we must learn to speak healing and deliverance. Since Jesus has come to heal and deliver, we must elevate our hearing, thinking and speaking. There is only one reason why God heals and delivers. It is because He loves us.

> *Jesus loves the little children, all the children of the world.*
> *Red and yellow, black and white, they are precious in His sight.*
> *Jesus loves the little children of the world.*

> *Jesus loves me this I know for the Bible tells me so.*
> *Little ones to Him belong, they are weak but He is strong.*
> *Yes, Jesus loves me for the Bible tells me so.*

Scripture references for our reading
Luke 4:14-22

[14] And Jesus returned in the power of the Spirit into Galilee: and there went out a fame of him through all the region round about. [15] And he taught in their synagogues, being glorified of all. [16] And he came to Nazareth, where he had been brought up: and, as his custom was, he went into the synagogue on the sabbath day, and stood up for

to read. [17] And there was delivered unto him the book of the prophet Esaias. And when he had opened the book, he found the place where it was written, [18] The Spirit of the Lord *is* upon me, because he hath anointed me to preach the gospel to the poor; he hath sent me to heal the brokenhearted, to preach deliverance to the captives, and recovering of sight to the blind, to set at liberty them that are bruised, [19] To preach the acceptable year of the Lord. [20] And he closed the book, and he gave *it* again to the minister, and sat down. And the eyes of all them that were in the synagogue were fastened on him. [21] And he began to say unto them, This day is this scripture fulfilled in your ears. [22] And all bare him witness, and wondered at the gracious words which proceeded out of his mouth. And they said, Is not this Joseph's son?

Matthew 4:23-24

[23] And Jesus went about all Galilee, teaching in their synagogues, and preaching the gospel of the kingdom, and healing all manner of sickness and all manner of disease among the people. [24] And his fame went throughout all Syria: and they brought unto him all sick people that were taken with divers diseases and torments, and those which were possessed with devils, and those which were lunatick, and those that had the palsy; and he healed them.

Isaiah 61

[1] The Spirit of the Lord GOD *is* upon me; because the LORD hath anointed me to preach good tidings unto the meek; he hath sent me to bind up the brokenhearted, to proclaim liberty to the captives, and the opening of the prison to *them that are* bound; [2] To proclaim the acceptable year of the LORD, and the day of vengeance of our God; to comfort all that mourn; [3] To appoint unto them that mourn in Zion, to give unto them beauty for ashes, the oil of joy for mourning, the garment of praise

for the spirit of heaviness; that they might be called trees of righteousness, the planting of the LORD, that he might be glorified.

⁴ And they shall build the old wastes, they shall raise up the former desolations, and they shall repair the waste cities, the desolations of many generations. ⁵ And strangers shall stand and feed your flocks, and the sons of the alien *shall be* your plowmen and your vinedressers. ⁶ But ye shall be named the Priests of the LORD: *men* shall call you the Ministers of our God: ye shall eat the riches of the Gentiles, and in their glory shall ye boast yourselves. ⁷ For your shame *ye shall have* double; and *for* confusion they shall rejoice in their portion: therefore in their land they shall possess the double: everlasting joy shall be unto them. ⁸ For I the LORD love judgment, I hate robbery for burnt offering; and I will direct their work in truth, and I will make an everlasting covenant with them. ⁹ And their seed shall be known among the Gentiles, and their offspring among the people: all that see them shall acknowledge them, that they *are* the seed *which* the LORD hath blessed.

¹⁰ I will greatly rejoice in the LORD, my soul shall be joyful in my God; for he hath clothed me with the garments of salvation, he hath covered me with the robe of righteousness, as a bridegroom decketh *himself* with ornaments, and as a bride adorneth *herself* with her jewels. ¹¹ For as the earth bringeth forth her bud, and as the garden causeth the things that are sown in it to spring forth; so the Lord GOD will cause righteousness and praise to spring forth before all the nations.

Isaiah 53

¹ Who hath believed our report ? and to whom is the arm of the LORD revealed? ² For he shall grow up before him as a tender plant, and as a root out of a dry ground: he hath no form nor comeliness; and when we shall see

him, *there is* no beauty that we should desire him. ³ He is despised and rejected of men; a man of sorrows, and acquainted with grief: and we hid as it were *our* faces from him; he was despised, and we esteemed him not.

⁴ Surely he hath borne our griefs, and carried our sorrows: yet we did esteem him stricken, smitten of God, and afflicted. ⁵ But he *was* wounded for our transgressions, *he was* bruised for our iniquities: the chastisement of our peace *was* upon him; and with his stripes we are healed. ⁶ All we like sheep have gone astray; we have turned every one to his own way; and the LORD hath laid on him the iniquity of us all. ⁷ He was oppressed, and he was afflicted, yet he opened not his mouth: he is brought as a lamb to the slaughter, and as a sheep before her shearers is dumb, so he openeth not his mouth. ⁸ He was taken from prison and from judgment: and who shall declare his generation? for he was cut off out of the land of the living: for the transgression of my people was he stricken. ⁹ And he made his grave with the wicked, and with the rich in his death; because he had done no violence, neither *was any* deceit in his mouth.

¹⁰ Yet it pleased the LORD to bruise him; he hath put *him* to grief: when thou shalt make his soul an offering for sin, he shall see *his* seed, he shall prolong *his* days, and the pleasure of the LORD shall prosper in his hand. ¹¹ He shall see of the travail of his soul, *and* shall be satisfied: by his knowledge shall my righteous servant justify many; for he shall bear their iniquities. ¹² Therefore will I divide him *a portion* with the great, and he shall divide the spoil with the strong; because he hath poured out his soul unto death: and he was numbered with the transgressors; and he bare the sin of many, and made intercession for the transgressors.

"The Healing and Deliverance Prescription,"
James 5:12-20; 1 John 1

I have discovered that it is a fact that good people do suffer. Job said man has but a few days to live and all those days are filled with misery. Yes, good people do suffer.

Sometimes our friends frustrate us.

When Job was going through his storm, his friends came to accuse him. They blamed Job's problems on him. "You must have made God mad. You must have sinned against God. You're suffering Job because of you." Friends do exacerbate our suffering. When they do not understand what we are going through they often make our lives worse. Sometimes when we need a friend the most, our friends do not appear friendly. So good people do suffer and are frustrated by friends.

Sometimes our family frustrates us.

Joseph was sold into slavery by his own brothers. What kind of family will sell its own into slavery? The top answer to the survey is a jealous family. The second best answer is a heartless family. It is a fact that while you can pick your friends, you cannot pick your family. We are born where we are born, when we are born, how we are born all without our choosing. We cannot choose our color, our culture, or our condition. When we are born, we are born where we are born and that is it. Yes, family will sometimes make us suffer. In a word, good people do suffer and are frustrated by family.

Sometimes our physicality frustrates us.

Our physicality includes how we look, how we are shaped, and how we feel. In the society we live in, we can do something about some of this. If we have enough money, we can do something about our looks. We can add hair, puff our lips, lift our face, bleach or darken our skin. With the right money, we can do something about our looks. Unfortunately, the poor people have to live with their looks. Yes, with enough money, we can do something about our looks.

Resources are the name of the game. We do more with the right resources. We can do something about our shape. We can augment this, reduce that, push up this, push down that, expand this, reduce that. There is even a machine that has a vacuum-like attachment that doctors can stick inside you to vacuum stuff out. For the right price, they will even let you use what has been vacuumed out to put back in someplace else. Yes, with the right money, we can do something about our shape. Unfortunately, the poor people have to live with their shape.

My questions though have to do with what happens outside the realm of surgical procedure. We may be able to pay for procedure after procedure but what about how we feel? Has any consideration been given concerning how our body works? What about a heart condition, kidney failure, liver disorder, or lung disease? Sometimes even the rich can't buy their way out of these. They might be able to buy their way up a donor list but they really cannot buy health. So it is true, good people suffer and are frustrated by friends, family or physicality.

For the good people who are going through a physical storm, I want to speak into your life today. Somebody has numbness in a place that should not be numb – God has a Word for you today. Somebody has pain in a place that should not be painful – God has a Word for you today. Somebody has malfunction in a place that should function as designed – God has a Word for you today. Somebody has something growing or spreading in a place that should not be there – God has a Word for you today. God has a healing and deliverance prescription for you.

Before going further, I am feeling led to ask you to do something unique. I hope you will use what you have learned thus far and simply have child-like faith at this juncture. Please place your hand on this page and pray with me.

> *Dear God, I thank You for giving me this book to read. It is a book about healing and deliverance. Lord, I have a pain (state the location) and I know this pain should not be where it is. Lord, I believe in Your Son Jesus Christ and that He died on the cross and rose from the dead for me. Lord, I believe in Your healing and in Your deliverance. Lord, I praise You for being Who You are.*

You are my Healer and my Deliverer. Lord, I need Your power over the enemy. I claim my healing the name of Jesus Christ. I also claim my deliverance in the name of Jesus Christ. I realize I am powerless without Your Son Jesus. I realize I have power in Jesus Christ. Lord as Your anointing overshadows me, I know Your healing will come as well. I plead the blood of Jesus on my case. Lord, I will tell everybody who will hear me about what You have done for me. You have to get the glory for Your miracle and the church will be edified. Lord, I will testify and I thank You in advance for my healing. I will not doubt one moment and I claim victory in Jesus' name. Amen.

I trust you are already feeling better. If you have

someone who is in the room with you and is in need, repeat this

prayer while touching this page and holding their hand.

Remember, it is not about you. It is always about God and what

He is doing. If anyone is suffering, God is interested. God

reminds us that the righteous do suffer in Psalm 34, particularly

in verses 11-22.

There is the praise (verses 1-3). "[1] I will bless the LORD at all

times: his praise *shall* continually *be* in my mouth. [2] My soul

shall make her boast in the LORD: the humble shall hear *thereof,* and be glad. ³ O magnify the LORD with me, and let us exalt his name together."

There is the petition (verses 4-7). "⁴ I sought the LORD, and he heard me, and delivered me from all my fears. ⁵ They looked unto him, and were lightened: and their faces were not ashamed. ⁶ This poor man cried, and the LORD heard *him*, and saved him out of all his troubles. ⁷ The angel of the LORD encampeth round about them that fear him, and delivereth them."

There is the prescription (verse 8-10). "⁸ O taste and see that the LORD *is* good: blessed *is* the man *that* trusteth in him. ⁹ O fear the LORD, ye his saints: for *there is* no want to them that fear him. ¹⁰ The young lions do lack, and suffer hunger: but they that seek the LORD shall not want any good *thing*."

There is the problem (verses 11-22).

> ¹¹ Come, ye children, hearken unto me: I will teach you the fear of the LORD. ¹² What man *is he that* desireth life, *and* loveth *many* days, that he may see good? ¹³ Keep thy tongue from evil, and thy lips from speaking guile. ¹⁴ Depart from evil, and do good; seek peace, and pursue it. ¹⁵ The eyes of the LORD *are* upon the

righteous, and his ears *are open* unto their cry. [16] The face of the LORD *is* against them that do evil, to cut off the remembrance of them from the earth. [17] *The righteous* cry, and the LORD heareth, and delivereth them out of all their troubles. [18] The LORD *is* nigh unto them that are of a broken heart; and saveth such as be of a contrite spirit. [19] Many *are* the afflictions of the righteous: but the LORD delivereth him out of them all. [20] He keepeth all his bones: not one of them is broken. [21] Evil shall slay the wicked: and they that hate the righteous shall be desolate. [22] The LORD redeemeth the soul of his servants: and none of them that trust in him shall be desolate.

Psalm 34 validates that the righteous people do suffer.

Beloved, sometimes well meaning people suffer or get sick because of behavior, belief and background problems. Sometimes our bodies do not function properly because of these issues. In particular, behavior problems link to sin.

Read the Word of the Lord in Psalm 107:17-22 concerning sickness, iniquity and sin.

[17] Fools because of their transgression, and because of their iniquities, are afflicted. [18] Their soul abhorreth all manner of meat; and they draw near unto the gates of death. [19] Then they cry unto the LORD in their trouble, *and* he saveth them out of their distresses. [20] He sent his word, and healed them, and delivered *them* from their destructions. [21] Oh that *men* would praise the LORD *for* his goodness, and *for* his wonderful works to the children of men! [22] And let them sacrifice the sacrifices of thanksgiving, and declare his works with rejoicing.

Read the Word of the Lord in Ephesians 4:17-32 concerning behavior matters.

[17] This I say therefore, and testify in the Lord, that ye henceforth walk not as other Gentiles walk, in the vanity of their mind, [18] Having the understanding darkened, being alienated from the life of God through the ignorance that is in them, because of the blindness of their heart: [19] Who being past feeling have given themselves over unto lasciviousness, to work all uncleanness with greediness. [20] But ye have not so learned Christ; [21] If so be that ye have heard him, and have been taught by him, as the truth is in Jesus: [22] That ye put off concerning the former conversation the old man, which is corrupt according to the deceitful lusts; [23] And be renewed in the spirit of your mind; [24] And that ye put on the new man, which after God is created in righteousness and true holiness. [25] Wherefore putting away lying, speak every man truth with his neighbour: for we are members one of another. [26] Be ye angry, and sin not: let not the sun go down upon your wrath: [27] Neither give place to the devil. [28] Let him that stole steal no more: but rather let him labour, working with *his* hands the thing which is good, that he may have to give to him that needeth. [29] Let no corrupt communication proceed out of your mouth, but that which is good to the use of edifying, that it may minister grace unto the hearers. [30] And grieve not the holy Spirit of God, whereby ye are sealed unto the day of redemption. [31] Let all bitterness, and wrath, and anger, and clamour, and evil speaking, be put away from you, with all malice: [32] And be ye kind one to another, tenderhearted, forgiving one another, even as God for Christ's sake hath forgiven you.

Read the Word of the Lord in James 4 which shares more about behavior.

[1] From whence *come* wars and fightings among you? *come they* not hence, *even* of your lusts that war in your members? [2] Ye lust, and have not: ye kill, and desire to have, and cannot obtain: ye fight and war, yet ye have not, because ye ask not. [3] Ye ask, and receive not, because ye ask amiss, that ye may consume *it* upon your lusts. [4] Ye adulterers and adulteresses, know ye not that the friendship of the world is enmity with God? whosoever therefore will be a friend of the world is the enemy of God. [5] Do ye think that the scripture saith in vain, The spirit that dwelleth in us lusteth to envy? [6] But he giveth more grace. Wherefore he saith, God resisteth the proud, but giveth grace unto the humble. [7] Submit yourselves therefore to God. Resist the devil, and he will flee from you. [8] Draw nigh to God, and he will draw nigh to you. Cleanse *your* hands, *ye* sinners; and purify *your* hearts, *ye* double minded. [9] Be afflicted, and mourn, and weep: let your laughter be turned to mourning, and *your* joy to heaviness. [10] Humble yourselves in the sight of the Lord, and he shall lift you up.

[11] Speak not evil one of another, brethren. He that speaketh evil of *his* brother, and judgeth his brother, speaketh evil of the law, and judgeth the law: but if thou judge the law, thou art not a doer of the law, but a judge. [12] There is one lawgiver, who is able to save and to destroy: who art thou that judgest another? [13] Go to now, ye that say, To day or to morrow we will go into such a city, and continue there a year, and buy and sell, and get gain: [14] Whereas ye know not what *shall be* on the morrow. For what *is* your life? It is even a vapour, that appeareth for a little time, and then vanisheth away. [15] For that ye *ought* to say, If the Lord will, we shall live, and do this, or that. [16] But now ye rejoice in your

boastings: all such rejoicing is evil. [17] Therefore to him that knoweth to do good, and doeth *it* not, to him it is sin. While behavior problems are linked to sin, there are also belief and background issues. As stated earlier, if what we believe is not a sin no matter what the Bible says about it, then our participation such an activity will be a sin. It does not matter how we feel about it, sin is sin. Concerning our background, no one will deny that a person reared in a house full of incest or Satanic Ritual Abuse is in a house with a good background. Let us go deeper. How many people know that hatred is a sin? Additionally, malice is a sin. Holding grudges is a sin. Game playing, backstabbing, and backbiting are all sins. Speaking badly about one another is a sin. Plotting against, lying on, ignoring, not speaking to, and disrespecting one another are all sins. When we give place to the devil and give him room to operate in our lives, he will infect us.

Sin causes infection.

When we consider sin, let us look at it this way. If we were to contract a cough, most of us would go to the pharmacist to purchase some cough medicine. If we were to catch a cold or come down with the flu, we would go get something for the same. Many of us would not think twice about getting our prescription filled to remedy our situation. When we consider sin, it is like an illness in the soul. If it goes unchecked, it can lead to infection. Infection often brings with it death. The precursors to death are sickness, disease, demonic infestation or demonic influence.

Read the Word of the Lord in Luke 11:23-26 and discover that demons need a host.

> [23] He that is not with me is against me: and he that gathereth not with me scattereth. [24] When the unclean spirit is gone out of a man, he walketh through dry places, seeking rest; and finding none, he saith, I will return unto my house whence I came out. [25] And when he cometh, he findeth *it* swept and garnished. [26] Then goeth he, and taketh *to him* seven other spirits more wicked than himself; and they enter in, and dwell there: and the last *state* of that man is worse than the first.

Read the Word of the Lord in Matthew 12:43-45 to find a similar statement concerning demons.

> [43] When the unclean spirit is gone out of a man, he walketh through dry places, seeking rest, and findeth none. [44] Then he saith, I will return into my house from whence I came out; and when he is come, he findeth *it* empty, swept, and garnished. [45] Then goeth he, and taketh with himself seven other spirits more wicked than

himself, and they enter in and dwell there: and the last *state* of that man is worse than the first. Even so shall it be also unto this wicked generation.

Sin causes infection which often brings with it infestation.

The devil gets a place and puts in a hook. Once he gets his hook

in, he aims to influence or control our behavior. One way the

devil controls us is by using guilt to affect our bodies with

sickness or disease. If we have sinned and have not been

forgiven, we may have some functional physical issues. Two

Scriptures bear this out.

Read the Word of the Lord in John 5:1-16.

Here we find healing by command and forgiveness. Pay

attention to verse fourteen.

[1] After this there was a feast of the Jews; and Jesus went up to Jerusalem. [2] Now
there is at Jerusalem by the sheep *market* a pool, which is called in the Hebrew tongue Bethesda, having five porches. [3] In these lay a great multitude of impotent folk, of blind, halt, withered, waiting for the moving of the water. [4] For an angel went down at a certain season into the pool, and troubled the water: whosoever then first after the troubling of the water stepped in was made whole of whatsoever disease he had. [5] And a certain man was there, which had an infirmity thirty and eight years. [6] When Jesus saw him lie, and knew that he had been now

a long time *in that case*, he saith unto him, Wilt thou be made whole? [7] The impotent man answered him, Sir, I have no man, when the water is troubled, to put me into the pool: but while I am coming, another steppeth down before me. [8] Jesus saith unto him, Rise, take up thy bed, and walk. [9] And immediately the man was made whole, and took up his bed, and walked: and on the same day was the sabbath. [10] The Jews therefore said unto him that was cured, It is the sabbath day: it is not lawful for thee to carry *thy* bed. [11] He answered them, He that made me whole, the same said unto me, Take up thy bed, and walk. [12] Then asked they him, What man is that which said unto thee, Take up thy bed, and walk? [13] And he that was healed wist not who it was: for Jesus had conveyed himself away, a multitude being in *that* place. [14] Afterward Jesus findeth him in the temple, and said unto him, Behold, thou art made whole: sin no more, lest a worse thing come unto thee. [15] The man departed, and told the Jews that it was Jesus, which had made him whole. [16] And therefore did the Jews persecute Jesus, and sought to slay him, because he had done these things on the sabbath day.

Sin causes infection, infestation and sometimes both.

Read the Word of the Lord in Luke 5:17-26.

A Man Borne by Four is Healed by Forgiveness. Pay attention to verse twenty.

[17] And it came to pass on a certain day, as he was teaching, that there were Pharisees and doctors of the law sitting by, which were come out of every town of Galilee, and Judaea, and Jerusalem: and the power of the Lord was *present* to heal them. [18] And, behold, men brought in

271

a bed a man which was taken with a palsy: and they sought *means* to bring him in, and to lay *him* before him. [19] And when they could not find by what *way* they might bring him in because of the multitude, they went upon the housetop, and let him down through the tiling with *his* couch into the midst before Jesus. [20] And when he saw their faith, he said unto him, Man, thy sins are forgiven thee. [21] And the scribes and the Pharisees began to reason, saying, Who is this which speaketh blasphemies? Who can forgive sins, but God alone? [22] But when Jesus perceived their thoughts, he answering said unto them, What reason ye in your hearts? [23] Whether is easier, to say, Thy sins be forgiven thee; or to say, Rise up and walk? [24] But that ye may know that the Son of man hath power upon earth to forgive sins,(he said unto the sick of the palsy,) I say unto thee, Arise, and take up thy couch, and go into thine house. [25] And immediately he rose up before them, and took up that whereon he lay, and departed to his own house, glorifying God. [26] And they were all amazed, and they glorified God, and were filled with fear, saying, We have seen strange things to day.

The healing and deliverance prescription to our sickness requires

forgiveness.

Sin causes infection, infestation and sometimes both.

The obvious question concerning infection and

infestation I how do we get healing? Well, one way is to stop

sinning. We need to learn how to straighten up and fly right.

Read the Word of the Lord in 1 John 1:5-10 concerning confession, cleansing and forgiveness. Pay close attention to verses eight through ten.

> [5] This then is the message which we have heard of him, and declare unto you, that God is light, and in him is no darkness at all. [6] If we say that we have fellowship with him, and walk in darkness, we lie, and do not the truth: [7] But if we walk in the light, as he is in the light, we have fellowship one with another, and the blood of Jesus Christ his Son cleanseth us from all sin.
>
> [8] If we say that we have no sin, we deceive ourselves, and the truth is not in us. [9] If we confess our sins, he is faithful and just to forgive us *our* sins, and to cleanse us from all unrighteousness. [10] If we say that we have not sinned, we make him a liar, and his word is not in us.

There are three remedies in the prescription of healing and

deliverance.

The remedy for sin which causes infection or infestation is confession.
A songwriter said it best.

> *God, it is me standing in the need of prayer.*
> *It's me, it is me oh Lord, standing in the need of prayer.*
> *Not my father, not my mother but it's me oh Lord,*
> *standing in the need of prayer.*
> *Not my sister, not my brother but it's me oh Lord,*
> *standing in the need of prayer.*

Confession is an "admission, especially of guilt or sin; also, a statement of religious belief. 'To confess' can mean to agree, to promise, or to admit something."[50] Confession denotes making a personal statement. Confession means I don't point at you but I point at me. Confession means I don't blame you but I blame me. The key to my healing or deliverance is confession. I have to be willing to confess. In order to confess I must be willing to do at least two things: Repent and Renounce. Repentance means "literally a change of mind, not about individual plans, intentions, or beliefs, but rather a change in the whole personality from a sinful course of action to God."[51] Repentance means a person changes his/her behavior from satisfying his/her own desires to satisfying God. Renouncing means to formally "declare one's abandonment of a claim, right, or possession."[52]

---

[50] W. A. Elwell and B. J. Beitzel, *Baker Encyclopedia of the Bible* (Grand Rapids, Mich.: Baker Book House, 1988), 505.

[51] Ibid., 1836.

[52] C. Soanes and A. Stevenson, *Concise Oxford English Dictionary – 11th Ed.* (Oxford: Oxford University Press, 2004), n. p.

To renounce something means to disassociate oneself from any and all behavior that led to a particular sin. To repent and renounce are two required steps of confession.

There are three remedies in the prescription of healing and deliverance, one of which is confession.

The remedy for sin which causes infection or infestation is correction.

I have to correct my ways, my thoughts, and my actions. Correction means that one engages in "learning that molds character and enforces correct behavior. Correction aims at getting instruction and/or training."[53] Correction requires that we discard and destroy whatever is connected to what caused us to sin.

Discarding is throwing away those things that influence sin. Influencers may be friends that are not going where we are headed. Influencers may be to websites we visit, the books we

---

[53] W. A. Elwell and B. J. Beitzel, *Baker Encyclopedia of the Bible* (Grand Rapids: Baker Book House, 1988), 631.

read, the places we go, the friends with whom we associate. It all depends. If it gets between God and ourselves, we need to discard it.

Destroying means to make something and render it unusable. This one takes some soul-searching. If we really want to remove something that causes us to sin, we have to destroy it. Think about this. Let us say that you want to stop drinking but you have a chest full of liquor. What do you do? Do you give it away? If you do, you're condoning drinking for those to whom you give it. Do you keep it around? If you do, it just verifies that you aren't serious with God. If you want to be successful and show God you mean business, you will pour it all out. Why? You pour it out because you aim to get rid of this problem and its influence on your life. Behavior uncorrected is behavior condoned. If I keep doing what I have been doing, I'm going to keep getting what I have been getting. If I keep sinning, I'm going to keep sinking. But if I stop sinning, I'll stop sinking.

I was sinking deep in sin far from the peaceful shore.

Very deeply stained within, sinking to rise no more.
But the Master of the sea heard my despairing cry.
From the waters lifted me, now safe am I.
When nothing else could help, love lifted me.

The key to my healing or deliverance is correction. Correction

includes discarding and destroying. I have to be willing to

discard and destroy everything that gets in the way of my

relationship with God. There are three remedies in the

prescription of healing and deliverance, two of which are

confession and correction.

The remedy for sin which causes infection or infestation is commitment.

I have to commit myself to God. The kind of

commitment God is looking for in us is to trust in His direction

and train in His discipleship. Proverbs 3:5-6 says, "Trust in the

Lord with all your heart and lean not to your own understanding;

in all your ways acknowledge Him and He shall direct your

path." We must be willing to go where He leads us. In that way

we show commitment to Him.

Not only must we be committed by trusting God's

direction, we must also train in His discipleship. Jesus said in

John 13:34-35, "A new commandment I give unto you, That ye love one another; as I have loved you, that ye also love one another. By this shall all *men* know that ye are my disciples, if ye have love one to another." Discipleship requires loving one another in the way that Jesus loved us. It is a sacrificial love. It is a love that puts others ahead of ourself. It is a love that verifies and validates that we are Christ's disciples. A committed person's ways and will must acquiesce to God's ways and will. A trained disciple thinks like God thinks, speak like God speaks, and love like God loves. Our walk will match our talk and our living will match our giving. When I am ready to commit my ways unto the Lord, He will be ready to commit His healing and deliverance unto me. The Scripture in James bears this out.

Read the Word of the Lord in James 5:12-20 concerning healing through prayer, confession, and forgiveness.

> [12] But above all things, my brethren, swear not, neither by heaven, neither by the earth, neither by any other oath: but let your yea be yea; and *your* nay, nay; lest ye fall into condemnation. [13] Is any among you afflicted? let him pray. Is any merry? let him sing psalms. [14] Is any sick

278

among you? let him call for the elders of the church; and let them pray over him, anointing him with oil in the name of the Lord: [15] And the prayer of faith shall save the sick, and the Lord shall raise him up; and if he have committed sins, they shall be forgiven him. [16] Confess *your* faults one to another, and pray one for another, that ye may be healed. The effectual fervent prayer of a righteous man availeth much. [17] Elias was a man subject to like passions as we are, and he prayed earnestly that it might not rain: and it rained not on the earth by the space of three years and six months. [18] And he prayed again, and the heaven gave rain, and the earth brought forth her fruit. [19] Brethren, if any of you do err from the truth, and one convert him; [20] Let him know, that he which converteth the sinner from the error of his way shall save a soul from death, and shall hide a multitude of sins.

The healing and deliverance prescription to our sickness requires forgiveness.

When we do wrong things, it causes wrong things within. Our thoughts and communication affect us within. When we sin against God and each other we need forgiveness. Hear this well: Unconfessed sin is sin unforgiven. Unrepented sin is sin unforgiven. The healing and deliverance prescription includes forgiveness. When we sin against God we need forgiveness from Him. When we sin against one another we need forgiveness from them. The Bible spells our forgiveness so plainly and so completely.

Read the Words of the Lord concerning forgiveness.

Luke 17:1-4 says,

> Then said he unto the disciples, It is impossible but that offences will come: but woe *unto him*, through whom they come! [2] It were better for him that a millstone were hanged about his neck, and he cast into the sea, than that he should offend one of these little ones. [3] Take heed to yourselves: If thy brother trespass against thee, rebuke him; and if he repent, forgive him. [4] And if he trespass against thee seven times in a day, and seven times in a day turn again to thee, saying, I repent; thou shalt forgive him.

When I have something against my brother, I have to go to him.

Matthew 18:15-20 says,

> [15] Moreover if thy brother shall trespass against thee, go and tell him his fault between thee and him alone: if he shall hear thee, thou hast gained thy brother. [16] But if he will not hear *thee, then* take with thee one or two more, that in the mouth of two or three witnesses every word may be established. [17] And if he shall neglect to hear them, tell *it* unto the church: but if he neglect to hear the church, let him be unto thee as an heathen man and a publican. [18] Verily I say unto you, Whatsoever ye shall bind on earth shall be bound in heaven: and whatsoever ye shall loose on earth shall be loosed in heaven. [19] Again I say unto you, That if two of you shall agree on earth as touching any thing that they shall ask, it shall be done for them of my Father which is in heaven. [20] For where two

or three are gathered together in my name, there am I in the midst of them.

When I have something against my brother, I have to go to him.

Matthew 5:23-27 says,

> [23] Therefore if thou bring thy gift to the altar, and there rememberest that thy brother hath ought against thee; [24] Leave there thy gift before the altar, and go thy way; first be reconciled to thy brother, and then come and offer thy gift. [25] Agree with thine adversary quickly, whiles thou art in the way with him; lest at any time the adversary deliver thee to the judge, and the judge deliver thee to the officer, and thou be cast into prison. [26] Verily I say unto thee, Thou shalt by no means come out thence, till thou hast paid the uttermost farthing.

When my brother has something against me, I need to go to him.

Reconciliation goes ahead of church ministry. We cannot do any ministry with issues hanging over our head. Reconciliation needs to happen before we do ministry. Reconciliation includes prayer.

Matthew 6:5-15 says,

> [5] And when thou prayest, thou shalt not be as the hypocrites *are*: for they love to pray standing in the synagogues and in the corners of the streets, that they may be seen of men. Verily I say unto you, They have their reward. [6] But thou, when thou prayest, enter into thy closet, and when thou hast shut thy door, pray to thy Father which is in secret; and thy Father which seeth in secret shall reward thee openly. [7] But when ye pray, use not vain repetitions, as the heathen *do*: for they think that they shall be heard for their much speaking. [8] Be not ye

therefore like unto them: for your Father knoweth what things ye have need of, before ye ask him. [9] After this manner therefore pray ye:

Our Father which art in heaven, Hallowed be thy name. [10] Thy kingdom come. Thy will be done in earth, as *it is* in heaven. [11] Give us this day our daily bread. [12] And forgive us our debts, as we forgive our debtors. [13] And lead us not into temptation, but deliver us from evil: For thine is the kingdom, and the power, and the glory, for ever. Amen.

[14] For if ye forgive men their trespasses, your heavenly Father will also forgive you: [15] But if ye forgive not men their trespasses, neither will your Father forgive your trespasses.

Whenever there is an issue we have with another person, we need to quickly reconcile. The best way to go to a person is to first pray. We must pray that God will prepare the heart of the one to whom we are going. Additionally, we must pray that God will prepare our hearts to say what we need to say. Our words must be sure words, loving words, kind words. Observe the rule of engagement for the forgiveness of sins: I can't get forgiveness until I ask for it. Repeated differently, God will not forgive me for my sins until I repent and ask for forgiveness. Better stated, we will not forgive others who sin against us until they repent and ask them for it. Our problem is that we want God to forgive us of all our sins without going to our brother, that's not biblical. When we sin against God, we go to Him and get forgiveness. When we sin against each other we have to go to them to get forgiveness. When we refuse to reconcile with our brother or sister, that sin is still on our account. When we die, that sin is still going to be charged against us.

It is time for me to do ministry through the written page. I know that sometimes it's hard to ask for forgiveness. Asking for forgiveness is a humbling experience. Jesus made it easy. He lived among us preaching and teaching about forgiveness. He shared stories about forgiveness.

He went to the cross for forgiveness. He hung there and died for forgiveness. He was buried in a borrowed tomb for forgiveness. He stayed there three long days for forgiveness. Early one Sunday morning, He got up with all power in His hands. His purpose was forgiveness. Jesus made it easy when He went to the cross for our transgressions, bruised for our iniquity, chastised for our peace. Jesus made it easy for by His stripes, we are healed. Beloved, we cannot have a good relationship with God until we are healed, delivered and made whole. We cannot do good ministry until we are healed, delivered and made whole.

Read the Word of the Lord in Luke 8:1-3.

> [1] And it came to pass afterward, that he went throughout every city and village, preaching and shewing the glad tidings of the kingdom of God: and the twelve *were* with him, [2] And certain women, which had been healed of evil spirits and infirmities, Mary called Magdalene, out of whom went seven devils, [3] And Joanna the wife of Chuza Herod's steward, and Susanna, and many others, which ministered unto him of their substance.

Effective ministry requires a clean host. If we want to do effective ministry for God, especially in the area of healing and deliverance, we must diligently keep our temples clean. There is no stumbling or falling when one stays postured on his or her knees. Our bodies are temples of the Most High God. He is Jeremiah's Potter ever molding, shaping and reshaping His clay. He is looking for willing and usable vessels.

Read the Word of the Lord in Romans 12

> I beseech you therefore, brethren, by the mercies of God, that ye present your bodies a living sacrifice, holy, acceptable unto God, *which is* your reasonable

service. [2] And be not conformed to this world: but be ye transformed by the renewing of your mind, that ye may prove what *is* that good, and acceptable, and perfect, will of God. [3] For I say, through the grace given unto me, to every man that is among you, not to think *of himself* more highly than he ought to think; but to think soberly, according as God hath dealt to every man the measure of faith. [4] For as we have many members in one body, and all members have not the same office: [5] So we, *being* many, are one body in Christ, and every one members one of another. [6] Having then gifts differing according to the grace that is given to us, whether prophecy, *let us prophesy* according to the proportion of faith; [7] Or ministry, *let us wait* on *our* ministering: or he that teacheth, on teaching; [8] Or he that exhorteth, on exhortation: he that giveth, *let him do it* with simplicity; he that ruleth, with diligence; he that sheweth mercy, with cheerfulness.

[9] *Let* love be without dissimulation. Abhor that which is evil; cleave to that which is good. [10] *Be* kindly affectioned one to another with brotherly love; in honour preferring one another; [11] Not slothful in business; fervent in spirit; serving the Lord; [12] Rejoicing in hope; patient in tribulation; continuing instant in prayer; [13] Distributing to the necessity of saints; given to hospitality. [14] Bless them which persecute you: bless, and curse not. [15] Rejoice with them that do rejoice, and weep with them that weep. [16] *Be* of the same mind one toward another. Mind not high things, but condescend to men of low estate. Be not wise in your own conceits. [17] Recompense to no man evil for evil. Provide things honest in the sight of all men. [18] If it be possible, as much as lieth in you, live peaceably with all men. [19] Dearly beloved, avenge not yourselves, but *rather* give place unto wrath: for it is written, Vengeance *is* mine; I will

repay, saith the Lord. [20] Therefore if thine enemy hunger, feed him; if he thirst, give him drink: for in so doing thou shalt heap coals of fire on his head. [21] Be not overcome of evil, but overcome evil with good.

Read the Word of the Lord in 2 Corinthians 5:17-21.

[17] Therefore if any man *be* in Christ, *he is* a new creature: old things are passed away; behold, all things are become new. [18] And all things *are* of God, who hath reconciled us to himself by Jesus Christ, and hath given to us the ministry of reconciliation; [19] To wit, that God was in Christ, reconciling the world unto himself, not imputing their trespasses unto them; and hath committed unto us the word of reconciliation. [20] Now then we are ambassadors for Christ, as though God did beseech *you* by us: we pray *you* in Christ's stead, be ye reconciled to God. [21] For he hath made him *to be* sin for us, who knew no sin; that we might be made the righteousness of God in him.

Read the Word of the Lord in 2 Corinthians 6:17-21 and pay close attention to verse seventeen.

We then, *as* workers together *with him*, beseech *you* also that ye receive not the grace of God in vain. [2] (For he saith, I have heard thee in a time accepted, and in the day of salvation have I succoured thee: behold, now *is* the accepted time; behold, now *is* the day of salvation.) [3] Giving no offence in any thing, that the ministry be not blamed: [4] But in all *things* approving ourselves as the ministers of God, in much patience, in afflictions, in necessities, in distresses, [5] In stripes, in imprisonments, in tumults, in labours, in watchings, in fastings; [6] By pureness, by knowledge, by longsuffering, by kindness, by the Holy Ghost, by love unfeigned, [7] By the word of truth, by the power of God, by the armour of righteousness on the right hand and on the left, [8] By honour and dishonour, by evil report and good report: as deceivers, and *yet* true; ⁹ As unknown, and *yet* well known; as dying, and, behold, we live; as chastened, and not killed; ¹⁰ As sorrowful, yet alway rejoicing; as poor, yet making many rich; as having nothing, and *yet* possessing all things.

¹¹ O *ye* Corinthians, our mouth is open unto you, our heart is enlarged. ¹² Ye are not straitened in us, but ye are straitened in your own bowels. ¹³ Now for a recompence in the same, (I speak as unto *my* children,) be ye also enlarged. ¹⁴ Be ye not unequally yoked together with unbelievers: for what fellowship hath righteousness with unrighteousness? and what communion hath light with darkness? ¹⁵ And what concord hath Christ with Belial? or what part hath he that believeth with an infidel? ¹⁶ And what agreement hath the temple of God with idols? for ye are the temple of the living God; as God hath said, I will dwell in them, and walk in *them*; and I will be their God, and they shall be my people. ¹⁷ Wherefore come out from among them, and be ye separate, saith the Lord, and touch not the unclean *thing*; and I will receive you, ¹⁸ And will be a Father unto you, and ye shall be my sons and daughters, saith the Lord Almighty.

God is looking for willing and usable vessels. Will you hear and

heed His call? Hear the songwriter's plea:

> *Give me a clean heart and renew a right spirit within me.*
> *Give me a clean heart that I might serve Thee.*
> *Lord, fix my heart so that I can be used by Thee.*
> *I am not worthy of all these blessings.*
> *Lord, give me a clean heart and I will follow Thee.*

If you have decided to hear and heed God's call, healing and deliverance ministry requires a basic system and some simple do's and don'ts. Let us take a look.

Chapter 9

Chapter Nine – Healing and Deliverance Systems

Healing and Deliverance Ministry by Creative Means, (Leprosy)
Numbers 12; 2 Kings 5; Mark 1:40-45; Luke 17

If there is one thing that is absolutely clear, it is the fact that God does not do miracles by a cookie-cutter approach. The healing and deliverance system is one that identifies that God's system is not always the same. No matter what condition a person has, God can and will fix them as He sees fit as in the case of leprosy. "Leprosy is a chronic infectious disease caused by *Mycobacterium leprae,* a bacterium similar to the tuberculosis bacillus. The disease is manifested by changes in the skin, mucous membranes, and peripheral nerves."[54] According to the Center for Disease Control, Leprosy is a

> "chronic infectious disease usually affects the skin and peripheral nerves but has a wide range of possible clinical manifestations. Its milder counterpart is Hansen's disease Patients are classified as having paucibacillary or multibacillary Hansen's disease and is associated with

---

[54] W. A. Elwell and B. J. Beitzel, *Baker Encyclopedia of the Bible* (Grand Rapids: Baker Book House, 1988) 1323.

symmetric skin lesions, nodules, plaques, thickened dermis, and frequent involvement of the nasal mucosa resulting in nasal congestion and epistaxis.[55]

Leprosy is considered contagious and is often spread person to person either by touch or through some form of air born bacteria. Because of its highly infectious nature, God stipulated how to deal with leprosy in Leviticus 13-15. These passages will be included at the end of this lesson for your convenience.

Three Old Testament passages share how a person can contract leprosy. In Numbers 12, we discover that Miriam gets leprosy from speaking evil against the Man of God. We know that Moses was Miriam's brother but he was still God's anointed. In 2 Kings 5, we discover that Gehazi lied on the Man of God. Gehazi couldn't understand how Elisha could turn down Naaman's freewill offering so he took it upon himself to go get a portion for himself on behalf of Elisha. Both Miriam and Gehazi could learn from Psalm 105:15 which states, "Touch not Mine

---

[55] http://www.cdc.gov/nczved/divisions/dfbmd/diseases/hansens_disease/technical.html/#clinical

anointed and do My prophets no harm." Speaking badly about the Man of God or lying on him can be damaging to one's health.

In 2 Kings 15, we find the King of Judah (Azariah) being stricken with leprosy because of the mandate of God. Azariah called Judah into reform and lived according to God's standards. His exception was that he did not remove the altars dedicated for worshipping false gods. That God gave each of these persons leprosy proves that leprosy is a curse. Miriam as the first prophetess, Gehazi as the servant of the prophet, and Azariah as King of Judah establish that no one is exempt from the wrath of God. Obedience is always better than sacrifice. We will discover as we read these passages on leprosy that whenever God is going to cleanse someone from this dreadful disease, there will usually be a request, requirement, remedy and rejoicing. *Request* is a transitive verb that aims to petition someone for a favor, privilege or special consideration.[56] The petitioner makes the request of someone capable of fulfilling the appeal. ***Requirement*** is a noun that mandates something essential to the existence or occurrence of something else.[57] A requirement is an item that is desired. This item comes in the form of a conditional contract where the person needing a particular item will have to do something to receive said item. ***Remedy*** is the restoration of a thing to a sound physical or psychological state or to the greatest degree.[58] A remedy is the miracle, which includes healing or deliverance. ***Rejoicing*** is a noun that identifies an instance, occasion, or expression of jubilation, joy or festivity.[59] Rejoicing means one is unashamed and unafraid to give praise and thanks for what someone has done for them. The scriptural model for

---

[56] *Merriam-Webster's Collegiate Dictionary 11th Ed.* (Springfield, Mass.: Merriam-Webster, Inc., 2003)

[57] Ibid., n. p.

[58] A. C. Myers, *The Eerdmans Bible Dictionary* (Grand Rapids: Eerdmans Publishers, 1987), 470.

[59] *Merriam-Webster's Collegiate Dictionary – 11th Ed.* (Springfield, MA: Merriam-Webster, Inc., 2003), n. p.

getting a miracle includes the request, the requirement, the

remedy and the rejoicing.

Read the Word of the Lord – 2 Kings 15:1-7 (Leprosy as Punishment)

15 In the twenty and seventh year of Jeroboam king of Israel began Azariah son of Amaziah king of Judah to reign. [2] Sixteen years old was he when he began to reign, and he reigned two and fifty years in Jerusalem. And his mother's name *was* Jecholiah of Jerusalem. [3] And he did *that which was* right in the sight of the LORD, according to all that his father Amaziah had done; [4] Save that the high places were not removed: the people sacrificed and burnt incense still on the high places. [5] And the LORD smote the king, so that he was a leper unto the day of his death, and dwelt in a several house. And Jotham the king's son *was* over the house, judging the people of the land. [6] And the rest of the acts of Azariah, and all that he did, *are* they not written in the book of the chronicles of the kings of Judah? [7] So Azariah slept with his fathers; and they buried him with his fathers in the city of David: and Jotham his son reigned in his stead.

Read the Word of the Lord – Numbers 12 (Leprosy as Punishment)

12 And Miriam and Aaron spake against Moses because of the Ethiopian woman whom he had married: for he had married an Ethiopian woman. [2] And they said, Hath the LORD indeed spoken only by Moses? hath he not spoken also by us? And the LORD heard *it*. [3] (Now the man Moses *was* very meek, above all the men which *were* upon the face of the earth.) [4] And the LORD spake suddenly unto Moses, and unto Aaron, and unto Miriam, Come out ye three unto the tabernacle of the congregation. And they three came out. [5] And the LORD came down in the pillar of the cloud, and stood *in* the door of the tabernacle, and called Aaron and Miriam: and they both came forth. [6] And he said, Hear now my words: If there be a prophet among you, *I* the LORD will make myself known unto him in a vision, *and* will speak unto him in a dream. [7] My servant Moses *is* not so, who *is* faithful in all mine house. [8] With him will I speak mouth to mouth, even apparently, and not in dark speeches; and the similitude of the LORD shall he behold: wherefore then were ye not afraid to speak against my servant Moses? [9] And the anger of the LORD was kindled against them; and he departed. [10] And the cloud departed from off the tabernacle; and, behold, Miriam *became* leprous, *white* as snow: and Aaron looked upon Miriam, and, behold, *she was* leprous. [11] And Aaron said unto Moses, Alas, my lord, I beseech thee, lay not the sin upon us, wherein we have done foolishly, and wherein we have sinned. [12] Let her not be as one dead, of whom the flesh is half consumed when he cometh out of his mother's womb. [13] And Moses cried unto the LORD, saying, Heal her now, O God, I beseech thee. [14] And the LORD said unto Moses, If her father had but spit in her face, should she not be ashamed seven days? let her be shut out from the camp seven days, and after that let her be received in *again.* [15] And Miriam was shut out from the camp seven days: and the people journeyed not till Miriam was brought in *again.* [16] And afterward the people removed from Hazeroth, and pitched in the wilderness of Paran.

Request

When Miriam and Aaron spoke negatively about the man of God (Moses), God got angry. Because Aaron was the high priest, God did not punish him. He chose to punish Miriam instead. By giving Miriam leprosy, God banished her from being in fellowship with the Children of Israel. Aaron repents to Moses and asks him to go to God for Miriam's cleansing to which Moses agrees. Miracles begin with a request.

Requirement

After Moses petitioned God for Miriam's cleansing, God gave the requirement. He would not allow her to get her miracle until she met the requirement of staying in her condition for seven days. The next step in gaining a miracle is the requirement.

Remedy

As soon as the seven days were complete, Miriam received her remedy by being cleansed. Her skin was returned as new. While it is not stated implicitly, her cleansing is implied because the people moved to Hazeroth after the seven days were completed. The remedy is always the requested miracle.

Rejoicing

Rejoicing is the thanking and praising God for answering the request with the remedy. While it is not stated in the passage, it is an obvious response to the miracle. Aaron would have rejoiced that his sister was cleansed. Moses would have rejoiced that God answered his request and cleansed his sister. Miriam would have rejoiced that God forgave her and remedied her situation. Finally, some of the people who would have been close to Miriam would have rejoiced to have her back in fellowship with the people. The last step in the miracle process is rejoicing. Rejoicing allows God to know that we appreciate Him for what He has done. Whenever we praise God for what He has done, we are likely to get another miracle from Him when we ask for it.

Read the Word of the Lord – 2 Kings 5 (Leprosy Cleansing and Punishment in Same Story)

5 Now Naaman, captain of the host of the king of Syria, was a great man with his master, and honourable, because by him the LORD had given deliverance unto Syria: he was also a mighty man in valour, *but he was* a leper. [2] And the Syrians had gone out by companies, and had brought away captive out of the land of Israel a little maid; and she waited on Naaman's wife. [3] And she said unto her mistress, Would God my lord *were* with the prophet that *is* in Samaria! for he would recover him of his leprosy. [4] And *one* went in, and told his lord, saying, Thus and thus said the maid that *is* of the land of Israel. [5] And the king of Syria said, Go to, go, and I will send a letter unto the king of Israel. And he departed, and took with him ten talents of silver, and six thousand *pieces* of gold, and ten changes of raiment. [6] And he brought the letter to the king of Israel, saying, Now when this letter is come unto thee, behold, I have *therewith* sent Naaman my servant to thee, that thou mayest recover him of his leprosy. [7] And it came to pass, when the king of Israel had read the letter, that he rent his clothes, and said, *Am* I God, to kill and to make alive, that this man doth send unto me to recover a man of his leprosy? wherefore consider, I pray you, and see how he seeketh a quarrel against me. [8] And it was *so*, when Elisha the man of God had heard that the king of Israel had rent his clothes, that he sent to the king, saying, Wherefore hast thou rent thy clothes? let him come now to me, and he shall know that there is a prophet in Israel. [9] So Naaman came with his horses and with his chariot, and stood at the door of the house of Elisha. [10] And Elisha sent a messenger unto him, saying, Go and wash in Jordan seven times, and thy flesh shall come again to thee, and thou shalt be clean. [11] But Naaman was wroth, and went away, and said, Behold, I thought, He will surely come out to me, and stand, and call on the name of the LORD his God, and strike his hand over the place, and recover the leper. [12] *Are* not Abana and Pharpar, rivers of Damascus, better than all the waters of Israel? may I not wash in them, and be clean? So he turned and went away in a rage. [13] And his servants came near, and spake unto him, and said, My father, *if* the prophet had bid thee *do some* great thing, wouldest thou not have done *it*? how much rather then, when he saith to thee, Wash, and be clean? [14] Then went he down, and dipped himself seven times in Jordan, according to the saying of the man of God: and his flesh came again like unto the flesh of a little child, and he was clean.

Request

The story of Naaman begins with a description of him. He is a great high ranking official with military status who has leprosy. The Children of Israel had been brought out of their land by Tiglath-pileser during the Syrian Captivity. One of his wife's Jewish handmaids recognized his condition and mentioned that Naaman could be cleansed if he went to petition Elisha, the man of God. When Naaman's wife gave him the news, he got the papers and finances prepared to go ask the man of God for the miracle. As soon as Naaman reached Elisha's location, Elisha sent his servant out to meet Naaman. This was not normal for someone of Naaman's status to not meet whomever he desired to meet. His high military ranking would have demanded the respect of whomever he was going to see. The fact that the man of God did not go to meet him is significant because one must go before God with humility to ask anything of Him. No one outranks God. Naaman had to make his request through a servant of the man of God rather than directly. The miracle begins with the request.

Requirement

Once the messenger received the request from Naaman, Elisha told his servant to have Naaman go dip in the Jordan River seven times. When Naaman receives the requirement, he is disappointed because there were other more appropriate things that could have taken place. He could have been given a clean bill of health directly by Elisha. There were other more convenient bodies of water available for him to dip in. The cleansing of Naaman hung in the balance. Had he not gone to the Jordan River to dip seven times, the story would read differently. The fact that Naaman did obey meant that he would get his remedy.

Remedy

After Naaman dipped in the Jordan River seven times, he was cleansed from leprosy. Naaman's skin became as new as a child's skin. The fact that Naaman received his miracle proves that a person does not have to be in the family of faith to receive a miracle. God only needs a willing participant and obedience and He will handle the rest of the details. While God does not need a person to be in the household of faith to receive a miracle, He usually uses those within the household of faith to perform or be conduits for the miracles He is going to perform. The vessel through which the requests come will generally be those with whom God has a strong relationship. These are the ones who know God's voice and are prone to follow His instructions completely.

Rejoicing

Rejoicing is the last step in the miracle process. Naaman appreciated what God did for him. As a consequence, Naaman offered the man of God a gift.

The story continues.

The Miracles of God Cannot be Purchased

[15] And he returned to the man of God, he and all his company, and came, and stood before him: and he said, Behold, now I know that *there is* no God in all the earth,

but in Israel: now therefore, I pray thee, take a blessing of thy servant. [16] But he said, *As* the LORD liveth, before whom I stand, I will receive none. And he urged him to take *it*; but he refused. [17] And Naaman said, Shall there not then, I pray thee, be given to thy servant two mules' burden of earth? for thy servant will henceforth offer neither burnt offering nor sacrifice unto other gods, but unto the LORD. [18] In this thing the LORD pardon thy servant, *that* when my master goeth into the house of Rimmon to worship there, and he leaneth on my hand, and I bow myself in the house of Rimmon: when I bow down myself in the house of Rimmon, the LORD pardon thy servant in this thing. [19] And he said unto him, Go in peace. So he departed from him a little way.

This is a good place to insert a word on giftings. While there is no indication that suggests that giving a gift to the man of God (or the church for that matter) is inappropriate, is it considered to be in poor taste in this particular lesson. The main reason receiving a gift is not accepted here is that the miracles of God cannot be purchased. There are persons today whom God uses to travel the world preaching the Word of God and performing His miracles. Many of these persons rely solely on the free-will offering of those who support their ministries. The best way to understand whether or not receiving a gift is appropriate is to seek the guidance of God. At best God will direct each person on a case by case basis. If God is okay with the vessel receiving a gift, He will let that vessel know. When receiving a gift is inappropriate, God will likewise let the vessel know. As we read further, we will discover what happens when a vessel disobeys God's instructions.

Disobedience will cause one to be punished.

^{20} But Gehazi, the servant of Elisha the man of God, said, Behold, my master hath spared Naaman this Syrian, in not receiving at his hands that which he brought: but, *as* the LORD liveth, I will run after him, and take somewhat of him. ^{21} So Gehazi followed after Naaman. And when Naaman saw *him* running after him, he lighted down from the chariot to meet him, and said, *Is* all well? ^{22} And he said, All *is* well. My master hath sent me, saying, Behold, even now there be come to me from mount Ephraim two young men of the sons of the prophets: give them, I pray thee, a talent of silver, and two changes of garments. ^{23} And Naaman said, Be content, take two talents. And he urged him, and bound two talents of silver in two bags, with two changes of garments, and laid *them* upon two of his servants; and they bare *them* before him. ^{24} And when he came to the tower, he took *them* from their hand, and bestowed *them* in the house: and he let the men go, and they departed. ^{25} But he went in, and stood before his master. And Elisha said unto him, Whence *comest thou*, Gehazi? And he said, Thy servant went no whither. ^{26} And he said unto him, Went not mine heart *with thee*, when the man turned again from his chariot to meet thee? *Is it* a time to receive money, and to receive garments, and oliveyards, and vineyards, and sheep, and oxen, and menservants, and maidservants? [27] The leprosy therefore of Naaman shall cleave unto thee, and unto thy seed for ever. And he went out from his presence a leper *as white* as snow.

Had Gehazi not lied on the Man of God or disobeyed him, Gehazi never would have contracted leprosy. The fact that he was greedy rather than gracious caused Gehazi to lose more than he thought he would. Obedience is better than sacrifice. God's anointed is not to be lied on or disobeyed. A interesting note to ponder is appropriate. The Man of God was the one responsible for transferring the leprosy of Naaman to Gehazi. God honors His anointed and empowers His anointed to speak things that come to pass. Elisha cursed Gehazi with leprosy and God did allow it to happen. Proverbs 18:21 says, "There is death and life in the power of the tongue." The tongue can be used for both good and evil. The fact that Elisha spoke leprosy on Gehazi proves that bad behavior gets bad results. A final word of warning is needed right here. Just because Elisha cursed Gehazi in a God-sanctioned environment does not give anyone license to go around cursing others. Remember God's promise to Abraham in Genesis 12:3, "I will bless those who bless you and I will curse those who curse you; and in you shall all the families of the earth be blessed." It is God's will that we bless people. Even though we have the power to curse, His will is that we bless.

More information on Gehazi – 2 Kings 8:1-6

8 Then spake Elisha unto the woman, whose son he had restored to life, saying, Arise, and go thou and thine household, and sojourn wheresoever thou canst sojourn: for the LORD hath called for a famine; and it shall also come upon the land seven years. [2] And the woman arose, and did after the saying of the man of God: and she went with her household, and sojourned in the land of the Philistines seven years. [3] And it came to pass at the seven years' end, that the woman returned out of the land of the Philistines: and she went forth to cry unto the king for her house and for her land. [4] And the king talked with Gehazi the servant of the man of God, saying, Tell me, I pray thee, all the great things that Elisha hath done. [5] And it came to pass, as he was telling the king how he had restored a dead body to life, that, behold, the woman, whose son he had restored to life, cried to the king for her house and for her land. And Gehazi said, My lord, O king, this *is* the woman, and this *is* her son, whom Elisha restored to life. [6] And when the king asked the woman, she told him. So the king appointed unto her a certain officer, saying, Restore all that *was* hers, and all the fruits of the field since the day that she left the land, even until now.

No one knows whether Gehazi is still leprous at the time he speaks with the king. Nothing reveals that he was cleansed from leprosy. The fact that Gehazi is speaking with the king within a reasonable proximity proves problematic at first glance. If we remember that Naaman addressed the king in chapter 5, then Gehazi's audience with the king in chapter 8 is not an issue. In addition, the fact that Gehazi is referred to as the servant of the Man of God bears in mind that his contracting leprosy may have occurred some time after his audience with the king was over. The truth of the matter is that Elisha would not have kept a leprous servant around. Gehazi would have either been dismissed or cleansed. There would not have been a leper serving the Man of God.

Each of these stories reflects a God who has a history of doing the miraculous. The Old Testament passages share how each person came to know this God of Miracles. Miriam knows about this God through direct experience. Naaman hears about this God through a servant who knows God directly. Miriam and

Naaman know about God from a direct source. The New Testament passages share differently how each person came to know this God of Miracles. Their stories reflect a more indirect knowledge of God.

Read the Word of the Lord – Luke 17:11-19 (Cleansing the Leprosy by Spoken Word)

[11] And it came to pass, as he went to Jerusalem that he passed through the midst of Samaria and Galilee. [12] And as he entered into a certain village, there met him ten men that were lepers, which stood afar off: [13] And they lifted up *their* voices, and said, Jesus, Master, have mercy on us. [14] And when he saw *them*, he said unto them, Go shew yourselves unto the priests. And it came to pass, that, as they went, they were cleansed. [15] And one of them, when he saw that he was healed, turned back, and with a loud voice glorified God, [16] And fell down on *his* face at his feet, giving him thanks: and he was a Samaritan. [17] And Jesus answering said, Were there not ten cleansed? but where *are* the nine? [18] There are not found that returned to give glory to God, save this stranger. [19] And he said unto him, Arise, go thy way: thy faith hath made thee whole.

Request

In this story Jesus is passing through a certain village and discovered ten lepers who stood afar off. These ten lepers petitioned Him for His mercy. Apparently, Jesus was known to be moved with compassion and miraculous works followed Him. While none of them specifically asked Jesus for the miracle of being cleansed from leprosy, they did know that Jesus had the power to remedy their situation.

Requirement

Jesus responded to their plea by making a requirement. He tells them to go show themselves to the priest. It was Jewish custom that only a priest can declare a leper to be clean. You will find that Leviticus 13 and 14 spell out all the details. A copy of the passage will be included at the end of this lesson. When the ten lepers heard Jesus' statement, they had a decision to make. Their miracle held in the balance. Their obedience of going to show themselves to the priests was the only requirement Jesus gave them to remedy their situation.

Remedy

When the ten lepers turned to go show themselves to the priests, they were obedient. At some point along their journey they received their miracle. Conjecture abounds as to how soon they received their miracle. Some suggest the miracle was immediate while others suggest it may have been a moment, two or several moments. The fact of the matter remains that the ten lepers received their remedy after they followed the instructions of Jesus.

Rejoicing

As they went on their way, at least one noticed that he was cleansed. While there is no indication that the others did not know, what is obvious is that only one returned to Jesus to give thanks. When Jesus inquired about the other nine, it seemed more a question of intrigue rather than a question of appreciation. There is no indication that the other nine would have lost their miracle for being unthankful. The fact that this one person returned showed an immense amount of gratitude and faith on his part.

A special note about gratitude is in order. It is always appropriate to thank God as soon as He grants a miracle. When we are grateful, we let God know that He can trust us with a miracle. When God can trust us, we are more than likely able to

receive a miracle again whenever we need one. An ungrateful

person is less likely to get another miracle from God. The history

of the Children of Israel bears this out.

Read the Word of the Lord – Mark 1:40-45 (Cleansing Leprosy by Word and Touch)

[40] And there came a leper to him, beseeching him, and kneeling down to him, and saying unto him, If thou wilt, thou canst make me clean. [41] And Jesus, moved with compassion, put forth *his* hand, and touched him, and saith unto him, I will; be thou clean. [42] And as soon as he had spoken, immediately the leprosy departed from him, and he was cleansed. [43] And he straitly charged him, and forthwith sent him away; [44] And saith unto him, See thou say nothing to any man: but go thy way, shew thyself to the priest, and offer for thy cleansing those things which Moses commanded, for a testimony unto them. [45] But he went out, and began to publish *it* much, and to blaze abroad the matter, insomuch that Jesus could no more openly enter into the city, but was without in desert places: and they came to him from every quarter.

Request

In this story a leper breaks with the rules of Jewish society and

approaches Jesus. He kneels down humbly and makes his

request. His request is to be cleansed and he knows Jesus can cleanse him. The choice was Jesus' and His alone. That he acknowledged that Jesus had the power showed great faith.

Remedy

In this case, Jesus puts forth His hand and does the unthinkable – He touches the leper. No Jew would ever touch a leper because the leper was ceremonially unclean. Any person who touched someone who was unclean was made unclean as well. That Jesus touched this man was unthinkable. Not only was this an unusual part of the story but Jesus gave the remedy before He gave the requirement. This proves that there is no cookie-cutter approach to the miraculous power of God.

Requirement

As in the previous story, Jesus gave to the man the requirement of going to the priest. Jesus sent the man to show himself to the priest so that he could be declared clean again and charged the man not to publish his miracle with anybody but to keep it to himself. While this requirement seems to challenge us at first glance, it does make sense when we review the sequence of the requested events. Looking closely at the text, the man was instructed to not stop and converse with anybody before going to the priest. His first stop was to the priest and no one else. As one who had been ceremonially unclean, it would have been careless of him to be seen conversing with anyone before having been declared clean by the priest. Being seen in close proximity to another before getting clearance from the priest would have been tantamount to breaking the law. He could have been placed in leper's prison for something as simple as testifying about his miracle from Jesus. Going to the priest first without stopping to speak to anyone was simply precautionary and right. Following his priestly visit would not have limited him to being in proximity to anyone.

Rejoicing

After having had an opportunity of showing himself to the priest, this former leper did what anybody who has received a miracle by God would do. He was thankful to God and told everybody his testimony. This man published the wondrous works of Jesus so much that Jesus could no longer do anonymous works there.

Jesus' notoriety spread all over and people came from

everywhere to see Him. I do not know about you but that appears

to be a great deal of talking. Here is a parting shot. How much

talking about the goodness of Jesus have you been sharing

lately? This man obviously told everybody he met about a

Miracle-worker named Jesus.

Read the Word of the Lord – Mark 14:1-11 (Leprosy as a Reminder)

     14 After two days was *the feast of* the passover, and of unleavened bread: and the chief priests and the scribes sought how they might take him by craft, and put *him* to death. ² But they said, Not on the feast *day*, lest there be an uproar of the people.

     ³ And being in Bethany in the house of Simon the leper, as he sat at meat, there came a woman having an alabaster box of ointment of spikenard very precious; and she brake the box, and poured *it* on his head. ⁴ And there were some that had indignation within themselves, and said, Why was this waste of the ointment made? ⁵ For it might have been sold for more than three hundred pence, and have been given to the poor. And they murmured against her. ⁶ And Jesus said, Let her alone; why trouble ye her? she hath wrought a good work on me. ⁷ For ye have the poor with you always, and whensoever ye will ye may do them good: but me ye have not always. ⁸ She hath done what she could: she is come aforehand to anoint my body to the burying. ⁹ Verily I say unto you,

Wheresoever this gospel shall be preached throughout the whole world, *this* also that she hath done shall be spoken of for a memorial of her.

¹⁰ And Judas Iscariot, one of the twelve, went unto the chief priests, to betray him unto them. ¹¹ And when they heard *it*, they were glad, and promised to give him money. And he sought how he might conveniently betray him.

Read the Word of the Lord – 2 Kings 7 (Leprosy as Preservation)

7 Then Elisha said, Hear ye the word of the LORD; Thus saith the LORD, To morrow about this time *shall* a measure of fine flour *be sold* for a shekel, and two measures of barley for a shekel, in the gate of Samaria. ² Then a lord on whose hand the king leaned answered the man of God, and said, Behold, *if* the LORD would make windows in heaven, might this thing be? And he said, Behold, thou shalt see *it* with thine eyes, but shalt not eat thereof.

³ And there were four leprous men at the entering in of the gate: and they said one to another, Why sit we here until we die? ⁴ If we say, We will enter into the city, then the famine *is* in the city, and we shall die there: and if we sit still here, we die also. Now therefore come, and let us fall unto the host of the Syrians: if they save us alive, we shall live; and if they kill us, we shall but die. ⁵ And they rose up in the twilight, to go unto the camp of the Syrians: and when they were come to the uttermost part of the camp of Syria, behold, *there was* no man there. ⁶ For the Lord had made the host of the Syrians to hear a noise of chariots, and a noise of horses, *even* the noise of a great host: and they said one to another, Lo, the king of

Israel hath hired against us the kings of the Hittites, and the kings of the Egyptians, to come upon us. ⁷ Wherefore they arose and fled in the twilight, and left their tents, and their horses, and their asses, even the camp as it *was*, and fled for their life. ⁸ And when these lepers came to the uttermost part of the camp, they went into one tent, and did eat and drink, and carried thence silver, and gold, and raiment, and went and hid *it*; and came again, and entered into another tent, and carried thence *also*, and went and hid *it*. ⁹ Then they said one to another, We do not well: this day *is* a day of good tidings, and we hold our peace: if we tarry till the morning light, some mischief will come upon us: now therefore come, that we may go and tell the king's household. ¹⁰ So they came and called unto the porter of the city: and they told them, saying, We came to the camp of the Syrians, and, behold, *there was* no man there, neither voice of man, but horses tied, and asses tied, and the tents as they *were*. ¹¹ And he called the porters; and they told *it* to the king's house within.

¹² And the king arose in the night, and said unto his servants, I will now shew you what the Syrians have done to us. They know that we *be* hungry; therefore are they gone out of the camp to hide themselves in the field, saying, When they come out of the city, we shall catch them alive, and get into the city. ¹³ And one of his servants answered and said, Let *some* take, I pray thee, five of the horses that remain, which are left in the city, (behold, they *are* as all the multitude of Israel that are left in it: behold, *I say*, they *are* even as all the multitude of the Israelites that are consumed:) and let us send and see. ¹⁴ They took therefore two chariot horses; and the king sent after the host of the Syrians, saying, Go and see. ¹⁵ And they went after them unto Jordan: and, lo, all the way *was* full of garments and vessels, which the Syrians had cast away in their haste. And the messengers

returned, and told the king. [16] And the people went out, and spoiled the tents of the Syrians. So a measure of fine flour was *sold* for a shekel, and two measures of barley for a shekel, according to the word of the LORD.

[17] And the king appointed the lord on whose hand he leaned to have the charge of the gate: and the people trode upon him in the gate, and he died, as the man of God had said, who spake when the king came down to him. [18] And it came to pass as the man of God had spoken to the king, saying, Two measures of barley for a shekel, and a measure of fine flour for a shekel, shall be to morrow about this time in the gate of Samaria: [19] And that lord answered the man of God, and said, Now, behold, *if* the LORD should make windows in heaven, might such a thing be? And he said, Behold, thou shalt see it with thine eyes, but shalt not eat thereof. [20] And so it fell out unto him: for the people trode upon him in the gate, and he died.

The Syrians had surrounded Samaria. No one could go in or come out. The city was closed up. On the outside were four lepers. They would have been outside because they were ceremonially unclean. In addition to the siege on the city, there was a famine in the land. Now there is neither sufficient food nor water. People had resorted to eating their children to stay alive. There is an interesting analogy to discover. The Syrians who were not the people of God were on the outside living in abundance. The Israelites who were the people of God were on the inside surviving outside of abundance. The fact that the people of God were not in abundance is too much to grasp in this small space of time and paper. Cutting to the chase, they were in this condition because of disobedience. When things deteriorated to the point that there appeared to be no hope God confused the Syrian Army to the point of deserting their tents, leaving all their substance. There was plenty food and resources to go around. The four lepers made the discovery and rather than being greedy, they were gracious. They went to Samaria and called unto the gatekeepers to share the good news. The gracious act of these four lepers of sharing the plunder of the Syrians preserved the city.

A Final Note on Leprosy

Each of these cases shares a different side of leprosy and that no matter how devastating a disease it is, God still can do something about it. A person is not healed or delivered from leprosy but cleansed. The most intriguing aspect of these stories

317

is that God did not remove the disease the same way from one person to the next. In Miriam's case, it took seven days of sequestration. In Naaman's case, it took seven dips of saturation. In the leper's (Mark 1) case, it took the Savior's words and touch. In the ten lepers' (Luke 17) case, it took the Savior's touching words. In all of these stories, one thing is absolutely clear – there is no cookie-cutter approach to the miracles of God. A Spirit-formed and Spirit-filled vessel will allow for Spirit-flow. God can heal, cleanse and deliver the same thing a multitude of ways. All that needs to be remembered is that the vessel must learn to hear God's voice and follow God's lead. God is looking for obedience in both the subject and the object. The passage in Mark 14 confirms that whatever condition we used to be in, God is good enough to remind us of what He has done. All of us are former whatevers. Whatever we used to have or whatever we used to be, God brought us out. We can be thankful that He healed, cleansed, delivered, saved and sanctified us. We can be thankful that we are new creatures. Old things

have passed away and all things are become new.

The Priest's Observations Concerning Leprosy (Leviticus 13-15)

13 And the LORD spake unto Moses and Aaron, saying, [2] When a man shall have in the skin of his flesh a rising, a scab, or bright spot, and it be in the skin of his flesh *like* the plague of leprosy; then he shall be brought unto Aaron the priest, or unto one of his sons the priests: [3] And the priest shall look on the plague in the skin of the flesh: and *when* the hair in the plague is turned white, and the plague in sight *be* deeper than the skin of his flesh, it *is* a plague of leprosy: and the priest shall look on him, and pronounce him unclean. [4] If the bright spot *be* white in the skin of his flesh, and in sight *be* not deeper than the skin, and the hair thereof be not turned white; then the priest shall shut up *him that hath* the plague seven days: [5] And the priest shall look on him the seventh day: and, behold, *if* the plague in his sight be at a stay, *and* the plague spread not in the skin; then the priest shall shut him up seven days more: [6] And the priest shall look on him again the seventh day: and, behold, *if* the plague *be* somewhat dark, *and* the plague spread not in the skin, the priest shall pronounce him clean: it *is but* a scab: and he shall wash his clothes, and be clean. [7] But if the scab spread much abroad in the skin, after that he hath been seen of the priest for his cleansing, he shall be seen of the priest again: [8] And *if* the priest see that, behold, the scab spreadeth in the skin, then the priest shall pronounce him unclean: it *is* a leprosy.

[9] When the plague of leprosy is in a man, then he shall be brought unto the priest; [10] And the priest shall see *him*: and, behold, *if* the rising *be* white in the skin,

and it have turned the hair white, and *there be* quick raw flesh in the rising; [11] It *is* an old leprosy in the skin of his flesh, and the priest shall pronounce him unclean, and shall not shut him up: for he *is* unclean. [12] And if a leprosy break out abroad in the skin, and the leprosy cover all the skin of *him that hath* the plague from his head even to his foot, wheresoever the priest looketh; [13] Then the priest shall consider: and, behold, *if* the leprosy have covered all his flesh, he shall pronounce *him* clean *that hath* the plague: it is all turned white: he *is* clean. [14] But when raw flesh appeareth in him, he shall be unclean [15] And the priest shall see the raw flesh, and pronounce him to be unclean: *for* the raw flesh *is* unclean: it *is* a leprosy. [16] Or if the raw flesh turn again, and be changed unto white, he shall come unto the priest; [17] And the priest shall see him: and, behold, *if* the plague be turned into white; then the priest shall pronounce *him* clean *that hath* the plague: he *is* clean.

[18] The flesh also, in which, *even* in the skin thereof, was a boil, and is healed, [19] And in the place of the boil there be a white rising, or a bright spot, white, and somewhat reddish, and it be shewed to the priest; [20] And if, when the priest seeth it, behold, it *be* in sight lower than the skin, and the hair thereof be turned white; the priest shall pronounce him unclean: it *is* a plague of leprosy broken out of the boil. [21] But if the priest look on it, and, behold, *there be* no white hairs therein, and *if* it *be* not lower than the skin, but *be* somewhat dark; then the priest shall shut him up seven days: [22] And if it spread much abroad in the skin, then the priest shall pronounce him unclean: it *is* a plague. [23] But if the bright spot stay in his place, *and* spread not, it *is* a burning boil; and the priest shall pronounce him clean.

[24] Or if there be *any* flesh, in the skin whereof *there is* a hot burning, and the quick *flesh* that burneth have a

white bright spot, somewhat reddish, or white; [25] Then the priest shall look upon it: and, behold, *if* the hair in the bright spot be turned white, and it *be in* sight deeper than the skin; it *is* a leprosy broken out of the burning: wherefore the priest shall pronounce him unclean: it *is* the plague of leprosy. [26] But if the priest look on it, and, behold, *there be* no white hair in the bright spot, and it *be* no lower than the *other* skin, but *be* somewhat dark; then the priest shall shut him up seven days: [27] And the priest shall look upon him the seventh day: *and* if it be spread much abroad in the skin, then the priest shall pronounce him unclean: it *is* the plague of leprosy. [28] And if the bright spot stay in his place, *and* spread not in the skin, but it *be* somewhat dark; it *is* a rising of the burning, and the priest shall pronounce him clean: for it *is* an inflammation of the burning.

[29] If a man or woman have a plague upon the head or the beard; [30] Then the priest shall see the plague: and, behold, if it *be* in sight deeper than the skin; *and there be* in it a yellow thin hair; then the priest shall pronounce him unclean: it *is* a dry scall, *even* a leprosy upon the head or beard. [31] And if the priest look on the plague of the scall, and, behold, it *be* not in sight deeper than the skin, and *that there is* no black hair in it; then the priest shall shut up *him that hath* the plague of the scall seven days: [32] And in the seventh day the priest shall look on the plague: and, behold, *if* the scall spread not, and there be in it no yellow hair, and the scall *be* not in sight deeper than the skin; [33] He shall be shaven, but the scall shall he not shave; and the priest shall shut up *him that hath* the scall seven days more: [34] And in the seventh day the priest shall look on the scall: and, behold, *if* the scall be not spread in the skin, nor *be* in sight deeper than the skin; then the priest shall pronounce him clean: and he shall wash his clothes, and be clean. [35] But if the scall

spread much in the skin after his cleansing; ³⁶ Then the priest shall look on him: and, behold, if the scall be spread in the skin, the priest shall not seek for yellow hair; he *is* unclean. ³⁷ But if the scall be in his sight at a stay, and *that* there is black hair grown up therein; the scall is healed, he *is* clean: and the priest shall pronounce him clean.

³⁸ If a man also or a woman have in the skin of their flesh bright spots, *even* white bright spots; ³⁹ Then the priest shall look: and, behold, *if* the bright spots in the skin of their flesh *be* darkish white; it *is* a freckled spot *that* groweth in the skin; he *is* clean. ⁴⁰ And the man whose hair is fallen off his head, he *is* bald; *yet is* he clean. ⁴¹ And he that hath his hair fallen off from the part of his head toward his face, he *is* forehead bald: *yet is* he clean. ⁴² And if there be in the bald head, or bald forehead, a white reddish sore; it *is* a leprosy sprung up in his bald head, or his bald forehead. ⁴³ Then the priest shall look upon it: and, behold, *if* the rising of the sore *be* white reddish in his bald head, or in his bald forehead, as the leprosy appeareth in the skin of the flesh; ⁴⁴ He is a leprous man, he *is* unclean: the priest shall pronounce him utterly unclean; his plague *is* in his head. ⁴⁵ And the leper in whom the plague *is*, his clothes shall be rent, and his head bare, and he shall put a covering upon his upper lip, and shall cry, Unclean, unclean. ⁴⁶ All the days wherein the plague *shall be* in him he shall be defiled; he *is* unclean: he shall dwell alone; without the camp *shall* his habitation *be*.

⁴⁷ The garment also that the plague of leprosy is in, *whether it be* a woollen garment, or a linen garment; ⁴⁸ Whether *it be* in the warp, or woof; of linen, or of woollen; whether in a skin, or in any thing made of skin; ⁴⁹ And if the plague be greenish or reddish in the garment, or in the skin, either in the warp, or in the woof,

or in any thing of skin; it *is* a plague of leprosy, and shall be shewed unto the priest: [50] And the priest shall look upon the plague, and shut up *it that hath* the plague seven days: [51] And he shall look on the plague on the seventh day: if the plague be spread in the garment, either in the warp, or in the woof, or in a skin, *or* in any work that is made of skin; the plague *is* a fretting leprosy; it *is* unclean. [52] He shall therefore burn that garment, whether warp or woof, in woollen or in linen, or any thing of skin, wherein the plague is: for it *is* a fretting leprosy; it shall be burnt in the fire. [53] And if the priest shall look, and, behold, the plague be not spread in the garment, either in the warp, or in the woof, or in any thing of skin; [54] Then the priest shall command that they wash *the thing* wherein the plague *is*, and he shall shut it up seven days more: [55] And the priest shall look on the plague, after that it is washed: and, behold, *if* the plague have not changed his colour, and the plague be not spread; it *is* unclean; thou shalt burn it in the fire; it *is* fret inward, *whether* it *be* bare within or without. [56] And if the priest look, and, behold, the plague *be* somewhat dark after the washing of it; then he shall rend it out of the garment, or out of the skin, or out of the warp, or out of the woof: [57] And if it appear still in the garment, either in the warp, or in the woof, or in any thing of skin; it *is* a spreading *plague*: thou shalt burn that wherein the plague *is* with fire. [58] And the garment, either warp, or woof, or whatsoever thing of skin *it be*, which thou shalt wash, if the plague be departed from them, then it shall be washed the second time, and shall be clean. [59] This *is* the law of the plague of leprosy in a garment of woollen or linen, either in the warp, or woof, or any thing of skins, to pronounce it clean, or to pronounce it unclean.

14 And the LORD spake unto Moses, saying, [2] This shall be the law of the leper in the day of his cleansing:

He shall be brought unto the priest: [3] And the priest shall go forth out of the camp; and the priest shall look, and, behold, *if* the plague of leprosy be healed in the leper; [4] Then shall the priest command to take for him that is to be cleansed two birds alive *and* clean, and cedar wood, and scarlet, and hyssop: [5] And the priest shall command that one of the birds be killed in an earthen vessel over running water: [6] As for the living bird, he shall take it, and the cedar wood, and the scarlet, and the hyssop, and shall dip them and the living bird in the blood of the bird *that was* killed over the running water: [7] And he shall sprinkle upon him that is to be cleansed from the leprosy seven times, and shall pronounce him clean, and shall let the living bird loose into the open field. [8] And he that is to be cleansed shall wash his clothes, and shave off all his hair, and wash himself in water, that he may be clean: and after that he shall come into the camp, and shall tarry abroad out of his tent seven days. [9] But it shall be on the seventh day, that he shall shave all his hair off his head and his beard and his eyebrows, even all his hair he shall shave off: and he shall wash his clothes, also he shall wash his flesh in water, and he shall be clean. [10] And on the eighth day he shall take two he lambs without blemish, and one ewe lamb of the first year without blemish, and three tenth deals of fine flour *for* a meat offering, mingled with oil, and one log of oil. [11] And the priest that maketh *him* clean shall present the man that is to be made clean, and those things, before the LORD, *at* the door of the tabernacle of the congregation: [12] And the priest shall take one he lamb, and offer him for a trespass offering, and the log of oil, and wave them *for* a wave offering before the LORD: [13] And he shall slay the lamb in the place where he shall kill the sin offering and the burnt offering, in the holy place: for as the sin offering *is* the priest's, *so is* the trespass offering: it *is* most holy: [14] And the priest shall take *some* of the blood of the trespass offering, and the priest shall put *it* upon the tip of the right ear of him that is to be cleansed, and upon the thumb of his right hand, and upon the great toe of his right foot: ¹⁵ And the priest shall take *some* of the log of oil, and pour *it* into the palm of his own left hand: ¹⁶ And the priest shall dip his right finger in the oil that *is* in his left hand, and shall sprinkle of the oil with his finger seven times before the LORD: ¹⁷ And of the rest of the oil that *is* in his hand shall the priest put upon the tip of the right ear of him that is to be cleansed, and upon the thumb of his right hand, and upon the great toe of his right foot, upon the blood of the trespass offering: ¹⁸ And the remnant of the oil that *is* in the priest's hand he shall pour upon the head of him that is to be cleansed: and the priest shall make an atonement for him before the LORD. ¹⁹ And the priest shall offer the sin offering, and make an atonement for him that is to be cleansed from his uncleanness; and afterward he shall kill the burnt offering: ²⁰ And the priest shall offer the burnt offering and the meat offering upon the altar: and the priest shall make an atonement for him, and he shall be clean.

²¹ And if he *be* poor, and cannot get so much; then he shall take one lamb *for* a trespass offering to be waved, to make an atonement for him, and one tenth deal of fine flour mingled with oil for a meat offering, and a log of oil; ²² And two turtledoves, or two young pigeons, such as he is able to get; and the one shall be a sin offering, and the other a burnt offering. ²³ And he shall bring them on the eighth day for his cleansing unto the priest, unto the door of the tabernacle of the congregation, before the LORD. ²⁴ And the priest shall take the lamb of the trespass offering, and the log of oil, and the priest shall wave them *for* a wave offering before the LORD: ²⁵ And he shall kill the lamb of the trespass offering, and the priest

shall take *some* of the blood of the trespass offering, and put *it* upon the tip of the right ear of him that is to be cleansed, and upon the thumb of his right hand, and upon the great toe of his right foot: ²⁶ And the priest shall pour of the oil into the palm of his own left hand: ²⁷ And the priest shall sprinkle with his right finger *some* of the oil that *is* in his left hand seven times before the LORD: ²⁸ And the priest shall put of the oil that *is* in his hand upon the tip of the right ear of him that is to be cleansed, and upon the thumb of his right hand, and upon the great toe of his right foot, upon the place of the blood of the trespass offering: ²⁹ And the rest of the oil that *is* in the priest's hand he shall put upon the head of him that is to be cleansed, to make an atonement for him before the LORD. ³⁰ And he shall offer the one of the turtledoves, or of the young pigeons, such as he can get; ³¹ *Even* such as he is able to get, the one *for* a sin offering, and the other *for* a burnt offering, with the meat offering: and the priest shall make an atonement for him that is to be cleansed before the LORD. ³² This *is* the law *of him* in whom *is* the plague of leprosy, whose hand is not able to get *that which pertaineth* to his cleansing.

³³ And the LORD spake unto Moses and unto Aaron, saying, ³⁴ When ye be come into the land of Canaan, which I give to you for a possession, and I put the plague of leprosy in a house of the land of your possession; ³⁵ And he that owneth the house shall come and tell the priest, saying, It seemeth to me *there is* as it were a plague in the house: ³⁶ Then the priest shall command that they empty the house, before the priest go *into it* to see the plague, that all that *is* in the house be not made unclean: and afterward the priest shall go in to see the house: ³⁷ And he shall look on the plague, and, behold, *if* the plague *be* in the walls of the house with hollow strakes, greenish or reddish, which in sight *are* lower

than the wall; ³⁸ Then the priest shall go out of the house
to the door of the house, and shut up the house seven
days: ³⁹ And the priest shall come again the seventh day,
and shall look: and, behold, *if* the plague be spread in the
walls of the house; ⁴⁰ Then the priest shall command that
they take away the stones in which the plague *is*, and
they shall cast them into an unclean place without the
city: ⁴¹ And he shall cause the house to be scraped within
round about, and they shall pour out the dust that they
scrape off without the city into an unclean place: ⁴² And
they shall take other stones, and put *them* in the place of
those stones; and he shall take other morter, and shall
plaister the house. ⁴³ And if the plague come again, and
break out in the house, after that he hath taken away the
stones, and after he hath scraped the house, and after it is
plaistered; ⁴⁴ Then the priest shall come and look, and,
behold, *if* the plague be spread in the house, it *is* a
fretting leprosy in the house: it *is* unclean. ⁴⁵ And he shall
break down the house, the stones of it, and the timber
thereof, and all the morter of the house; and he shall carry
them forth out of the city into an unclean place.
⁴⁶ Moreover he that goeth into the house all the while that
it is shut up shall be unclean until the even. ⁴⁷ And he that
lieth in the house shall wash his clothes; and he that
eateth in the house shall wash his clothes. ⁴⁸ And if the
priest shall come in, and look *upon it*, and, behold, the
plague hath not spread in the house, after the house was
plaistered: then the priest shall pronounce the house
clean, because the plague is healed. ⁴⁹ And he shall take
to cleanse the house two birds, and cedar wood, and
scarlet, and hyssop: ⁵⁰ And he shall kill the one of the
birds in an earthen vessel over running water: ⁵¹ And he
shall take the cedar wood, and the hyssop, and the scarlet,
and the living bird, and dip them in the blood of the slain
bird, and in the running water, and sprinkle the house

seven times: [52] And he shall cleanse the house with the blood of the bird, and with the running water, and with the living bird, and with the cedar wood, and with the hyssop, and with the scarlet: [53] But he shall let go the living bird out of the city into the open fields, and make an atonement for the house: and it shall be clean.

[54] This *is* the law for all manner of plague of leprosy, and scall, [55] And for the leprosy of a garment, and of a house, [56] And for a rising, and for a scab, and for a bright spot: [57] To teach when *it is* unclean, and when *it is* clean: this *is* the law of leprosy.

15 And the LORD spake unto Moses and to Aaron, saying, [2] Speak unto the children of Israel, and say unto them, When any man hath a running issue out of his flesh, *because of* his issue he *is* unclean. [3] And this shall be his uncleanness in his issue: whether his flesh run with his issue, or his flesh be stopped from his issue, it *is* his uncleanness. [4] Every bed, whereon he lieth that hath the issue, is unclean: and every thing, whereon he sitteth, shall be unclean. [5] And whosoever toucheth his bed shall wash his clothes, and bathe *himself* in water, and be unclean until the even. [6] And he that sitteth on *any* thing whereon he sat that hath the issue shall wash his clothes, and bathe *himself* in water, and be unclean until the even. [7] And he that toucheth the flesh of him that hath the issue shall wash his clothes, and bathe *himself* in water, and be unclean until the even. [8] And if he that hath the issue spit upon him that is clean; then he shall wash his clothes, and bathe *himself* in water, and be unclean until the even. [9] And what saddle soever he rideth upon that hath the issue shall be unclean. [10] And whosoever toucheth any thing that was under him shall be unclean until the even: and he that beareth *any of* those things shall wash his clothes, and bathe *himself* in water, and be unclean until the even. [11] And whomsoever he toucheth that hath the issue, and hath not rinsed his hands in water, he shall wash his clothes, and bathe *himself* in water, and be unclean until the even. [12] And the vessel of earth, that he toucheth which hath the issue, shall be broken: and every vessel of wood shall be rinsed in water. [13] And when he that hath an issue is cleansed of his issue; then he shall number to himself seven days for his cleansing, and wash his clothes, and bathe his flesh in running water, and shall be clean. [14] And on the eighth day he shall take to him two turtledoves, or two young pigeons, and come before the LORD unto the door of the tabernacle of the congregation, and give them unto the priest: [15] And the priest shall offer them, the one *for* a sin offering, and the other *for* a burnt offering; and the priest shall make an atonement for him before the LORD for his issue. [16] And if any man's seed of copulation go out from him, then he shall wash all his flesh in water, and be unclean until the even. [17] And every garment, and every skin, whereon is the seed of copulation, shall be washed with water, and be unclean until the even. [18] The woman also with whom man shall lie *with* seed of copulation, they shall *both* bathe *themselves* in water, and be unclean until the even.

[19] And if a woman have an issue, *and* her issue in her flesh be blood, she shall be put apart seven days: and whosoever toucheth her shall be unclean until the even. [20] And every thing that she lieth upon in her separation shall be unclean: every thing also that she sitteth upon shall be unclean. [21] And whosoever toucheth her bed shall wash his clothes, and bathe *himself* in water, and be unclean until the even. [22] And whosoever toucheth any thing that she sat upon shall wash his clothes, and bathe *himself* in water, and be unclean until the even. [23] And if it *be* on *her* bed, or on any thing whereon she sitteth, when he toucheth it, he shall be unclean until the even. [24] And if any man lie with her at all, and her flowers be

upon him, he shall be unclean seven days; and all the bed whereon he lieth shall be unclean. ²⁵ And if a woman have an issue of her blood many days out of the time of her separation, or if it run beyond the time of her separation; all the days of the issue of her uncleanness shall be as the days of her separation: she *shall be* unclean. ²⁶ Every bed whereon she lieth all the days of her issue shall be unto her as the bed of her separation: and whatsoever she sitteth upon shall be unclean, as the uncleanness of her separation. ²⁷ And whosoever toucheth those things shall be unclean, and shall wash his clothes, and bathe *himself* in water, and be unclean until the even. ²⁸ But if she be cleansed of her issue, then she shall number to herself seven days, and after that she shall be clean. ²⁹ And on the eighth day she shall take unto her two turtles, or two young pigeons, and bring them unto the priest, to the door of the tabernacle of the congregation. ³⁰ And the priest shall offer the one *for* a sin offering, and the other *for* a burnt offering; and the priest shall make an atonement for her before the LORD for the issue of her uncleanness.

³¹ Thus shall ye separate the children of Israel from their uncleanness; that they die not in their uncleanness, when they defile my tabernacle that *is* among them. ³² This *is* the law of him that hath an issue, and *of him* whose seed goeth from him, and is defiled therewith; ³³ And of her that is sick of her flowers, and of him that hath an issue, of the man, and of the woman, and of him that lieth with her that is unclean.

You may wonder why there are not any more stories shared in

this book. Certainly there are many other miracles worthy of our attention. I have accomplished my purpose. This final lesson concerning leprosy lets us know that God has a simple system. All we have to do is listen to Him and He will give us all the direction we need. Learning to listen to God means we have to get close to Him. The closer we are, the better we can hear His voice. Healing and deliverance are environments where we really have to pay attention to the voice of God. When we do this, we will be on our way to being used by God. Hallelujah.

A Recap of God's System for Producing Miracles

Praying to God for His Power Provides Enablement
- Miracles happen by God's power.

Praising God brings His Presence which Prepares the Environment
- Miracles happen in God's presence.

Partnership with God Produces Employment
- God is willing to use us as conduits for His miracles.

Potential for Godly Usefulness Positions Endowment
- *Spirit-formed.* We must be saved and sanctified.
- *Spirit-filled.* We must be filled with His Spirit exhibiting God's Fruit and Gifts.

- ***Spirit-flow.*** We must be available to God so He can use our *observation, operation* and *obedience* to flow through us.

Speak in Authority
- *Invoke the Name of Jesus*
- We must submit the **Request**, satisfy the **Requirement**, secure the **Remedy** and specify the **Rejoicing**. We must speak authoritatively with **unwavering faith**.
- Here is a special note on the requirement. Often, this is the place where God may reveal why the person is in a particular condition. There could any number of reasons why they are in the state you find them. God may use the Word of Wisdom, the Word of Knowledge or Prophecy to get the information to them. It is our job to simply present to them what God presents to us and leave the rest up to Him.

Speaking Accurately
- *Look them in the eyes and speak directly to the condition and tell it what to do. It does not matter if they have an illness or a demon.*
- Here is a simple word of warning. Whenever we are addressing a demon or demons, it is best to secure a team. Demons are unlike illnesses in that they speak back. They are stubborn and unpredictable. Having a team gives the best opportunity for success. During the casting out of the demon, one can pray while the other observes and takes notes on what is happening. Before addressing the demonic realm, make sure everyone on the team is covered by the *Blood of Jesus*. This protects them against the tricks of the enemy.

Secure an Assessment
- *Ask them to do what they could not do before.*
- If there is a sin involved they may have to **Confess** *(Repent and Renounce)*, **Correct** *(Discard and Destroy)* and **Commit** *(Walk, Talk, Live and Give)* according to God's Standards.
- *Invoke the Blood of Jesus*

Remember: The *Name of Jesus* gets the miracle and the *Blood of Jesus* keeps the miracle.

Simple Do's and Don'ts

The right way is to be used by God to affect the lives of His hurting children. The wrong way is to move without God's help. You must go under the power of the Holy Spirit and His anointing and not on your own agenda. Make sure you get their permission to touch them before putting your hands on them. Even something as simple as a hug can set someone off in the wrong direction. Make sure you maintain gender specificity in one on one situations. Men can pray for men and women for women whenever there's no one else around. Whenever there's a male/female praying environment, find another person who is the same gender of the one in need. This way, if the healing requires touching, the one who is the same gender can be asked to do the touching. If you cannot find another person and the situation warrants a prayer, make sure you are in an open space and not behind a closed door, and remember that Jesus often prayed for healing or deliverance from a distance. He did not touch everybody He healed. If God is going to heal or deliver them, He can do it without your being at risk. You must maintain the confidence of anyone who tells you anything that could damage their reputation. Do not tell what you hear no matter how "juicy" it is. If you find out that a crime has been committed, you must advise the person to speak to the proper authorities about the crime if they are the perpetrators. Their sickness may be tied to the crime. Do not go to the authorities for them unless you have exhausted all available options to get them to go first. By all means, follow the laws of your immediate jurisdiction. If your jurisdiction requires you to keep the confidence of those with whom you have counseled, please do so. If you are at no obligation to hold the information in confidence, make sure they know what the law requires you to do. By all means keep prayer and seeking God's direction first and foremost in your life and you cannot go wrong. Sometimes letting them know that you will go with them is enough to get them to come clean. If they refuse, they need to know that you will make the report. These simple do's and don'ts will help you do well in this area of ministry. These do not exhaust all the possible scenarios you will face. When in doubt, seek wise counsel from your pastor, a seasoned prayer counselor or a licensed therapist. Remember, safety is the best policy.

The abused, marginalized and sinned against cannot be approached as though their issues need quick fixes. There are often years of turmoil and mountains of pain to sift through. To help those with deep-seeded issues can take years to overcome and in many cases the services of a seasoned pastor and/or a skilled licensed therapist. It is advisable that whoever feels God's call in this area should pray earnestly, seek God's whole counsel and be prepared to read as much material as possible on the subjects of healing, deliverance, counseling, mission, and ministry. One can benefit greatly from being well read, spiritually led and God fed.

As I close this book I offer a simple prayer:

God, I ask that You prepare the heart of the person reading this book. You know the people who are hurting and demonized. You know every issue affecting their capacity to love, forgive, maintain fellowship, and grow in faith. Lord, please send Your angels to minister to them that they would return to a right relationship with You. Please anoint and prepare your servant who will be dispatched to Your healing assignment. Grant them discernment, patience, love, faith, grace, and Your abiding presence. Allow Your Word to reach the soul of mankind that real healing and wholeness can be found and sustained so that we once again can approach You naked and unashamed. For those who have sinned against You and have been demonized, I pray that they are led to confession, repentance, renouncement, and return to a right fellowship with You. Please grant Your vessels knowledge of the authority they have in You and the capacity to command the illness to be gone and the demonic presence to leave in the Name of Jesus. Please remind them that the Blood of Jesus comes against all evil and has defeated it to the end.

Lord, I thank You for inspiring me to write this book. I hope Your people will read it and get something from it. I hope that Your glory shines through these feeble pages. I trust that Your anointing is on every page because there are those who will receive this book and scrutinize it from page to page. Let them feel Your anointing so that they dare not question what You have given me. Lord, it has been a long journey. Thank You for keeping me until the very end. You are worthy to receive all worship and honor. Finally, I pray for Your ambassadors who will travel around the world with this book and be conduits for miracles, healings and deliverances. Let Your name be exalted. You alone are worthy to be praised.

Your Humble Servant

APPENDIX

APPENDIX

In the following pages there are passages of Scripture that address healing and deliverance. They have been categorized so that all stories with similar conditions are linked together. I trust that you will appreciate the scholasticism that went into this study. Please be aware that some stories are found in multiple categories. It is not a misprint.

Healing and Deliverance by Authority and Command

Matthew 12:9-13 (Man with the Withered Hand)
[9] And when he was departed thence, he went into their synagogue: [10] And, behold, there was a man which had *his* hand withered. And they asked him, saying, Is it lawful to heal on the Sabbath days? that they might accuse him. [11] And he said unto them, What man shall there be among you, that shall have one sheep, and if it fall into a pit on the Sabbath day, will he not lay hold on it, and lift *it* out? [12] How much then is a man better than a sheep? Wherefore it is lawful to do well on the Sabbath days. [13] Then saith he to the man, Stretch forth thine hand. And he stretched *it* forth; and it was restored whole, like as the other.

Mark 3:1-8 (Withered Hand)
[1] And he entered again into the synagogue; and there was a man there which had a withered hand. [2] And they watched him, whether he would heal him on the Sabbath day; that they might accuse him. [3] And he saith unto the man which had the withered hand, Stand forth. [4] And he saith unto them, Is it lawful to do good on the Sabbath days, or to do evil? to save life, or to kill?

But they held their peace. [5] And when he had looked round about on them with anger, being grieved for the hardness of their hearts, he saith unto the man, Stretch forth thine hand. And he stretched *it* out: and his hand was restored whole as the other. [6] And the Pharisees went forth, and straightway took counsel with the Herodians against him, how they might destroy him. [7] But Jesus withdrew himself with his disciples to the sea: and a great multitude from Galilee followed him, and from Judaea, [8] And from Jerusalem, and from Idumaea, and *from* beyond Jordan; and they about Tyre and Sidon, a great multitude, when they had heard what great things he did, came unto him.

Luke 6:6-11 (Withered Hand)

[6] And it came to pass also on another Sabbath, that he entered into the synagogue and taught: and there was a man whose right hand was withered. [7] And the scribes and Pharisees watched him, whether he would heal on the Sabbath day; that they might find an accusation against him. [8] But he knew their thoughts, and said to the man which had the withered hand, Rise up, and stand forth in the midst. And he arose and stood forth. [9] Then said Jesus unto them, I will ask you one thing; Is it lawful on the Sabbath days to do good, or to do evil? to save life, or to destroy *it*? [10] And looking round about upon them all, he said unto the man, Stretch forth thy hand. And he did so: and his hand was restored whole as the other. [11] And they were filled with madness; and communed one with another what they might do to Jesus.

Luke 13:10-17 (Woman Bound and Bent Over)

[10] And he was teaching in one of the synagogues on the Sabbath. [11] And, behold, there was a woman which had a spirit of infirmity eighteen years, and was bowed together, and could in no wise lift up *herself.* [12] And when Jesus saw her, he called *her to him*, and said unto her, Woman, thou art loosed from thine infirmity. [13] And he laid *his* hands on her: and immediately she was made straight, and glorified God. [14] And the ruler of the synagogue answered with indignation, because that Jesus had

healed on the Sabbath day, and said unto the people, There are six days in which men ought to work: in them therefore come and be healed, and not on the Sabbath day. [15] The Lord then answered him, and said, *Thou* hypocrite, doth not each one of you on the Sabbath loose his ox or *his* ass from the stall, and lead *him* away to watering? [16] And ought not this woman, being a daughter of Abraham, whom Satan hath bound, lo, these eighteen years, be loosed from this bond on the Sabbath day? [17] And when he had said these things, all his adversaries were ashamed: and all the people rejoiced for all the glorious things that were done by him.

Matthew 8:1-4 (A Leper is Cleansed by Jesus' Touch, Command and Authority)

[1] When he was come down from the mountain, great multitudes followed him. [2] And, behold, there came a leper and worshipped him, saying, Lord, if thou wilt, thou canst make me clean. [3] And Jesus put forth *his* hand, and touched him, saying, I will; be thou clean. And immediately his leprosy was cleansed. [4] And Jesus saith unto him, See thou tell no man; but go thy way, shew thyself to the priest, and offer the gift that Moses commanded, for a testimony unto them.

Luke 4:7-13 (Disciples Cast Out Demons)

[7] And he called *unto him* the twelve, and began to send them forth by two and two; and gave them power over unclean spirits; [8] And commanded them that they should take nothing for *their* journey, save a staff only; no scrip, no bread, no money in *their* purse: [9] But *be* shod with sandals; and not put on two coats. [10] And he said unto them, In what place soever ye enter into an house, there abide till ye depart from that place. [11] And whosoever shall not receive you, nor hear you, when ye depart thence, shake off the dust under your feet for a testimony against them. Verily I say unto you, It shall be more tolerable for Sodom and Gomorrha in the day of judgment, than for that city. [12] And they went out, and preached that men should repent. [13] And they

cast out many devils, and anointed with oil many that were sick, and healed *them.*

John 5:1-16 (Healing by Command and Forgiveness)

[1] After this there was a feast of the Jews; and Jesus went up to Jerusalem. [2] Now there is at Jerusalem by the sheep *market* a pool, which is called in the Hebrew tongue Bethesda, having five porches. [3] In these lay a great multitude of impotent folk, of blind, halt, withered, waiting for the moving of the water. [4] For an angel went down at a certain season into the pool, and troubled the water: whosoever then first after the troubling of the water stepped in was made whole of whatsoever disease he had. [5] And a certain man was there, which had an infirmity thirty and eight years. [6] When Jesus saw him lie, and knew that he had been now a long time *in that case,* he saith unto him, Wilt thou be made whole? [7] The impotent man answered him, Sir, I have no man, when the water is troubled, to put me into the pool: but while I am coming, another steppeth down before me. [8] Jesus saith unto him, Rise, take up thy bed, and walk. [9] And immediately the man was made whole, and took up his bed, and walked: and on the same day was the Sabbath. [10] The Jews therefore said unto him that was cured, It is the Sabbath day: it is not lawful for thee to carry *thy* bed. [11] He answered them, He that made me whole, the same said unto me, Take up thy bed, and walk. [12] Then asked they him, What man is that which said unto thee, Take up thy bed, and walk? [13] And he that was healed wist not who it was: for Jesus had conveyed himself away, a multitude being in *that* place. [14] Afterward Jesus findeth him in the temple, and said unto him, Behold, thou art made whole: sin no more, lest a worse thing come unto thee. [15] The man departed, and told the Jews that it was Jesus, which had made him whole. [16] And therefore did the Jews persecute Jesus, and sought to slay him, because he had done these things on the Sabbath day.

[37] And it came to pass, that on the next day, when they were come down from the hill, much people met him. [38] And, behold, a man of the company cried out, saying, Master, I beseech thee,

look upon my son: for he is mine only child. ³⁹ And, lo, a spirit
taketh him, and he suddenly crieth out; and it teareth him that he
foameth again, and bruising him hardly departeth from him. ⁴⁰
And I besought thy disciples to cast him out; and they could not.
⁴¹ And Jesus answering said, O faithless and perverse generation,
how long shall I be with you, and suffer you? Bring thy son
hither. ⁴² And as he was yet a coming, the devil threw him down,
and tare *him*. And Jesus rebuked the unclean spirit, and healed
the child, and delivered him again to his father.

Luke 4:31-44 (Healing and Deliverance by Command)

³¹ And came down to Capernaum, a city of Galilee, and
taught them on the Sabbath days. ³² And they were astonished at
his doctrine: for his word was with power. ³³ And in the
synagogue there was a man, which had a spirit of an unclean
devil, and cried out with a loud voice, ³⁴ Saying, Let *us* alone;
what have we to do with thee, *thou* Jesus of Nazareth? art thou
come to destroy us? I know thee who thou art; the Holy One of
God. ³⁵ And Jesus rebuked him, saying, Hold thy peace, and
come out of him. And when the devil had thrown him in the
midst, he came out of him, and hurt him not. ³⁶ And they were all
amazed, and spake among themselves, saying, What a word *is*
this! for with authority and power he commandeth the unclean
spirits, and they come out. ³⁷ And the fame of him went out into
every place of the country round about. ³⁸ And he arose out of
the synagogue, and entered into Simon's house. And Simon's
wife's mother was taken with a great fever; and they besought
him for her. ³⁹ And he stood over her, and rebuked the fever; and
it left her: and immediately she arose and ministered unto them.
⁴⁰ Now when the sun was setting, all they that had any sick with
divers diseases brought them unto him; and he laid his hands on
every one of them, and healed them. ⁴¹ And devils also came out
of many, crying out, and saying, Thou art Christ the Son of God.
And he rebuking *them* suffered them not to speak: for they knew
that he was Christ. ⁴² And when it was day, he departed and went
into a desert place: and the people sought him, and came unto

him, and stayed him, that he should not depart from them. [43] And he said unto them, I must preach the kingdom of God to other cities also: for therefore am I sent. [44] And he preached in the synagogues of Galilee.

Mark 1:23-28 (Deliverance by Command)

[23] And there was in their synagogue a man with an unclean spirit; and he cried out, [24] Saying, Let *us* alone; what have we to do with thee, thou Jesus of Nazareth? art thou come to destroy us? I know thee who thou art, the Holy One of God. [25] And Jesus rebuked him, saying, Hold thy peace, and come out of him. [26] And when the unclean spirit had torn him, and cried with a loud voice, he came out of him. [27] And they were all amazed, insomuch that they questioned among themselves, saying, What thing is this? what new doctrine *is* this? for with authority commandeth he even the unclean spirits, and they do obey him. [28] And immediately his fame spread abroad throughout all the region round about Galilee.

Matthew 9:31-34 (Deliverance by Command and Authority)

[31] But they, when they were departed, spread abroad his fame in all that country. [32] As they went out, behold, they brought to him a dumb man possessed with a devil. [33] And when the devil was cast out, the dumb spake: and the multitudes marvelled, saying, It was never so seen in Israel. [34] But the Pharisees said, He casteth out devils through the prince of the devils.

Matthew 12:22-37 (Healing and Deliverance by Command and Authority)

[22] Then was brought unto him one possessed with a devil, blind, and dumb: and he healed him, insomuch that the blind and dumb both spake and saw. [23] And all the people were amazed, and said, Is not this the son of David? [24] But when the Pharisees heard *it*, they said, This *fellow* doth not cast out devils, but by Beelzebub the prince of the devils. [25] And Jesus knew their thoughts, and said unto them, Every kingdom divided against itself is brought to desolation; and every city or house divided against itself shall not stand: [26] And if Satan cast out Satan, he is divided against

himself; how shall then his kingdom stand? [27] And if I by Beelzebub cast out devils, by whom do your children cast *them* out? therefore they shall be your judges. [28] But if I cast out devils by the Spirit of God, then the kingdom of God is come unto you. [29] Or else how can one enter into a strong man's house, and spoil his goods, except he first bind the strong man? and then he will spoil his house. [30] He that is not with me is against me; and he that gathereth not with me scattereth abroad. [31] Wherefore I say unto you, All manner of sin and blasphemy shall be forgiven unto men: but the blasphemy *against* the *Holy* Ghost shall not be forgiven unto men. [32] And whosoever speaketh a word against the Son of man, it shall be forgiven him: but whosoever speaketh against the Holy Ghost, it shall not be forgiven him, neither in this world, neither in the *world* to come. [33] Either make the tree good, and his fruit good; or else make the tree corrupt, and his fruit corrupt: for the tree is known by *his* fruit. [34] O generation of vipers, how can ye, being evil, speak good things? for out of the abundance of the heart the mouth speaketh. [35] A good man out of the good treasure of the heart bringeth forth good things: and an evil man out of the evil treasure bringeth forth evil things. [36] But I say unto you, That every idle word that men shall speak, they shall give account thereof in the day of judgment. [37] For by thy words thou shalt be justified, and by thy words thou shalt be condemned.

Mark 5:1-20 (Deliverance by Command – Legion)

[1] And they came over unto the other side of the sea, into the country of the Gadarenes. [2] And when he was come out of the ship, immediately there met him out of the tombs a man with an unclean spirit, [3] Who had *his* dwelling among the tombs; and no man could bind him, no, not with chains: [4] Because that he had been often bound with fetters and chains, and the chains had been plucked asunder by him, and the fetters broken in pieces: neither could any *man* tame him. [5] And always, night and day, he was in the mountains, and in the tombs, crying, and cutting himself with stones. [6] But when he saw Jesus afar off, he ran and

worshipped him, [7] And cried with a loud voice, and said, What have I to do with thee, Jesus, *thou* Son of the most high God? I adjure thee by God, that thou torment me not. [8] For he said unto him, Come out of the man, *thou* unclean spirit. [9] And he asked him, What *is* thy name? And he answered, saying, My name *is* Legion: for we are many. [10] And he besought him much that he would not send them away out of the country. [11] Now there was there nigh unto the mountains a great herd of swine feeding. [12] And all the devils besought him, saying, Send us into the swine, that we may enter into them. [13] And forthwith Jesus gave them leave. And the unclean spirits went out, and entered into the swine: and the herd ran violently down a steep place into the sea, (they were about two thousand;) and were choked in the sea. [14] And they that fed the swine fled, and told *it* in the city, and in the country. And they went out to see what it was that was done. [15] And they come to Jesus, and see him that was possessed with the devil, and had the legion, sitting, and clothed, and in his right mind: and they were afraid. [16] And they that saw *it* told them how it befell to him that was possessed with the devil, and *also* concerning the swine. [17] And they began to pray him to depart out of their coasts. [18] And when he was come into the ship, he that had been possessed with the devil prayed him that he might be with him. [19] Howbeit Jesus suffered him not, but saith unto him, Go home to thy friends, and tell them how great things the Lord hath done for thee, and hath had compassion on thee. [20] And he departed, and began to publish in Decapolis how great things Jesus had done for him: and all *men* did marvel.

Luke 8:22-39 (Deliverance by Command – Legion)

[22] Now it came to pass on a certain day, that he went into a ship with his disciples: and he said unto them, Let us go over unto the other side of the lake. And they launched forth. [23] But as they sailed he fell asleep: and there came down a storm of wind on the lake; and they were filled *with water*, and were in jeopardy. [24] And they came to him, and awoke him, saying, Master, master, we perish. Then he arose, and rebuked the wind and the

raging of the water: and they ceased, and there was a calm. ²⁵ And he said unto them, Where is your faith? And they being afraid wondered, saying one to another, What manner of man is this! for he commandeth even the winds and water, and they obey him. ²⁶ And they arrived at the country of the Gadarenes, which is over against Galilee. ²⁷ And when he went forth to land, there met him out of the city a certain man, which had devils long time, and ware no clothes, neither abode in *any* house, but in the tombs. ²⁸ When he saw Jesus, he cried out, and fell down before him, and with a loud voice said, What have I to do with thee, Jesus, *thou* Son of God most high? I beseech thee, torment me not. ²⁹ (For he had commanded the unclean spirit to come out of the man. For oftentimes it had caught him: and he was kept bound with chains and in fetters; and he brake the bands, and was driven of the devil into the wilderness.) ³⁰ And Jesus asked him, saying, What is thy name? And he said, Legion: because many devils were entered into him. ³¹ And they besought him that he would not command them to go out into the deep. ³² And there was there an herd of many swine feeding on the mountain: and they besought him that he would suffer them to enter into them. And he suffered them. ³³ Then went the devils out of the man, and entered into the swine: and the herd ran violently down a steep place into the lake, and were choked. ³⁴ When they that fed *them* saw what was done, they fled, and went and told *it* in the city and in the country. ³⁵ Then they went out to see what was done; and came to Jesus, and found the man, out of whom the devils were departed, sitting at the feet of Jesus, clothed, and in his right mind: and they were afraid. ³⁶ They also which saw *it* told them by what means he that was possessed of the devils was healed. ³⁷ Then the whole multitude of the country of the Gadarenes round about besought him to depart from them; for they were taken with great fear: and he went up into the ship, and returned back again. ³⁸ Now the man out of whom the devils were departed besought him that he might be with him: but Jesus sent him away, saying, ³⁹ Return to thine own house, and shew how great things God hath done unto thee. And he went his way, and published throughout the whole city how great things Jesus had done unto him.

Mark 9:14-29 (Healing and Deliverance by Command)

[14] And when he came to *his* disciples, he saw a great multitude about them, and the scribes questioning with them. [15] And straightway all the people, when they beheld him, were greatly amazed, and running to *him* saluted him. [16] And he asked the scribes, What question ye with them? [17] And one of the multitude answered and said, Master, I have brought unto thee my son, which hath a dumb spirit; [18] And wheresoever he taketh him, he teareth him: and he foameth, and gnasheth with his teeth, and pineth away: and I spake to thy disciples that they should cast him out; and they could not. [19] He answereth him, and saith, O faithless generation, how long shall I be with you? how long shall I suffer you? bring him unto me. [20] And they brought him unto him: and when he saw him, straightway the spirit tare him; and he fell on the ground, and wallowed foaming. [21] And he asked his father, How long is it ago since this came unto him? And he said, Of a child. [22] And ofttimes it hath cast him into the fire, and into the waters, to destroy him: but if thou canst do any thing, have compassion on us, and help us. [23] Jesus said unto him, If thou canst believe, all things *are* possible to him that believeth. [24] And straightway the father of the child cried out, and said with tears, Lord, I believe; help thou mine unbelief. [25] When Jesus saw that the people came running together, he rebuked the foul spirit, saying unto him, *Thou* dumb and deaf spirit, I charge thee, come out of him, and enter no more into him. [26] And *the spirit* cried, and rent him sore, and came out of him: and he was as one dead; insomuch that many said, He is dead. [27] But Jesus took him by the hand, and lifted him up; and he arose. [28] And when he was come into the house, his disciples asked him privately, Why could not we cast him out? [29] And he said unto them, This kind can come forth by nothing, but by prayer and fasting.

Luke 9:37-42 (Healing and Deliverance by Command)

[37] And it came to pass, that on the next day, when they were come down from the hill, much people met him. [38] And, behold, a man of the company cried out, saying, Master, I beseech thee, look upon my son: for he is mine only child. [39] And, lo, a spirit taketh him, and he suddenly crieth out; and it teareth him that he foameth again, and bruising him hardly departeth from him. [40] And I besought thy disciples to cast him out; and they could not. [41] And Jesus answering said, O faithless and perverse generation, how long shall I be with you, and suffer you? Bring thy son hither. [42] And as he was yet a coming, the devil threw him down, and tare *him*. And Jesus rebuked the unclean spirit, and healed the child, and delivered him again to his father.

John 11 (Lazarus is Raised from the Dead by Jesus' Command and Authority)

[1] Now a certain *man* was sick, *named* Lazarus, of Bethany, the town of Mary and her sister Martha. [2] (It was *that* Mary which anointed the Lord with ointment, and wiped his feet with her hair, whose brother Lazarus was sick.) [3] Therefore his sisters sent unto him, saying, Lord, behold, he whom thou lovest is sick. [4] When Jesus heard *that*, he said, This sickness is not unto death, but for the glory of God, that the Son of God might be glorified thereby. [5] Now Jesus loved Martha, and her sister, and Lazarus. [6] When he had heard therefore that he was sick, he abode two days still in the same place where he was. [7] Then after that saith he to *his* disciples, Let us go into Judaea again. [8] *His* disciples say unto him, Master, the Jews of late sought to stone thee; and goest thou thither again? [9] Jesus answered, Are there not twelve hours in the day? If any man walk in the day, he stumbleth not, because he seeth the light of this world. [10] But if a man walk in the night, he stumbleth, because there is no light in him. [11] These things said he: and after that he saith unto them, Our friend Lazarus sleepeth; but I go, that I may awake him out of sleep. [12] Then said his disciples, Lord, if he sleep, he shall do well. [13] Howbeit Jesus spake of his death: but they thought that he had

spoken of taking of rest in sleep. [14] Then said Jesus unto them plainly, Lazarus is dead. [15] And I am glad for your sakes that I was not there, to the intent ye may believe; nevertheless let us go unto him. [16] Then said Thomas, which is called Didymus, unto his fellow disciples, Let us also go, that we may die with him.

[17] Then when Jesus came, he found that he had *lain* in the grave four days already. [18] Now Bethany was nigh unto Jerusalem, about fifteen furlongs off: [19] And many of the Jews came to Martha and Mary, to comfort them concerning their brother. [20] Then Martha, as soon as she heard that Jesus was coming, went and met him: but Mary sat *still* in the house. [21] Then said Martha unto Jesus, Lord, if thou hadst been here, my brother had not died. [22] But I know, that even now, whatsoever thou wilt ask of God, God will give *it* thee. [23] Jesus saith unto her, Thy brother shall rise again. [24] Martha saith unto him, I know that he shall rise again in the resurrection at the last day. [25] Jesus said unto her, I am the resurrection, and the life: he that believeth in me, though he were dead, yet shall he live: [26] And whosoever liveth and believeth in me shall never die. Believest thou this? [27] She saith unto him, Yea, Lord: I believe that thou art the Christ, the Son of God, which should come into the world. [28] And when she had so said, she went her way, and called Mary her sister secretly, saying, The Master is come, and calleth for thee. [29] As soon as she heard *that*, she arose quickly, and came unto him. [30] Now Jesus was not yet come into the town, but was in that place where Martha met him. [31] The Jews then which were with her in the house, and comforted her, when they saw Mary, that she rose up hastily and went out, followed her, saying, She goeth unto the grave to weep there. [32] Then when Mary was come where Jesus was, and saw him, she fell down at his feet, saying unto him, Lord, if thou hadst been here, my brother had not died.

[33] When Jesus therefore saw her weeping, and the Jews also weeping which came with her, he groaned in the spirit, and was troubled, [34] And said, Where have ye laid him? They said unto

him, Lord, come and see. ³⁵ Jesus wept. ³⁶ Then said the Jews, Behold how he loved him! ³⁷ And some of them said, Could not this man, which opened the eyes of the blind, have caused that even this man should not have died? ³⁸ Jesus therefore again groaning in himself cometh to the grave. It was a cave, and a stone lay upon it. ³⁹ Jesus said, Take ye away the stone. Martha, the sister of him that was dead, saith unto him, Lord, by this time he stinketh: for he hath been *dead* four days. ⁴⁰ Jesus saith unto her, Said I not unto thee, that, if thou wouldest believe, thou shouldest see the glory of God? ⁴¹ Then they took away the stone *from the place* where the dead was laid. And Jesus lifted up *his* eyes, and said, Father, I thank thee that thou hast heard me. ⁴² And I knew that thou hearest me always: but because of the people which stand by I said *it*, that they may believe that thou hast sent me. ⁴³ And when he thus had spoken, he cried with a loud voice, Lazarus, come forth. ⁴⁴ And he that was dead came forth, bound hand and foot with grave clothes: and his face was bound about with a napkin. Jesus saith unto them, Loose him, and let him go.

Healing and Deliverance by Control

Mark 1:33-35 (Demons are Quieted)
And all the city was gathered together at the door. ³⁴ And he healed many that were sick of divers diseases, and cast out many devils; and suffered not the devils to speak, because they knew him. ³⁵ And in the morning, rising up a great while before day, he went out, and departed into a solitary place, and there prayed.

Mark 3:7-12 (People are Healed and Demons are Quieted)
⁷ But Jesus withdrew himself with his disciples to the sea: and a great multitude from Galilee followed him, and from Judaea, ⁸ And from Jerusalem, and from Idumaea, and *from* beyond Jordan; and they about Tyre and Sidon, a great multitude, when they had heard what great things he did, came unto him. ⁹ And

he spake to his disciples, that a small ship should wait on him because of the multitude, lest they should throng him. [10] For he had healed many; insomuch that they pressed upon him for to touch him, as many as had plagues. [11] And unclean spirits, when they saw him, fell down before him, and cried, saying, Thou art the Son of God. [12] And he straitly charged them that they should not make him known.

Luke 4:7-13 (Power over the Demonic)

[7] And he called *unto him* the twelve, and began to send them forth by two and two; and gave them power over unclean spirits; [8] And commanded them that they should take nothing for *their* journey, save a staff only; no scrip, no bread, no money in *their* purse: [9] But *be* shod with sandals; and not put on two coats. [10] And he said unto them, In what place soever ye enter into an house, there abide till ye depart from that place. [11] And whosoever shall not receive you, nor hear you, when ye depart thence, shake off the dust under your feet for a testimony against them. Verily I say unto you, It shall be more tolerable for Sodom and Gomorrha in the day of judgment, than for that city. [12] And they went out, and preached that men should repent. [13] And they cast out many devils, and anointed with oil many that were sick, and healed *them*.

"Healing and Deliverance by Faith"

Scriptures Concerning Faith
Hebrews 11

[1] Now faith is the substance of things hoped for, the evidence of things not seen. [2] For by it the elders obtained a good report. [3] Through faith we understand that the worlds were framed by the word of God, so that things which are seen were not made of things which do appear.

[4] By faith Abel offered unto God a more excellent sacrifice than Cain, by which he obtained witness that he was righteous,

God testifying of his gifts: and by it he being dead yet speaketh. [5] By faith Enoch was translated that he should not see death; and was not found, because God had translated him: for before his translation he had this testimony, that he pleased God. [6] But without faith *it is* impossible to please *him*: for he that cometh to God must believe that he is, and *that* he is a rewarder of them that diligently seek him. [7] By faith Noah, being warned of God of things not seen as yet, moved with fear, prepared an ark to the saving of his house; by the which he condemned the world, and became heir of the righteousness which is by faith. [8] By faith Abraham, when he was called to go out into a place which he should after receive for an inheritance, obeyed; and he went out, not knowing whither he went. [9] By faith he sojourned in the land of promise, as *in* a strange country, dwelling in tabernacles with Isaac and Jacob, the heirs with him of the same promise: [10] For he looked for a city which hath foundations, whose builder and maker *is* God. [11] Through faith also Sara herself received strength to conceive seed, and was delivered of a child when she was past age, because she judged him faithful who had promised. [12] Therefore sprang there even of one, and him as good as dead, *so many* as the stars of the sky in multitude, and as the sand which is by the sea shore innumerable. [13] These all died in faith, not having received the promises, but having seen them afar off, and were persuaded of *them*, and embraced *them*, and confessed that they were strangers and pilgrims on the earth. [14] For they that say such things declare plainly that they seek a country. [15] And truly, if they had been mindful of that *country* from whence they came out, they might have had opportunity to have returned. [16] But now they desire a better *country*, that is, an heavenly: wherefore God is not ashamed to be called their God: for he hath prepared for them a city. [17] By faith Abraham, when he was tried, offered up Isaac: and he that had received the promises offered up his only begotten *son*, [18] Of whom it was said, That in Isaac shall thy seed be called: [19] Accounting that God *was* able to raise *him* up, even from the dead; from whence also he received him in a figure. [20] By faith Isaac blessed Jacob and Esau concerning things to come. [21] By faith Jacob, when he was a dying, blessed both the sons of Joseph; and worshipped, *leaning* upon the top of his staff. [22] By faith Joseph, when he died, made mention of the departing of the children of Israel; and gave commandment concerning his bones. [23] By faith Moses, when he was born, was hid three months of his parents, because they saw *he was* a proper child; and they were not afraid of the king's commandment. [24] By faith Moses, when he was come to years, refused to be called the son of Pharaoh's daughter; [25] Choosing rather to suffer affliction with the people of God, than to enjoy the pleasures of sin for a season; [26] Esteeming the reproach of Christ greater riches than the treasures in Egypt: for he had respect unto the recompence of the reward. [27] By faith he forsook Egypt, not fearing the wrath of the king: for he endured, as seeing him who is invisible. [28] Through faith he kept the passover, and the sprinkling of blood, lest he that destroyed the firstborn should touch them. [29] By faith they passed through the Red sea as by dry *land*: which the Egyptians assaying to do were drowned. [30] By faith the walls of Jericho fell down, after they were compassed about seven days. [31] By faith the harlot Rahab perished not with them that believed not, when she had received the spies with peace.

[32] And what shall I more say? for the time would fail me to tell of Gedeon, and *of* Barak, and *of* Samson, and *of* Jephthae; *of* David also, and Samuel, and *of* the prophets: [33] Who through faith subdued kingdoms, wrought righteousness, obtained promises, stopped the mouths of lions, [34] Quenched the violence of fire, escaped the edge of the sword, out of weakness were made strong, waxed valiant in fight, turned to flight the armies of the aliens. [35] Women received their dead raised to life again: and others were tortured, not accepting deliverance; that they might obtain a better resurrection: [36] And others had trial of *cruel* mockings and scourgings, yea, moreover of bonds and imprisonment: [37] They were stoned, they were sawn asunder,

were tempted, were slain with the sword: they wandered about in sheepskins and goatskins; being destitute, afflicted, tormented; [38] (Of whom the world was not worthy:) they wandered in deserts, and *in* mountains, and *in* dens and caves of the earth. [39] And these all, having obtained a good report through faith, received not the promise: [40] God having provided some better thing for us, that they without us should not be made perfect.

1 Corinthians 12:1-11

[1] Now concerning spiritual *gifts*, brethren, I would not have you ignorant. [2] Ye know that ye were Gentiles, carried away unto these dumb idols, even as ye were led. [3] Wherefore I give you to understand, that no man speaking by the Spirit of God calleth Jesus accursed: and *that* no man can say that Jesus is the Lord, but by the Holy Ghost. [4] Now there are diversities of gifts, but the same Spirit. [5] And there are differences of administrations, but the same Lord. [6] And there are diversities of operations, but it is the same God which worketh all in all. [7] But the manifestation of the Spirit is given to every man to profit withal. [8] For to one is given by the Spirit the word of wisdom; to another the word of knowledge by the same Spirit; [9] To another faith by the same Spirit; to another the gifts of healing by the same Spirit; [10] To another the working of miracles; to another prophecy; to another discerning of spirits; to another *divers* kinds of tongues; to another the interpretation of tongues: [11] But all these worketh that one and the selfsame Spirit, dividing to every man severally as he will.

Galatians 5:22-26

[22] But the fruit of the Spirit is love, joy, peace, longsuffering, gentleness, goodness, faith, [23] Meekness, temperance: against such there is no law. [24] And they that are Christ's have crucified the flesh with the affections and lusts. [25] If we live in the Spirit, let us also walk in the Spirit. [26] Let us not be desirous of vain glory, provoking one another, envying one another.

Luke 7:1-10 (Healing the Centurion's Servant According to Faith)

[1] Now when he had ended all his sayings in the audience of the people, he entered into Capernaum. [2] And a certain centurion's servant, who was dear unto him, was sick, and ready to die. [3] And when he heard of Jesus, he sent unto him the elders of the Jews, beseeching him that he would come and heal his servant. [4] And when they came to Jesus, they besought him instantly, saying, That he was worthy for whom he should do this: [5] For he loveth our nation, and he hath built us a synagogue. [6] Then Jesus went with them. And when he was now not far from the house, the centurion sent friends to him, saying unto him, Lord, trouble not thyself: for I am not worthy that thou shouldest enter under my roof: [7] Wherefore neither thought I myself worthy to come unto thee: but say in a word, and my servant shall be healed. [8] For I also am a man set under authority, having under me soldiers, and I say unto one, Go, and he goeth; and to another, Come, and he cometh; and to my servant, Do this, and he doeth *it*. [9] When Jesus heard these things, he marvelled at him, and turned him about, and said unto the people that followed him, I say unto you, I have not found so great faith, no, not in Israel. [10] And they that were sent, returning to the house, found the servant whole that had been sick.

Mathew 8:5-13 (Healing the Centurion's Servant According to Faith)

[5] And when Jesus was entered into Capernaum, there came unto him a centurion, beseeching him, [6] And saying, Lord, my servant lieth at home sick of the palsy, grievously tormented. [7] And Jesus saith unto him, I will come and heal him. [8] The centurion answered and said, Lord, I am not worthy that thou shouldest come under my roof: but speak the word only, and my servant shall be healed. [9] For I am a man under authority, having soldiers under me: and I say to this *man*, Go, and he goeth; and to

another, Come, and he cometh; and to my servant, Do this, and he doeth *it*. [10] When Jesus heard *it*, he marvelled, and said to them that followed, Verily I say unto you, I have not found so great faith, no, not in Israel. [11] And I say unto you, That many shall come from the east and west, and shall sit down with Abraham, and Isaac, and Jacob, in the kingdom of heaven. [12] But the children of the kingdom shall be cast out into outer darkness: there shall be weeping and gnashing of teeth. [13] And Jesus said unto the centurion, Go thy way; and as thou hast believed, *so* be it done unto thee. And his servant was healed in the selfsame hour.

Matthew 15:21-28 (Syro-Phoenician Woman's Daughter Healed)

[21] Then Jesus went thence, and departed into the coasts of Tyre and Sidon. [22] And, behold, a woman of Canaan came out of the same coasts, and cried unto him, saying, Have mercy on me, O Lord, *thou* Son of David; my daughter is grievously vexed with a devil. [23] But he answered her not a word. And his disciples came and besought him, saying, Send her away; for she crieth after us. [24] But he answered and said, I am not sent but unto the lost sheep of the house of Israel. [25] Then came she and worshipped him, saying, Lord, help me. [26] But he answered and said, It is not meet to take the children's bread, and to cast *it* to dogs. [27] And she said, Truth, Lord: yet the dogs eat of the crumbs which fall from their masters' table. [28] Then Jesus answered and said unto her, O woman, great *is* thy faith: be it unto thee even as thou wilt. And her daughter was made whole from that very hour.

Mark 7:24-30 (Syro-Phoenician Woman's Daughter Healed)

[24] And from thence he arose, and went into the borders of Tyre and Sidon, and entered into an house, and would have no man know *it*: but he could not be hid. [25] For a *certain* woman, whose young daughter had an unclean spirit, heard of him, and came and fell at his feet: [26] The woman was a Greek, a Syrophenician

by nation; and she besought him that he would cast forth the devil out of her daughter. [27] But Jesus said unto her, Let the children first be filled: for it is not meet to take the children's bread, and to cast *it* unto the dogs. [28] And she answered and said unto him, Yes, Lord: yet the dogs under the table eat of the children's crumbs. [29] And he said unto her, For this saying go thy way; the devil is gone out of thy daughter. [30] And when she was come to her house, she found the devil gone out, and her daughter laid upon the bed.

Matthew 9:27-30 (Jesus Heals by Faith and Touch)

[27] And when Jesus departed thence, two blind men followed him, crying, and saying, *Thou* Son of David, have mercy on us. [28] And when he was come into the house, the blind men came to him: and Jesus saith unto them, Believe ye that I am able to do this? They said unto him, Yea, Lord. [29] Then touched he their eyes, saying, According to your faith be it unto you. [30] And their eyes were opened; and Jesus straitly charged them, saying, See *that* no man know *it.*

Luke 17:11-19 (Ten Lepers Healed by Faith)

[11] And it came to pass, as he went to Jerusalem, that he passed through the midst of Samaria and Galilee. [12] And as he entered into a certain village, there met him ten men that were lepers, which stood afar off: [13] And they lifted up *their* voices, and said, Jesus, Master, have mercy on us. [14] And when he saw *them*, he said unto them, Go shew yourselves unto the priests. And it came to pass, that, as they went, they were cleansed. [15] And one of them, when he saw that he was healed, turned back, and with a loud voice glorified God, [16] And fell down on *his* face at his feet, giving him thanks: and he was a Samaritan. [17] And Jesus answering said, Were there not ten cleansed? but where *are* the nine? [18] There are not found that returned to give glory to God, save this stranger. [19] And he said unto him, Arise, go thy way: thy faith hath made thee whole.

Mark 10:46-52 (Jesus Heals Blind Bartimaeus by Faith)

[46] And they came to Jericho: and as he went out of Jericho with his disciples and a great number of people, blind Bartimaeus, the son of Timaeus, sat by the highway side begging. [47] And when he heard that it was Jesus of Nazareth, he began to cry out, and say, Jesus, *thou* Son of David, have mercy on me. [48] And many charged him that he should hold his peace: but he cried the more a great deal, *Thou* Son of David, have mercy on me. [49] And Jesus stood still, and commanded him to be called. And they call the blind man, saying unto him, Be of good comfort, rise; he calleth thee. [50] And he, casting away his garment, rose, and came to Jesus. [51] And Jesus answered and said unto him, What wilt thou that I should do unto thee? The blind man said unto him, Lord, that I might receive my sight. [52] And Jesus said unto him, Go thy way; thy faith hath made thee whole. And immediately he received his sight, and followed Jesus in the way.

Luke 8:40-56 (Healing by the Touch of Jesus)

[40] And it came to pass, that, when Jesus was returned, the people *gladly* received him: for they were all waiting for him. [41] And, behold, there came a man named Jairus, and he was a ruler of the synagogue: and he fell down at Jesus' feet, and besought him that he would come into his house: [42] For he had one only daughter, about twelve years of age, and she lay a dying. But as he went the people thronged him. [43] And a woman having an issue of blood twelve years, which had spent all her living upon physicians, neither could be healed of any, [44] Came behind *him*, and touched the border of his garment: and immediately her issue of blood stanched. [45] And Jesus said, Who touched me? When all denied, Peter and they that were with him said, Master, the multitude throng thee and press *thee*, and sayest thou, Who touched me? [46] And Jesus said, Somebody hath touched me: for I perceive that virtue is gone out of me. [47] And when the woman saw that she was not hid, she came trembling, and falling down before him, she declared unto him before all the people for what cause she had touched him, and how she was healed

immediately. [48] And he said unto her, Daughter, be of good comfort: thy faith hath made thee whole; go in peace. [49] While he yet spake, there cometh one from the ruler of the synagogue's *house*, saying to him, Thy daughter is dead; trouble not the Master. [50] But when Jesus heard *it*, he answered him, saying, Fear not: believe only, and she shall be made whole. [51] And when he came into the house, he suffered no man to go in, save Peter, and James, and John, and the father and the mother of the maiden. [52] And all wept, and bewailed her: but he said, Weep not; she is not dead, but sleepeth. [53] And they laughed him to scorn, knowing that she was dead. [54] And he put them all out, and took her by the hand, and called, saying, Maid, arise. [55] And her spirit came again, and she arose straightway: and he commanded to give her meat. [56] And her parents were astonished: but he charged them that they should tell no man what was done.

Healing and Deliverance by Obedience

Luke 17:11-18 (Cleansing the Lepers by their Obedience and Faith)

[11] And it came to pass, as he went to Jerusalem, that he passed through the midst of Samaria and Galilee. [12] And as he entered into a certain village, there met him ten men that were lepers, which stood afar off: [13] And they lifted up *their* voices, and said, Jesus, Master, have mercy on us. [14] And when he saw *them*, he said unto them, Go shew yourselves unto the priests. And it came to pass, that, as they went, they were cleansed. [15] And one of them, when he saw that he was healed, turned back, and with a loud voice glorified God, [16] And fell down on *his* face at his feet, giving him thanks: and he was a Samaritan. [17] And Jesus answering said, Were there not ten cleansed? but where *are* the nine? [18] There are not found that returned to give glory to God,

save this stranger. ¹⁹ And he said unto him, Arise, go thy way: thy faith hath made thee whole.

2 Kings 5 (Cleansing of Leprosy by Dipping in Jordan River – Naaman)

¹ Now Naaman, captain of the host of the king of Syria, was a great man with his master, and honourable, because by him the LORD had given deliverance unto Syria: he was also a mighty man in valour, *but he was* a leper. ² And the Syrians had gone out by companies, and had brought away captive out of the land of Israel a little maid; and she waited on Naaman's wife. ³ And she said unto her mistress, Would God my lord *were* with the prophet that *is* in Samaria! for he would recover him of his leprosy. ⁴ And *one* went in, and told his lord, saying, Thus and thus said the maid that *is* of the land of Israel. ⁵ And the king of Syria said, Go to, go, and I will send a letter unto the king of Israel. And he departed, and took with him ten talents of silver, and six thousand *pieces* of gold, and ten changes of raiment. ⁶ And he brought the letter to the king of Israel, saying, Now when this letter is come unto thee, behold, I have *therewith* sent Naaman my servant to thee, that thou mayest recover him of his leprosy. ⁷ And it came to pass, when the king of Israel had read the letter, that he rent his clothes, and said, *Am* I God, to kill and to make alive, that this man doth send unto me to recover a man of his leprosy? wherefore consider, I pray you, and see how he seeketh a quarrel against me. ⁸ And it was *so*, when Elisha the man of God had heard that the king of Israel had rent his clothes, that he sent to the king, saying, Wherefore hast thou rent thy clothes? let him come now to me, and he shall know that there is a prophet in Israel.

⁹ So Naaman came with his horses and with his chariot, and stood at the door of the house of Elisha. ¹⁰ And Elisha sent a messenger unto him, saying, Go and wash in Jordan seven times, and thy flesh shall come again to thee, and thou shalt be clean. ¹¹ But Naaman was wroth, and went away, and said, Behold, I thought, He will surely come out to me, and stand, and call on

the name of the LORD his God, and strike his hand over the place, and recover the leper. [12] *Are* not Abana and Pharpar, rivers of Damascus, better than all the waters of Israel? may I not wash in them, and be clean? So he turned and went away in a rage. [13] And his servants came near, and spake unto him, and said, My father, *if* the prophet had bid thee *do some* great thing, wouldest thou not have done *it*? how much rather then, when he saith to thee, Wash, and be clean? [14] Then went he down, and dipped himself seven times in Jordan, according to the saying of the man of God: and his flesh came again like unto the flesh of a little child, and he was clean.

[15] And he returned to the man of God, he and all his company, and came, and stood before him: and he said, Behold, now I know that *there is* no God in all the earth, but in Israel: now therefore, I pray thee, take a blessing of thy servant. [16] But he said, *As* the LORD liveth, before whom I stand, I will receive none. And he urged him to take *it*; but he refused. [17] And Naaman said, Shall there not then, I pray thee, be given to thy servant two mules' burden of earth? for thy servant will henceforth offer neither burnt offering nor sacrifice unto other gods, but unto the LORD. [18] In this thing the LORD pardon thy servant, *that* when my master goeth into the house of Rimmon to worship there, and he leaneth on my hand, and I bow myself in the house of Rimmon: when I bow down myself in the house of Rimmon, the LORD pardon thy servant in this thing. [19] And he said unto him, Go in peace. So he departed from him a little way.

[20] But Gehazi, the servant of Elisha the man of God, said, Behold, my master hath spared Naaman this Syrian, in not receiving at his hands that which he brought: but, *as* the LORD liveth, I will run after him, and take somewhat of him. [21] So Gehazi followed after Naaman. And when Naaman saw *him* running after him, he lighted down from the chariot to meet him, and said, *Is* all well? [22] And he said, All *is* well. My master hath sent me, saying, Behold, even now there be come to me from mount Ephraim two young men of the sons of the prophets: give

them, I pray thee, a talent of silver, and two changes of garments. ²³ And Naaman said, Be content, take two talents. And he urged him, and bound two talents of silver in two bags, with two changes of garments, and laid *them* upon two of his servants; and they bare *them* before him. ²⁴ And when he came to the tower, he took *them* from their hand, and bestowed *them* in the house: and he let the men go, and they departed. ²⁵ But he went in, and stood before his master. And Elisha said unto him, Whence *comest thou*, Gehazi? And he said, Thy servant went no whither. ²⁶ And he said unto him, Went not mine heart *with thee*, when the man turned again from his chariot to meet thee? *Is it* a time to receive money, and to receive garments, and oliveyards, and vineyards, and sheep, and oxen, and menservants, and maidservants? ²⁷ The leprosy therefore of Naaman shall cleave unto thee, and unto thy seed for ever. And he went out from his presence a leper *as white* as snow.

John 4:43-54 (Healing a Sick Boy by the Father's Obedience)

⁴³ Now after two days he departed thence, and went into Galilee. ⁴⁴ For Jesus himself testified, that a prophet hath no honour in his own country. ⁴⁵ Then when he was come into Galilee, the Galilaeans received him, having seen all the things that he did at Jerusalem at the feast: for they also went unto the feast. ⁴⁶ So Jesus came again into Cana of Galilee, where he made the water wine. And there was a certain nobleman, whose son was sick at Capernaum. ⁴⁷ When he heard that Jesus was come out of Judaea into Galilee, he went unto him, and besought him that he would come down, and heal his son: for he was at the point of death. ⁴⁸ Then said Jesus unto him, Except ye see signs and wonders, ye will not believe. ⁴⁹ The nobleman saith unto him, Sir, come down ere my child die. ⁵⁰ Jesus saith unto him, Go thy way; thy son liveth. And the man believed the word that Jesus had spoken unto him, and he went his way. ⁵¹ And as he was now going down, his servants met him, and told *him*, saying, Thy son liveth. ⁵² Then enquired he of them the hour when he began to amend. And they said unto him, Yesterday at

the seventh hour the fever left him. [53] So the father knew that *it was* at the same hour, in the which Jesus said unto him, Thy son liveth: and himself believed, and his whole house. [54] This *is* again the second miracle *that* Jesus did, when he was come out of Judaea into Galilee.

John 9 (Healing by Touch – A Blind Man from Birth Washes in the Pool of Siloam)

[1] And as *Jesus* passed by, he saw a man which was blind from *his* birth. [2] And his disciples asked him, saying, Master, who did sin, this man, or his parents, that he was born blind? [3] Jesus answered, Neither hath this man sinned, nor his parents: but that the works of God should be made manifest in him. [4] I must work the works of him that sent me, while it is day: the night cometh, when no man can work. [5] As long as I am in the world, I am the light of the world. [6] When he had thus spoken, he spat on the ground, and made clay of the spittle, and he anointed the eyes of the blind man with the clay, [7] And said unto him, Go, wash in the pool of Siloam, (which is by interpretation, Sent.) He went his way therefore, and washed, and came seeing.

[8] The neighbours therefore, and they which before had seen him that he was blind, said, Is not this he that sat and begged? [9] Some said, This is he: others *said*, He is like him: *but* he said, I am *he*. [10] Therefore said they unto him, How were thine eyes opened? [11] He answered and said, A man that is called Jesus made clay, and anointed mine eyes, and said unto me, Go to the pool of Siloam, and wash: and I went and washed, and I received sight. [12] Then said they unto him, Where is he? He said, I know not.

[13] They brought to the Pharisees him that aforetime was blind. [14] And it was the sabbath day when Jesus made the clay, and opened his eyes. [15] Then again the Pharisees also asked him how he had received his sight. He said unto them, He put clay upon mine eyes, and I washed, and do see. [16] Therefore said some of the Pharisees, This man is not of God, because he keepeth not the sabbath day. Others said, How can a man that is

a sinner do such miracles? And there was a division among them. [17] They say unto the blind man again, What sayest thou of him, that he hath opened thine eyes? He said, He is a prophet. [18] But the Jews did not believe concerning him, that he had been blind, and received his sight, until they called the parents of him that had received his sight. [19] And they asked them, saying, Is this your son, who ye say was born blind? how then doth he now see? [20] His parents answered them and said, We know that this is our son, and that he was born blind: [21] But by what means he now seeth, we know not; or who hath opened his eyes, we know not: he is of age; ask him: he shall speak for himself. [22] These *words* spake his parents, because they feared the Jews: for the Jews had agreed already, that if any man did confess that he was Christ, he should be put out of the synagogue. [23] Therefore said his parents, He is of age; ask him. [24] Then again called they the man that was blind, and said unto him, Give God the praise: we know that this man is a sinner. [25] He answered and said, Whether he be a sinner *or no*, I know not: one thing I know, that, whereas I was blind, now I see. [26] Then said they to him again, What did he to thee? how opened he thine eyes? [27] He answered them, I have told you already, and ye did not hear: wherefore would ye hear *it* again? will ye also be his disciples? [28] Then they reviled him, and said, Thou art his disciple; but we are Moses' disciples. [29] We know that God spake unto Moses: *as for* this *fellow*, we know not from whence he is. [30] The man answered and said unto them, Why herein is a marvellous thing, that ye know not from whence he is, and *yet* he hath opened mine eyes. [31] Now we know that God heareth not sinners: but if any man be a worshipper of God, and doeth his will, him he heareth. [32] Since the world began was it not heard that any man opened the eyes of one that was born blind. [33] If this man were not of God, he could do nothing. [34] They answered and said unto him, Thou wast altogether born in sins, and dost thou teach us? And they cast him out.

[35] Jesus heard that they had cast him out; and when he had found him, he said unto him, Dost thou believe on the Son of God? [36] He answered and said, Who is he, Lord, that I might believe on him? [37] And Jesus said unto him, Thou hast both seen him, and it is he that talketh with thee. [38] And he said, Lord, I believe. And he worshipped him.

[39] And Jesus said, For judgment I am come into this world, that they which see not might see; and that they which see might be made blind. [40] And *some* of the Pharisees which were with him heard these words, and said unto him, Are we blind also? [41] Jesus said unto them, If ye were blind, ye should have no sin: but now ye say, We see; therefore your sin remaineth.

Healing and Deliverance by Touch

Mark 3:7-12 (Healing by Touching Jesus)
[7] But Jesus withdrew himself with his disciples to the sea: and a great multitude from Galilee followed him, and from Judaea, [8] And from Jerusalem, and from Idumaea, and *from* beyond Jordan; and they about Tyre and Sidon, a great multitude, when they had heard what great things he did, came unto him. [9] And he spake to his disciples, that a small ship should wait on him because of the multitude, lest they should throng him. [10] For he had healed many; insomuch that they pressed upon him for to touch him, as many as had plagues. [11] And unclean spirits, when they saw him, fell down before him, and cried, saying, Thou art the Son of God. [12] And he straitly charged them that they should not make him known.

Luke 8:40-56 (Healing by the Touch of Jesus)
[40] And it came to pass, that, when Jesus was returned, the people *gladly* received him: for they were all waiting for him. [41] And, behold, there came a man named Jairus, and he was a ruler of the synagogue: and he fell down at Jesus' feet, and besought

him that he would come into his house: [42] For he had one only daughter, about twelve years of age, and she lay a dying. But as he went the people thronged him. [43] And a woman having an issue of blood twelve years, which had spent all her living upon physicians, neither could be healed of any, [44] Came behind *him*, and touched the border of his garment: and immediately her issue of blood stanched. [45] And Jesus said, Who touched me? When all denied, Peter and they that were with him said, Master, the multitude throng thee and press *thee*, and sayest thou, Who touched me? [46] And Jesus said, Somebody hath touched me: for I perceive that virtue is gone out of me. [47] And when the woman saw that she was not hid, she came trembling, and falling down before him, she declared unto him before all the people for what cause she had touched him, and how she was healed immediately. [48] And he said unto her, Daughter, be of good comfort: thy faith hath made thee whole; go in peace. [49] While he yet spake, there cometh one from the ruler of the synagogue's *house*, saying to him, Thy daughter is dead; trouble not the Master. [50] But when Jesus heard *it*, he answered him, saying, Fear not: believe only, and she shall be made whole. [51] And when he came into the house, he suffered no man to go in, save Peter, and James, and John, and the father and the mother of the maiden. [52] And all wept, and bewailed her: but he said, Weep not; she is not dead, but sleepeth. [53] And they laughed him to scorn, knowing that she was dead. [54] And he put them all out, and took her by the hand, and called, saying, Maid, arise. [55] And her spirit came again, and she arose straightway: and he commanded to give her meat. [56] And her parents were astonished: but he charged them that they should tell no man what was done.

Matthew 8:1-4 (A Leper is Cleansed by Jesus' Touch, Command and Authority)

[1] When he was come down from the mountain, great multitudes followed him. [2] And, behold, there came a leper and worshipped him, saying, Lord, if thou wilt, thou canst make me clean. [3] And

Jesus put forth *his* hand, and touched him, saying, I will; be thou clean. And immediately his leprosy was cleansed. [4] And Jesus saith unto him, See thou tell no man; but go thy way, shew thyself to the priest, and offer the gift that Moses commanded, for a testimony unto them.

Mark 6:7-13 (The Twelve Heal by Anointing)

[7] And he called *unto him* the twelve, and began to send them forth by two and two; and gave them power over unclean spirits; [8] And commanded them that they should take nothing for *their* journey, save a staff only; no scrip, no bread, no money in *their* purse: [9] But *be* shod with sandals; and not put on two coats. [10] And he said unto them, In what place soever ye enter into an house, there abide till ye depart from that place. [11] And whosoever shall not receive you, nor hear you, when ye depart thence, shake off the dust under your feet for a testimony against them. Verily I say unto you, It shall be more tolerable for Sodom and Gomorrha in the day of judgment, than for that city. [12] And they went out, and preached that men should repent. [13] And they cast out many devils, and anointed with oil many that were sick, and healed *them*.

Matthew 9:27-30 (Jesus Heals by Faith and Touch)

[27] And when Jesus departed thence, two blind men followed him, crying, and saying, *Thou* Son of David, have mercy on us. [28] And when he was come into the house, the blind men came to him: and Jesus saith unto them, Believe ye that I am able to do this? They said unto him, Yea, Lord. [29] Then touched he their eyes, saying, According to your faith be it unto you. [30] And their eyes were opened; and Jesus straitly charged them, saying, See *that* no man know *it*.

Healing and Deliverance by Touch

Mark 7:31-37 (Healing by Touch, Command and Unusual Means)

[31] And again, departing from the coasts of Tyre and Sidon, he came unto the sea of Galilee, through the midst of the coasts of Decapolis. [32] And they bring unto him one that was deaf, and had an impediment in his speech; and they beseech him to put his hand upon him. [33] And he took him aside from the multitude, and put his fingers into his ears, and he spit, and touched his tongue; [34] And looking up to heaven, he sighed, and saith unto him, Ephphatha, that is, Be opened. [35] And straightway his ears were opened, and the string of his tongue was loosed, and he spake plain. [36] And he charged them that they should tell no man: but the more he charged them, so much the more a great deal they published *it*; [37] And were beyond measure astonished, saying, He hath done all things well: he maketh both the deaf to hear, and the dumb to speak.

Acts 5:12-16 (Healing and Deliverance by Unusual Means)

[12] And by the hands of the apostles were many signs and wonders wrought among the people; (and they were all with one accord in Solomon's porch. [13] And of the rest durst no man join himself to them: but the people magnified them. [14] And believers were the more added to the Lord, multitudes both of men and women.) [15] Insomuch that they brought forth the sick into the streets, and laid *them* on beds and couches, that at the least the shadow of Peter passing by might overshadow some of them. [16] There came also a multitude *out* of the cities round about unto Jerusalem, bringing sick folks, and them which were vexed with unclean spirits: and they were healed every one.

Acts 28:1-10 (Paul Healed a Man by Touch)

[1] And when they were escaped, then they knew that the island was called Melita. [2] And the barbarous people shewed us no little kindness: for they kindled a fire, and received us every one, because of the present rain, and because of the cold. [3] And when Paul had gathered a bundle of sticks, and laid *them* on the fire,

there came a viper out of the heat, and fastened on his hand. [4] And when the barbarians saw the *venomous* beast hang on his hand, they said among themselves, No doubt this man is a murderer, whom, though he hath escaped the sea, yet vengeance suffereth not to live. [5] And he shook off the beast into the fire, and felt no harm. [6] Howbeit they looked when he should have swollen, or fallen down dead suddenly: but after they had looked a great while, and saw no harm come to him, they changed their minds, and said that he was a god. [7] In the same quarters were possessions of the chief man of the island, whose name was Publius; who received us, and lodged us three days courteously. [8] And it came to pass, that the father of Publius lay sick of a fever and of a bloody flux: to whom Paul entered in, and prayed, and laid his hands on him, and healed him. [9] So when this was done, others also, which had diseases in the island, came, and were healed: [10] Who also honoured us with many honours; and when we departed, they laded *us* with such things as were necessary.

Acts 3-4 (Peter and John Heal by Touch)

[1] Now Peter and John went up together into the temple at the hour of prayer, *being* the ninth *hour*. [2] And a certain man lame from his mother's womb was carried, whom they laid daily at the gate of the temple which is called Beautiful, to ask alms of them that entered into the temple; [3] Who seeing Peter and John about to go into the temple asked an alms. [4] And Peter, fastening his eyes upon him with John, said, Look on us. [5] And he gave heed unto them, expecting to receive something of them. [6] Then Peter said, Silver and gold have I none; but such as I have give I thee: In the name of Jesus Christ of Nazareth rise up and walk. [7] And he took him by the right hand, and lifted *him* up: and immediately his feet and ankle bones received strength. [8] And he leaping up stood, and walked, and entered with them into the temple, walking, and leaping, and praising God. [9] And all the people saw him walking and praising God: [10] And they knew that it was he which sat for alms at the Beautiful gate of the

temple: and they were filled with wonder and amazement at that which had happened unto him. [11] And as the lame man which was healed held Peter and John, all the people ran together unto them in the porch that is called Solomon's, greatly wondering.

[12] And when Peter saw *it*, he answered unto the people, Ye men of Israel, why marvel ye at this? or why look ye so earnestly on us, as though by our own power or holiness we had made this man to walk? [13] The God of Abraham, and of Isaac, and of Jacob, the God of our fathers, hath glorified his Son Jesus; whom ye delivered up, and denied him in the presence of Pilate, when he was determined to let *him* go. [14] But ye denied the Holy One and the Just, and desired a murderer to be granted unto you; [15] And killed the Prince of life, whom God hath raised from the dead; whereof we are witnesses. [16] And his name through faith in his name hath made this man strong, whom ye see and know: yea, the faith which is by him hath given him this perfect soundness in the presence of you all. [17] And now, brethren, I wot that through ignorance ye did *it*, as *did* also your rulers. [18] But those things, which God before had shewed by the mouth of all his prophets, that Christ should suffer, he hath so fulfilled. [19] Repent ye therefore, and be converted, that your sins may be blotted out, when the times of refreshing shall come from the presence of the Lord; [20] And he shall send Jesus Christ, which before was preached unto you: [21] Whom the heaven must receive until the times of restitution of all things, which God hath spoken by the mouth of all his holy prophets since the world began. [22] For Moses truly said unto the fathers, A prophet shall the Lord your God raise up unto you of your brethren, like unto me; him shall ye hear in all things whatsoever he shall say unto you. [23] And it shall come to pass, *that* every soul, which will not hear that prophet, shall be destroyed from among the people. [24] Yea, and all the prophets from Samuel and those that follow after, as many as have spoken, have likewise foretold of these days. [25] Ye are the children of the prophets, and of the covenant which God made with our fathers, saying unto Abraham, And in thy seed

shall all the kindreds of the earth be blessed. ²⁶ Unto you first God, having raised up his Son Jesus, sent him to bless you, in turning away every one of you from his iniquities.

Chapter 4

¹ And as they spake unto the people, the priests, and the captain of the temple, and the Sadducees, came upon them, ² Being grieved that they taught the people, and preached through Jesus the resurrection from the dead. ³ And they laid hands on them, and put *them* in hold unto the next day: for it was now eventide. ⁴ Howbeit many of them which heard the word believed; and the number of the men was about five thousand.

⁵ And it came to pass on the morrow, that their rulers, and elders, and scribes, ⁶ And Annas the high priest, and Caiaphas, and John, and Alexander, and as many as were of the kindred of the high priest, were gathered together at Jerusalem. ⁷ And when they had set them in the midst, they asked, By what power, or by what name, have ye done this? ⁸ Then Peter, filled with the Holy Ghost, said unto them, Ye rulers of the people, and elders of Israel, ⁹ If we this day be examined of the good deed done to the impotent man, by what means he is made whole; ¹⁰ Be it known unto you all, and to all the people of Israel, that by the name of Jesus Christ of Nazareth, whom ye crucified, whom God raised from the dead, *even* by him doth this man stand here before you whole. ¹¹ This is the stone which was set at nought of you builders, which is become the head of the corner. ¹² Neither is there salvation in any other: for there is none other name under heaven given among men, whereby we must be saved. ¹³ Now when they saw the boldness of Peter and John, and perceived that they were unlearned and ignorant men, they marvelled; and they took knowledge of them, that they had been with Jesus. ¹⁴ And beholding the man which was healed standing with them, they could say nothing against it.

¹⁵ But when they had commanded them to go aside out of the council, they conferred among themselves, ¹⁶ Saying, What shall we do to these men? for that indeed a notable miracle hath been

done by them *is* manifest to all them that dwell in Jerusalem; and we cannot deny *it*. [17] But that it spread no further among the people, let us straitly threaten them, that they speak henceforth to no man in this name. [18] And they called them, and commanded them not to speak at all nor teach in the name of Jesus. [19] But Peter and John answered and said unto them, Whether it be right in the sight of God to hearken unto you more than unto God, judge ye. [20] For we cannot but speak the things which we have seen and heard. [21] So when they had further threatened them, they let them go, finding nothing how they might punish them, because of the people: for all *men* glorified God for that which was done. [22] For the man was above forty years old, on whom this miracle of healing was shewed.

John 9 (Healing by Touch – A Blind Man from Birth Washes in the Pool of Siloam)

[1] And as *Jesus* passed by, he saw a man which was blind from *his* birth. [2] And his disciples asked him, saying, Master, who did sin, this man, or his parents, that he was born blind? [3] Jesus answered, Neither hath this man sinned, nor his parents: but that the works of God should be made manifest in him. [4] I must work the works of him that sent me, while it is day: the night cometh, when no man can work. [5] As long as I am in the world, I am the light of the world. [6] When he had thus spoken, he spat on the ground, and made clay of the spittle, and he anointed the eyes of the blind man with the clay, [7] And said unto him, Go, wash in the pool of Siloam, (which is by interpretation, Sent.) He went his way therefore, and washed, and came seeing.

[8] The neighbours therefore, and they which before had seen him that he was blind, said, Is not this he that sat and begged? [9] Some said, This is he: others *said*, He is like him: *but* he said, I am *he*. [10] Therefore said they unto him, How were thine eyes opened? [11] He answered and said, A man that is called Jesus made clay, and anointed mine eyes, and said unto me, Go to the pool of Siloam, and wash: and I went and washed, and I received

sight. [12] Then said they unto him, Where is he? He said, I know not.

[13] They brought to the Pharisees him that aforetime was blind. [14] And it was the sabbath day when Jesus made the clay, and opened his eyes. [15] Then again the Pharisees also asked him how he had received his sight. He said unto them, He put clay upon mine eyes, and I washed, and do see. [16] Therefore said some of the Pharisees, This man is not of God, because he keepeth not the sabbath day. Others said, How can a man that is a sinner do such miracles? And there was a division among them. [17] They say unto the blind man again, What sayest thou of him, that he hath opened thine eyes? He said, He is a prophet. [18] But the Jews did not believe concerning him, that he had been blind, and received his sight, until they called the parents of him that had received his sight. [19] And they asked them, saying, Is this your son, who ye say was born blind? how then doth he now see? [20] His parents answered them and said, We know that this is our son, and that he was born blind: [21] But by what means he now seeth, we know not; or who hath opened his eyes, we know not: he is of age; ask him: he shall speak for himself. [22] These *words* spake his parents, because they feared the Jews: for the Jews had agreed already, that if any man did confess that he was Christ, he should be put out of the synagogue. [23] Therefore said his parents, He is of age; ask him. [24] Then again called they the man that was blind, and said unto him, Give God the praise: we know that this man is a sinner. [25] He answered and said, Whether he be a sinner *or no*, I know not: one thing I know, that, whereas I was blind, now I see. [26] Then said they to him again, What did he to thee? how opened he thine eyes? [27] He answered them, I have told you already, and ye did not hear: wherefore would ye hear *it* again? will ye also be his disciples? [28] Then they reviled him, and said, Thou art his disciple; but we are Moses' disciples. [29] We know that God spake unto Moses: *as for* this *fellow*, we know not from whence he is. [30] The man answered and said unto them, Why herein is a marvellous thing, that ye know not from

whence he is, and *yet* he hath opened mine eyes. [31] Now we know that God heareth not sinners: but if any man be a worshipper of God, and doeth his will, him he heareth. [32] Since the world began was it not heard that any man opened the eyes of one that was born blind. [33] If this man were not of God, he could do nothing. [34] They answered and said unto him, Thou wast altogether born in sins, and dost thou teach us? And they cast him out.

[35] Jesus heard that they had cast him out; and when he had found him, he said unto him, Dost thou believe on the Son of God? [36] He answered and said, Who is he, Lord, that I might believe on him? [37] And Jesus said unto him, Thou hast both seen him, and it is he that talketh with thee. [38] And he said, Lord, I believe. And he worshipped him.

[39] And Jesus said, For judgment I am come into this world, that they which see not might see; and that they which see might be made blind. [40] And *some* of the Pharisees which were with him heard these words, and said unto him, Are we blind also? [41] Jesus said unto them, If ye were blind, ye should have no sin: but now ye say, We see; therefore your sin remaineth.

Acts 19:1-12 (Healing and Deliverance by Touching Paul's Handkerchief)

[1] And it came to pass, that, while Apollos was at Corinth, Paul having passed through the upper coasts came to Ephesus: and finding certain disciples, [2] He said unto them, Have ye received the Holy Ghost since ye believed? And they said unto him, We have not so much as heard whether there be any Holy Ghost. [3] And he said unto them, Unto what then were ye baptized? And they said, Unto John's baptism. [4] Then said Paul, John verily baptized with the baptism of repentance, saying unto the people, that they should believe on him which should come after him, that is, on Christ Jesus. [5] When they heard *this*, they were baptized in the name of the Lord Jesus. [6] And when Paul had laid *his* hands upon them, the Holy Ghost came on them; and

they spake with tongues, and prophesied. [7] And all the men were about twelve.

[8] And he went into the synagogue, and spake boldly for the space of three months, disputing and persuading the things concerning the kingdom of God. [9] But when divers were hardened, and believed not, but spake evil of that way before the multitude, he departed from them, and separated the disciples, disputing daily in the school of one Tyrannus. [10] And this continued by the space of two years; so that all they which dwelt in Asia heard the word of the Lord Jesus, both Jews and Greeks. [11] And God wrought special miracles by the hands of Paul: [12] So that from his body were brought unto the sick handkerchiefs or aprons, and the diseases departed from them, and the evil spirits went out of them.

Healing and Deliverance by Unusual Means

Acts 5:12-16 (Healing and Deliverance by Peter's Shadow)
[12] And by the hands of the apostles were many signs and wonders wrought among the people; (and they were all with one accord in Solomon's porch. [13] And of the rest durst no man join himself to them: but the people magnified them. [14] And believers were the more added to the Lord, multitudes both of men and women.) [15] Insomuch that they brought forth the sick into the streets, and laid *them* on beds and couches, that at the least the shadow of Peter passing by might overshadow some of them. [16] There came also a multitude *out* of the cities round about unto Jerusalem, bringing sick folks, and them which were vexed with unclean spirits: and they were healed every one.

2 Kings 20:1-11 (Healing by Prayer and Fig Leaves – Hezekiah)
[1] In those days was Hezekiah sick unto death. And the prophet Isaiah the son of Amoz came to him, and said unto him, Thus saith the LORD, Set thine house in order; for thou shalt die, and

not live. [2] Then he turned his face to the wall, and prayed unto the LORD, saying, [3] I beseech thee, O LORD, remember now how I have walked before thee in truth and with a perfect heart, and have done *that which is* good in thy sight. And Hezekiah wept sore. [4] And it came to pass, afore Isaiah was gone out into the middle court, that the word of the LORD came to him, saying, [5] Turn again, and tell Hezekiah the captain of my people, Thus saith the LORD, the God of David thy father, I have heard thy prayer, I have seen thy tears: behold, I will heal thee: on the third day thou shalt go up unto the house of the LORD. [6] And I will add unto thy days fifteen years; and I will deliver thee and this city out of the hand of the king of Assyria; and I will defend this city for mine own sake, and for my servant David's sake. [7] And Isaiah said, Take a lump of figs. And they took and laid *it* on the boil, and he recovered. [8] And Hezekiah said unto Isaiah, What *shall be* the sign that the LORD will heal me, and that I shall go up into the house of the LORD the third day? [9] And Isaiah said, This sign shalt thou have of the LORD, that the LORD will do the thing that he hath spoken: shall the shadow go forward ten degrees, or go back ten degrees? [10] And Hezekiah answered, It is a light thing for the shadow to go down ten degrees: nay, but let the shadow return backward ten degrees. [11] And Isaiah the prophet cried unto the LORD: and he brought the shadow ten degrees backward, by which it had gone down in the dial of Ahaz.

2 Kings 5 (Cleansing of Leprosy by Dipping in Jordan River – Naaman)

[1] Now Naaman, captain of the host of the king of Syria, was a great man with his master, and honourable, because by him the LORD had given deliverance unto Syria: he was also a mighty man in valour, *but he was* a leper. [2] And the Syrians had gone out by companies, and had brought away captive out of the land

of Israel a little maid; and she waited on Naaman's wife. [3] And she said unto her mistress, Would God my lord *were* with the prophet that *is* in Samaria! for he would recover him of his leprosy. [4] And *one* went in, and told his lord, saying, Thus and thus said the maid that *is* of the land of Israel. [5] And the king of Syria said, Go to, go, and I will send a letter unto the king of Israel. And he departed, and took with him ten talents of silver, and six thousand *pieces* of gold, and ten changes of raiment. [6] And he brought the letter to the king of Israel, saying, Now when this letter is come unto thee, behold, I have *therewith* sent Naaman my servant to thee, that thou mayest recover him of his leprosy [7] And it came to pass, when the king of Israel had read the letter, that he rent his clothes, and said, *Am* I God, to kill and to make alive, that this man doth send unto me to recover a man of his leprosy? wherefore consider, I pray you, and see how he seeketh a quarrel against me. [8] And it was *so*, when Elisha the man of God had heard that the king of Israel had rent his clothes, that he sent to the king, saying, Wherefore hast thou rent thy clothes? let him come now to me, and he shall know that there is a prophet in Israel.

[9] So Naaman came with his horses and with his chariot, and stood at the door of the house of Elisha. [10] And Elisha sent a messenger unto him, saying, Go and wash in Jordan seven times, and thy flesh shall come again to thee, and thou shalt be clean. [11] But Naaman was wroth, and went away, and said, Behold, I thought, He will surely come out to me, and stand, and call on the name of the LORD his God, and strike his hand over the place, and recover the leper. [12] *Are* not Abana and Pharpar, rivers of Damascus, better than all the waters of Israel? may I not wash in them, and be clean? So he turned and went away in a rage. [13] And his servants came near, and spake unto him, and said, My father, *if* the prophet had bid thee *do some* great thing, wouldest thou not have done *it*? how much rather then, when he saith to thee, Wash, and be clean? [14] Then went he down, and dipped himself seven times in Jordan, according to the saying of the

man of God: and his flesh came again like unto the flesh of a little child, and he was clean.

¹⁵ And he returned to the man of God, he and all his company, and came, and stood before him: and he said, Behold, now I know that *there is* no God in all the earth, but in Israel: now therefore, I pray thee, take a blessing of thy servant. ¹⁶ But he said, *As* the LORD liveth, before whom I stand, I will receive none. And he urged him to take *it*; but he refused. ¹⁷ And Naaman said, Shall there not then, I pray thee, be given to thy servant two mules' burden of earth? for thy servant will henceforth offer neither burnt offering nor sacrifice unto other gods, but unto the LORD. ¹⁸ In this thing the LORD pardon thy servant, *that* when my master goeth into the house of Rimmon to worship there, and he leaneth on my hand, and I bow myself in the house of Rimmon: when I bow down myself in the house of Rimmon, the LORD pardon thy servant in this thing. ¹⁹ And he said unto him, Go in peace. So he departed from him a little way.

²⁰ But Gehazi, the servant of Elisha the man of God, said, Behold, my master hath spared Naaman this Syrian, in not receiving at his hands that which he brought: but, *as* the LORD liveth, I will run after him, and take somewhat of him. ²¹ So Gehazi followed after Naaman. And when Naaman saw *him* running after him, he lighted down from the chariot to meet him, and said, *Is* all well? ²² And he said, All *is* well. My master hath sent me, saying, Behold, even now there be come to me from mount Ephraim two young men of the sons of the prophets: give them, I pray thee, a talent of silver, and two changes of garments. ²³ And Naaman said, Be content, take two talents. And he urged him, and bound two talents of silver in two bags, with two changes of garments, and laid *them* upon two of his servants; and they bare *them* before him. ²⁴ And when he came to the tower, he took *them* from their hand, and bestowed *them* in the house: and he let the men go, and they departed. ²⁵ But he went in, and stood before his master. And Elisha said unto him, Whence *comest thou*, Gehazi? And he said, Thy servant went no whither. ²⁶ And

he said unto him, Went not mine heart *with thee*, when the man turned again from his chariot to meet thee? *Is it* a time to receive money, and to receive garments, and oliveyards, and vineyards, and sheep, and oxen, and menservants, and maidservants? [27] The leprosy therefore of Naaman shall cleave unto thee, and unto thy seed for ever. And he went out from his presence a leper *as white* as snow.

John 4:43-54 (Healing a Sick Boy by the Father's Obedience)

[43] Now after two days he departed thence, and went into Galilee. [44] For Jesus himself testified, that a prophet hath no honour in his own country. [45] Then when he was come into Galilee, the Galilaeans received him, having seen all the things that he did at Jerusalem at the feast: for they also went unto the feast. [46] So Jesus came again into Cana of Galilee, where he made the water wine. And there was a certain nobleman, whose son was sick at Capernaum. [47] When he heard that Jesus was come out of Judaea into Galilee, he went unto him, and besought him that he would come down, and heal his son: for he was at the point of death. [48] Then said Jesus unto him, Except ye see signs and wonders, ye will not believe. [49] The nobleman saith unto him, Sir, come down ere my child die. [50] Jesus saith unto him, Go thy way; thy son liveth. And the man believed the word that Jesus had spoken unto him, and he went his way. [51] And as he was now going down, his servants met him, and told *him*, saying, Thy son liveth. [52] Then enquired he of them the hour when he began to amend. And they said unto him, Yesterday at the seventh hour the fever left him. [53] So the father knew that *it was* at the same hour, in the which Jesus said unto him, Thy son liveth: and himself believed, and his whole house. [54] This *is* again the second miracle *that* Jesus did, when he was come out of Judaea into Galilee.

Acts 19:1-12 (Healing and Deliverance by Touching Paul's Handkerchief)

[1] And it came to pass, that, while Apollos was at Corinth, Paul having passed through the upper coasts came to Ephesus:

and finding certain disciples, [2] He said unto them, Have ye received the Holy Ghost since ye believed? And they said unto him, We have not so much as heard whether there be any Holy Ghost. [3] And he said unto them, Unto what then were ye baptized? And they said, Unto John's baptism. [4] Then said Paul, John verily baptized with the baptism of repentance, saying unto the people, that they should believe on him which should come after him, that is, on Christ Jesus. [5] When they heard *this*, they were baptized in the name of the Lord Jesus. [6] And when Paul had laid *his* hands upon them, the Holy Ghost came on them; and they spake with tongues, and prophesied. [7] And all the men were about twelve.

[8] And he went into the synagogue, and spake boldly for the space of three months, disputing and persuading the things concerning the kingdom of God. [9] But when divers were hardened, and believed not, but spake evil of that way before the multitude, he departed from them, and separated the disciples, disputing daily in the school of one Tyrannus. [10] And this continued by the space of two years; so that all they which dwelt in Asia heard the word of the Lord Jesus, both Jews and Greeks. [11] And God wrought special miracles by the hands of Paul: [12] So that from his body were brought unto the sick handkerchiefs or aprons, and the diseases departed from them, and the evil spirits went out of them.

BIBLIOGRAPHY

BIBLIOGRAPHY

Books

Anderson, Neil T. *The Bondage Breaker – Overcoming Negative Thoughts, Irrational Feelings and Habitual Sins,* Eugene, OR: Harvest House Publishers, 1995.

Barry, William A. and William J. Connolly *The Practice of Spiritual Direction,* New York: HarperCollins Books, 1982.

Brand, Chad, Charles Draper Archie England et al. *Holman Illustrated Bible Dictionary*, Nashville: Holman Bible Publishers, 2003.

Bullinger, Ethelbert William *Figures of Speech Used in the Bible*, London; New York: Eyre & Spottiswoode; E. & J. B. Young & Co., 1898.

Carpenter, Eugene E. and Philip W. Comfort *Holman Treasury of Key Bible Words: 200 Greek and 200 Hebrew Words Defined and Explained*, Nashville: Broadman & Holman Publishers, 2000.

Ciarrocchi, Joseph W. A Minister's Handbook of Mental Disorders, Mahwah, NJ: Paulist Press, 1993.

Coulter, Leah *Rediscovering the Power of Repentance – Finding Healing and Justice for Reconcilable and Irreconcilable Wrongs,* Atlanta: Ampelon Publishing, 2006.

Crabb, Larry *Connecting – Healing for Ourselves and Our Relationships,* Nashville: W Publishing Group, 1997.

Cross, F. L. and Elizabeth A. Livingstone *The Oxford Dictionary of the Christian Church, 3rd ed. rev.,* Oxford; New York: Oxford University Press, 2005.

Dean Jr., Robert and Thomas Ice *What the Bible Teaches About Spiritual Warfare,* Grand Rapids: Kregel Publications, 2000.

Duffield, Guy P. and Nathaniel M. Van Cleave *Foundations of Pentecostal Theology,* Los Angeles: L.I.F.E. Bible College, 1983.

Easley, K. H., *Holman Quick Source Guide to Understanding the Bible,* Nashville: Holman Bible Publishers, 2002.

Easton, M.G. *Easton's Bible Dictionary*, Oak Harbor, WA: Logos Research Systems, Inc., 1996.

Elwell, Walter A. and Philip Wesley Comfort *Tyndale Bible Dictionary – Tyndale Reference Library,* Wheaton: Tyndale House Publishers, 2001.

Elwell, Walter A. ed. *Baker Theological Dictionary of the Bible,* Grand Rapids: Baker Books, 1996.

Enns, Paul P. *The Moody Handbook of Theology*, Chicago: Moody Press, 1997.

Ervin, Howard M. *Healing – Sign of the Kingdom,* Peabody, MA: Hendrickson Publishers, 2002.

Erickson, Millard J. *Christian Theology,* Grand Rapids: Baker Academics, 1998.

Fahlbusch, Erwin and Geoffrey William Bromiley, eds., *The Encyclopedia of Christianity*, Grand Rapids; Leiden, Netherlands: William. B. Eerdmans Publishing, 2003.

Friesen, James G. *Uncovering the Mystery of M.P.D – Its Shocking Origins…Its Shocking Cure,* San Bernardino: Here's Life Publishers, 1991.

Ferguson, Sinclair B., David F. Wright, and J. I. Packer, eds., *New Dictionary of Theology,* Downers Grove, IL: InterVarsity Press, 1978.

Hayford, Jack, W. *The Finger of God,* Van Nuys: Living Way Ministries, 1993.

Hayford, Jack, W. *Invading the Impossible,* Alachua, FL: Bridge Logos Publishers, 1977.

Hayford, Jack, W. and Rebecca Hayford Bauer *Penetrating the Darkness – Discovering the Power of the Cross against Unseen Evil,* Grand Rapids: Chosen Books, 2011.

Hayward, Chris *God's Cleansing Stream,* Ventura: Regal Books, 2004.

Hodge, Charles *Systematic Theology*, Oak Harbor, WA: Logos Research Systems, Inc., 1997.

Jamieson, Robert, A. R. Fausset and David Brown *Critical and Explanatory Commentary on the Whole Bible*, Oak Harbor, WA: Logos Research Systems, Inc., 1997.

Karkkainen, Veli-Matti *Pneumatology – The Holy Spirit in Ecumenical, International and Contextual Perspective,* Grand Rapids: Baker Academic, 2002.

Koch, Kurt *Between Christ and Satan,* Grand Rapids: Kregel Publications, 1981.

Kraft, Charles H. *Christianity with Power,* Ann Arbor: Vine Books, 1989.

Kraft, Charles H. *I Give You Authority,* Grand Rapids: Chosen Books, 1997,

Lindsay, D. G. *Harmony of Science and Scripture,* /Dallas: Christ for the Nations, 1998.

McNutt, Francis *Deliverance from Evil Spirits,* Grand Rapids: Chosen Books, 2009.

Merriam-Webster, Inc. *The Merriam-Webster Collegiate Dictionary,* 10th ed. Springfield, MA: Merriam-Webster, 1996.

Morgan, J. Vyrnwy *Theology at the Dawn of the Twentieth Century – Essays on the Present Status of Christianity and Its Doctrines,* Boston: Small, Maynard & Company, 1900.

Murphy, Edward F. *The Handbook for Spiritual Warfare,* Nashville: Thomas Nelson Publishers, Inc., 1992.

Nouwen, Henri J.M. *The Wounded Healer,* New York: Doubleday, 1972

Oxford University Press, Inc. *The Oxford Dictionary and Thesaurus,* Oxford; New York: Oxford University Press, 1996.

Pfeiffer, Charles F., Howard F. Vos and John Rea, eds., *The Wycliffe Bible Encyclopedia – Volumes I & II,* Chicago: Moody Press, 1975.

Pierce, Larry *Tense Voice Mood.* Bellingham, WA: Logos Bible Software, n.d.

Preston, Gary D. *Character Forged from Conflict – Staying Connected to God During Controversy: The Pastor's Soul Series,* Minneapolis: Bethany House, 1999.

Rankin, Jerry and Ed Stetzer *Spiritual Warfare and Missions – The Battle for God's Glory among the Nations,* Nashville: B & H Publishing Group, 2010.

Richards, Lawrence O., ed., *New International Encyclopedia of Biblical Words,* Grand Rapids: Zondervan Publishing House, 1996.

Robyn, Kathryn L. *Spiritual Housecleaning – Healing the Space Within by Beautifying the Space around You,* Oakland: New Harbinger Publications, 2001.

Scazzero, Peter and Bird, Warren *The Emotionally Healthy Church – A Strategy for Discipleship that Actually Changes Lives,* Grand Rapids: Zondervan Publishing House, 2003.

Strong, Augustus Hopkins *Systematic Theology,* Bellingham, WA: Logos Research Systems, Inc., 2004.

Tan, Paul Lee *Encyclopedia of 7700 Illustrations – Signs of the Times*, Garland, TX: Bible Communications, Inc., 1996.

Thomas, Robert L. *New American Standard Hebrew-Aramaic and Greek Dictionaries – Updated Edition,* Anaheim: Foundation Publications, Inc., 1998.

Trudeau, Kevin *More Natural Cures Revealed,* Elk Grove Village, IL: Alliance Publishing Group, Inc., 2006.

Trudeau, Kevin *Natural Cures "They" Don't Want You to Know About,* Elk Grove Village, IL: Alliance Publishing Group, Inc., 2004.

Vine, W. E., Merrill F. Unger and William White, Jr., eds., *Vine's Expository Dictionary of Biblical Words,* Nashville: Thomas Nelson Publishers, 1985.

Walvoord, John E., Donald K. Campbell and Roy B. Zuck, eds., *Lewis Sperry Chafer Systematic Theology – Volumes I & II,* Wheaton: Victor Books, 1984.

Williams, J. Rodman *Renewal Theology,* Grand Rapids: Zondervan Publishing House, 1996.

Willmington, H.L. *Willmington's Book of Bible Lists,* Wheaton: Tyndale, 1987.

Wimber, John and Springer, Kevin *Power Healing,* New York: HarperCollins, 1987.

Zodhiates, Spiros *The Complete Word Study Dictionary – New Testament, electronic ed.,* Chattanooga: AMG Publishers, 2000.

Periodicals

Elsevier, B.V. "Information Solutions for Science and Health."
American Journal of Medicine. http://elsevier.com
(June16, 2011)

Schaff, Philip *The Nicene and Post-Nicene Fathers Second
Series Vol. X*, Oak Harbor, WA: Logos Research
Systems, 1997.

Schlitz, Marilyn "Consciousness and Healing." October 2004,
*The American Journal of Medicine – Book Index on
Healing 2005*
http://www.elsevier.com/wps/find/simple_search.cws_ho
me?boost=true&needs_keyword=true&adv=false&action
=simple_search&default=default&keywords=healing
(April 2011)

E-Forms

CDC, *Center for Disease Control and Prevention.*
http://www.cdc.gov. (June 17, 2011)

Gondwe, Eric "Fundamentals of Christian Deliverance and
Healing." *Book Index,* 2008.
http://www.spiritualwarfaredeliverance.com/html/deliver
ance-and-healing-01.html (May 2011)

Greiner Jr., Max "Healing and Deliverance." *Unfinished Draft,
October 15, 2007.*
http://www.maxgrenierart.com/healing_deliverance.html
(May 2011)

Moody, Gene and Earlene Moody "Gene and Earlene
    Deliverance Manual."
    http://www.moodymanual.demonbuster.com/preambl1.ht
    ml (May 2011)

NAMI, "National Alliance on Mental Illness."
    http://www.nami.org (n.d.)

Order Form
Virgil Jones/VVJones Ministries
2219 W. Olive Ave., #272
Burbank, CA 91506
310-418-0582
vvjones@msn.com

Name: _____

Address: _____

City _____ State _____ Zip _____

Primary Phone _____

Secondary Phone _____

Quantity	Title	Price	Total
	Healing and Deliverance by the Finger of God – Book		
	Healing and Deliverance by the Finger of God – Workbook		
	Healing and Deliverance by the Finger of God – CD Sermon Series		
	Healing and Deliverance by the Finger of God – DVD Sermon Series		
Total	Shipping and handling is $3.00 per item.		